Discoveries through Meditation

(MahaMudra)

JULIEN BOUCHARD

Sherrington (Québec) Canada

julien@julienbouchard.com

Order this book online at www.trafford.com
or email orders@trafford.com

Most Trafford titles are also available at major online book retailers.

Printed in the United States of America.

ISBN: 978-1-4669-0195-7 (sc)
ISBN: 978-1-4669-0194-0 (hc)
ISBN: 978-1-4669-0193-3 (e)

Library of Congress Control Number: 2011919114

Trafford rev. 10/22/2011

 www.trafford.com

North America & International
toll-free: 1 888 232 4444 (USA & Canada)
phone: 250 383 6864 ♦ fax: 812 355 4082

When meditation (the search for truth) becomes a priority in one's life, the impact of material experiences is reduced accordingly.

J.B.

Foreword

After more than 45 years of study, research, reflection and meditation, I wish to share with honest searchers of truth the results of my efforts to reach a higher level of understanding of life, humanity and finally oneself.

I must thank all the Great Wise Searchers of the past and present for their help in keeping open the path leading to the ultimate truth. Because of them, those who are no longer satisfied with the material world can travel beyond illusion.

Anyone who can see, sees, and anyone who can understand, understands. I take the liberty to present this document, which, I hope, will be beneficial to those who, like me, are looking for a greater understanding of the universe in which we all live.

This book is composed of my points of views, my understanding and my truth. The word truth is in itself an important statement, and when stated in the material world context, can be defined in hundreds of thousands, maybe millions of different ways. This is possible because of the fact that, in the material world, nothing is stable, nothing is permanent, everything changes, and everything is transformed. What was truth yesterday is lie today, what was good the day before yesterday will be evil tomorrow.

But the ultimate truth remains and will always remain; the VOID of meditation will always be emptiness because it is immutable and eternal. Only the words used to define it, to interpret it will change. The whole content of this book can be interpreted in as many ways as there are human beings in the universe. Even my personal understanding will change with time and it is very likely that in a more or less distant future I will need to update this work because I will have evolved toward another level of understanding.

I am not asking the reader to believe or accept what I wrote in the following pages, quite the contrary. The searcher must develop a critical mind, question everything and believe only what he experiences himself.

Meditation is the greatest tool ever given to the world. Anyone using it can abolish all the limitations of the created world, see through the veil of illusion and perceive what really is our world and our reason for being in this great cosmic machine.

In silence, the mind rests in its natural state and, in this state communicates directly with its source. In silence, the truth makes itself known.

I wish the reader a good journey on the road to ultimate truth. The truth that comes as a lightning, and illuminates the onlooker. I hope that my researches will help daring researchers in their progress toward the real truth.

Julien Bouchard

Reading Method

This book was written in a dictionary format because the quest for truth is mainly composed of research, analysis and discovery. This format also allowed me to avoid the trap of the prose and to go directly to the subject's core. This collection of words gives the reader the opportunity to easily go from one word, definition or teaching to another. It makes it easy for him to find again a particularly interesting passage, definition or reflection.

This book can be read from the beginning to the end, or consulted by choosing a word or expression from the following list that the reader wishes to discover. The reader can make a mark (X) in the first box appearing on the left of a word or expression in order to remember that he has already consulted this particular word. After reading, he also can make a mark in the second box to remember that he wishes to read this particular passage again, for deeper analysis for example. Furthermore, if he wants, he can comment on a particular passage by writing on the line following the word.

First, a short definition is given for each word or expression in order to set the reader in a particular mental context. A section where the author shares with the reader his personal understanding of the subject inspired by the defined word or expression follows this definition.

The author has provided each point of view with a question. It is recommended to first read the question and to answer it immediately without reflecting on it. This answer can be very interesting for the searcher. This is a way to probe one's own deep spiritual knowledge. These questions can also be used as reflection topics.

Good reading

Reading Follow-up

Read	Reread	Word or expression	Comments
O	O	Abandon _____	
O	O	Absence of thought _____	
O	O	Absolute knowledge _____	
O	O	Absolution _____	
O	O	Accelerated path _____	
O	O	Accomplishment _____	
O	O	Acquisition _____	
O	O	Action _____	
O	O	Action/reaction _____	
O	O	Adept _____	
O	O	Aggregate _____	
O	O	Alert _____	
O	O	Alone _____	
O	O	Altruism _____	
O	O	Analytical meditation _____	
O	O	Anchor point _____	
O	O	Animal _____	
O	O	Annihilation _____	
O	O	Apparition _____	
O	O	Application _____	
O	O	Aspect _____	

O	O	Aspiration _____
O	O	Attachment _____
O	O	Attention _____
O	O	Attraction _____
O	O	Awakened _____
O	O	Awakening _____
O	O	Awakening path _____
O	O	Awareness _____
O	O	Bad _____
O	O	Become (to) _____
O	O	Behaviour _____
O	O	Benefits _____
O	O	Benevolence _____
O	O	Beyond _____
O	O	Block _____
O	O	Body _____
O	O	Bondage _____
O	O	Boredom _____
O	O	Brain _____
O	O	Breathing _____
O	O	Capability _____
O	O	Cause _____
O	O	Cell _____
O	O	Centre _____
O	O	Centre path _____
O	O	Charge _____
O	O	Charity _____
O	O	Chastity _____
O	O	Collective past _____
O	O	Commitment _____
O	O	Communication _____

O	O	Comparison _____
O	O	Compassion _____
O	O	Composed _____
O	O	Comprehension _____
O	O	Concentration _____
O	O	Concentration on an object _____
O	O	Concentration on emptiness _____
O	O	Concentration on the breathing _____
O	O	Conception _____
O	O	Confusion _____
O	O	Conqueror _____
O	O	Conquest _____
O	O	Consciousness _____
O	O	Consciousness in time _____
O	O	Contemplation _____
O	O	Contentment _____
O	O	Control _____
O	O	Convergence _____
O	O	Corporal distraction _____
O	O	Creation _____
O	O	Curiosity _____
O	O	Death _____
O	O	Decision _____
O	O	Deep view _____
O	O	Deliverance _____
O	O	Description _____
O	O	Desire _____
O	O	Desire-reject _____
O	O	Destiny _____
O	O	Destruction _____
O	O	Development _____

9

O	O	Difference _____
O	O	Different _____
O	O	Disappearance _____
O	O	Discipline _____
O	O	Disillusion _____
O	O	Dispatch _____
O	O	Dissipation _____
O	O	Distance _____
O	O	Distinction _____
O	O	Distraction _____
O	O	Disunity _____
O	O	Do (to) _____
O	O	Dogmatism _____
O	O	Dominating aggregate _____
O	O	Domination _____
O	O	Door _____
O	O	Doubt _____
O	O	Dream _____
O	O	Drowsiness _____
O	O	Duality _____
O	O	Duration _____
O	O	Easiness _____
O	O	Education _____
O	O	Effect _____
O	O	Ego _____
O	O	Elation _____
O	O	Emergence of thoughts _____
O	O	Emotion _____
O	O	Emotional relativity _____
O	O	Empathy _____
O	O	End of breath _____

O O Enemy _____

O O Entity _____

O O Envy _____

O O Error _____

O O Escape _____

O O Eternity _____

O O Evolution _____

O O Excess _____

O O Exclusion _____

O O Existence _____

O O Experience _____

O O Express way _____

O O Expression _____

O O External self-analysis _____

O O Extraordinary love _____

O O Extreme _____

O O Extremist _____

O O Extrospection _____

O O Failure _____

O O Faith _____

O O Feeding _____

O O First principle _____

O O Flexibility _____

O O Fluctuation _____

O O Force _____

O O Forgiveness _____

O O Form _____

O O Four great truths _____

O O Friendship _____

O O Fruit _____

O O Function _____

O	O	Future _____
O	O	Glimpse _____
O	O	Gluttony _____
O	O	Goal _____
O	O	Good _____
O	O	Good-bad _____
O	O	Great difference (the) _____
O	O	Great purificator _____
O	O	Great teaching _____
O	O	Guide _____
O	O	Hallucination _____
O	O	Happiness _____
O	O	Happiness-sorrow _____
O	O	Hate _____
O	O	Hindrance _____
O	O	Honesty _____
O	O	Human being _____
O	O	Humanity _____
O	O	Humility _____
O	O	Identification _____
O	O	Ignorance _____
O	O	Ignorant being _____
O	O	Illness _____
O	O	Illumination _____
O	O	Illusion _____
O	O	Illusory _____
O	O	Immateriality _____
O	O	Immobility _____
O	O	Impartiality _____
O	O	Imperfection _____
O	O	Impermanent _____

O   O   Importance _____

O   O   Impostor _____

O   O   Impulse _____

O   O   Incredulous _____

O   O   Indifference _____

O   O   Individual mind _____

O   O   Individual past _____

O   O   Inevitable _____

O   O   Inexplicable _____

O   O   Influence _____

O   O   Inner presence _____

O   O   Insensible _____

O   O   Inseparable _____

O   O   Insomnia _____

O   O   Instantaneity _____

O   O   Instinct _____

O   O   Integrity _____

O   O   Intellect _____

O   O   Intellectual analysis _____

O   O   Intensity _____

O   O   Interference _____

O   O   Interpretation _____

O   O   Introspection _____

O   O   Intuition _____

O   O   Invading thoughts _____

O   O   Invulnerable _____

O   O   Irreligious _____

O   O   Irritation _____

O   O   Isolation _____

O   O   Justice _____

O   O   Knower _____

O	O	Knowledge _____
O	O	Knowledge of self _____
O	O	Law _____
O	O	Liberated _____
O	O	Liberation _____
O	O	Life _____
O	O	Light _____
O	O	Limited intelligence _____
O	O	Live (to) _____
O	O	Love _____
O	O	Markers _____
O	O	Master _____
O	O	Mastery of emotions _____
O	O	Material relativity _____
O	O	Me _____
O	O	Meditation _____
O	O	Meditation on death _____
O	O	Meditation on emptiness _____
O	O	Meditation on matter _____
O	O	Meditation on the mind _____
O	O	Meditation on time _____
O	O	Meditation point _____
O	O	Memory _____
O	O	Metamorphosis _____
O	O	Mind _____
O	O	Misery _____
O	O	Misinterpretation _____
O	O	Moment of rest _____
O	O	Movement _____
O	O	Myself _____
O	O	Natural _____

O   O   Natural state _____

O   O   Nature of meditation _____

O   O   Need _____

O   O   Negative emotion _____

O   O   Neutrality _____

O   O   Noise _____

O   O   Non-attachment _____

O   O   Non-dominating aggregate _____

O   O   Non-intervention _____

O   O   Now _____

O   O   Observation _____

O   O   Observer _____

O   O   Obsession _____

O   O   Obstacle _____

O   O   Opportunity _____

O   O   Ordinary love _____

O   O   Origin _____

O   O   Paradox _____

O   O   Parasite _____

O   O   Parent _____

O   O   Passing thoughts _____

O   O   Passion _____

O   O   Path _____

O   O   Patience _____

O   O   Peace _____

O   O   Pendulum _____

O   O   Perception _____

O   O   Perfection _____

O   O   Permanent _____

O   O   Permanent meditation _____

O   O   Perseverance _____

O   O   Personality _____

O   O   Place _____

O   O   Planning _____

O   O   Point of concentration _____

O   O   Point of view _____

O   O   Pollution _____

O   O   Positive emotion _____

O   O   Possession _____

O   O   Posture _____

O   O   Poverty _____

O   O   Power _____

O   O   Practical knowledge _____

O   O   Practice _____

O   O   Practising person _____

O   O   Prayer _____

O   O   Preacher _____

O   O   Prerequisite _____

O   O   Presence _____

O   O   Present _____

O   O   Pretension _____

O   O   Pride _____

O   O   Problem _____

O   O   Progeny _____

O   O   Program _____

O   O   Progress _____

O   O   Progression _____

O   O   Projection _____

O   O   Provenance _____

O   O   Punishment _____

O   O   Pure _____

O   O   Purpose _____

O	O	Quiescence _____
O	O	Reaction _____
O	O	Reality _____
O	O	Reality of the illusion _____
O	O	Reality-illusion _____
O	O	Realization _____
O	O	Realization of reality _____
O	O	Rebirth _____
O	O	Recall _____
O	O	Recognition of emptiness _____
O	O	Reflection _____
O	O	Reform _____
O	O	Refuge _____
O	O	Regret _____
O	O	Reject _____
O	O	Relationships _____
O	O	Religion _____
O	O	Renouncement _____
O	O	Repetition _____
O	O	Research _____
O	O	Result _____
O	O	Retreat _____
O	O	Riches _____
O	O	Ritual _____
O	O	Satisfaction _____
O	O	Science _____
O	O	Searcher _____
O	O	Security _____
O	O	Self-confidence _____
O	O	Self-observation _____
O	O	Selfishness _____

O O Sensations _____

O O Separation _____

O O Servitude _____

O O Setting point _____

O O Short cut _____

O O Silence _____

O O Simple things _____

O O Simplicity _____

O O Singularity _____

O O Slander _____

O O Slave _____

O O Sleep _____

O O Sleeper _____

O O Small-teaching _____

O O Solitude _____

O O Sorrow _____

O O Source _____

O O Spark _____

O O Spiritual analysis _____

O O Stable data _____

O O Stage _____

O O Step _____

O O Stop _____

O O Study _____

O O Superior being _____

O O Superior consciousness _____

O O Superiority _____

O O Technology _____

O O Temporal relativity _____

O O Tendency _____

O O Tension _____

O   O   Theoretical knowledge _____

O   O   Thought _____

O   O   Thought process _____

O   O   Thought-matter _____

O   O   Three views _____

O   O   Time _____

O   O   Tolerance _____

O   O   Tonality _____

O   O   Tool _____

O   O   Training _____

O   O   Tranquillity _____

O   O   Transcendence _____

O   O   Transcendental knowledge _____

O   O   Transformation _____

O   O   Transitory _____

O   O   Trilogy of happiness _____

O   O   Truth _____

O   O   Unconsciousness _____

O   O   Uncreated _____

O   O   Union _____

O   O   Unity _____

O   O   Universal balance _____

O   O   Universal body _____

O   O   Universal mind _____

O   O   Universal voice _____

O   O   Universality _____

O   O   Universe _____

O   O   Unlimited intelligence _____

O   O   Unpredictable _____

O   O   Vehicle _____

O   O   Vice _____

O	O	Vigilance _____
O	O	Virtue _____
O	O	Void _____
O	O	Volubility _____
O	O	Voyage _____
O	O	Wandering _____
O	O	Waste _____
O	O	Wisdom _____
O	O	Wise one _____
O	O	Word _____
O	O	World _____

A

ABANDON

The action of not wishing a thing anymore and to renounce it.

It is very difficult for people in general to abandon one thing or another. It is always difficult to leave the native village, or to abandon a stable position. To quit one's country is hard and to divorce is simply painful. The relinquishment of a part of oneself is practically impossible for those who have not opened their eyes yet to another vision of the world. The arrogant clings to his pride, the liar to his illusions, the humble to his humility, the strong to his power, the weak to something else, etc. It is difficult for anyone to abandon what is interpreted as an integral part of one's entity. The ignorant believes that he will be diminished if he relinquishes some of his emotions and that he will disappear if he abandons them all. The wise man who looks within discovers that he is not the sum of his emotions, envy, jealousy, attachment, humility, goodness, charity, etc., but rather a being free of any form of feeling. Then he begins to study his behaviour, an activity that encourages him to better himself. In order to improve himself, he abandons his emotions, his false interpretations, and his false values, to keep only the pure light of observation. The more the relinquishment is complete, the more peace and serenity are overwhelming. The wise man acknowledges that the abandonment is a path to happiness.

Why does one cling to what will disappear tomorrow?

ABSENCE OF THOUGHT

Period of mental emptiness during which the observer is not distracted by thoughts.

People who do not practice meditation do not know what inner silence is. During their whole life their head is filled with thoughts to which they identify. They live in this unending cacophony that prevents them from realizing that they are something else than thoughts. One has to reach inner silence in order to acknowledge an individual existence outside of the thought process. A human being is not thoughts he is consciousness. When the adept closes his eyes, he experiences a short moment of silence, then thoughts emerge from nothingness and attempt to take possession of the consciousness. The seasoned adept ignores thoughts that he sees passing before his inner eye. Then, little by little even those signs vanish and silence takes over, the persevering adept has reached the state of absence of thought. At this very moment meditation starts, all that has been done before was only preliminary work. Meditation is total silence. The adept is there and contemplates the eternal void, he realizes that only emptiness is permanent, all that he has experienced until now in his life has had a beginning, a duration and an end, but not the void of meditation. The more often and the longer he visits this «space», the closer he gets to the eternal truth.

What would the world resemble if human beings were not there to look at it?

ABSOLUTE KNOWLEDGE

Complete knowledge by itself without comparison with anything external.

It is impossible to acquire absolute knowledge in the dualistic world of illusion. An extreme such as implied by the word absolute is unrealizable in the material world because it cannot exist between the two positive and negative poles. It is impossible to find an absolute temperature, an absolute situation, an absolute truth or anything else with an absolute characteristic in our world of illusion, where everything is always more or less pure or impure, more or less true or false. Absolute knowledge does not depend on an analytical technique. It is a perfect knowledge that can be experienced during deep meditation. But this knowledge experienced during a short or long period will vanish as soon as the adept comes out of his state of quiescence. It is possible to experience a moment of absolute truth only if the mental process is suspended, otherwise all that is perceived would be analyzed and rationalized according to material world parameters. Thus the wise man, after coming out of meditation, will feel the slow vanishing of the absolute certainty he felt earlier, and after a while there will remain only an intellectualization of the experience itself. No longer will there be an absolute memory. It is only in the final stage of illumination that the wise one will experience the ultimate absolute knowledge that will remain with him forever. Then he will have reached his goal.

Why, when stating that he is rich, is the poor more sincere than the rich saying that he is poor?

ABSOLUTION

Forgiveness and erasing of faults, which follow their confession.

Most human beings know when they have committed a reprehensible action and the fact that they know drives them to look for forgiveness. They do so by confessing their faults to those they hurt or simply to a superior being in the hope that He will forgive them. But the most sought after form of forgiveness is the one coming from within oneself. Numerous people refuse to forgive themselves for things they have done and by doing so they destroy their chance to find serenity in their life. Any action whose memory is not harmonious can be considered as a fault needing to be forgiven. Human beings are what they think they are, therefore they must pay particular attention to what is happening in their own head. Negative memories hinder the evolution of people. The wise man knows that any action produces a result and that he will be subjected to the results of all his past faults. But he also knows that the initiator of an action is only vulnerable to its returning impact if he is still subjected to matter. Anyone will no longer be affected by illusions once they are finally transcended. The wise one sees this moment as a great absolution of all the negative actions he has performed during this life and the previous ones. The liberated wise man is no longer enslaved to matter because he has no more desire for it. Since he does not want anything from illusion anymore, illusion has no more hold on him; he is now a being free from the burden of illusion.

Why are some people not able to forgive themselves?

ACCELERATED PATH

A way that leads more rapidly to the goal.

All beings in the universe are on the path leading to the ultimate confrontation with reality. Choice has no part in this. Human beings emerge from a long chain of evolution, which started with inanimate aggregates evolving into animate aggregates, then intellectual aggregates, and finally spiritual ones. These aggregates, which in fact are only thoughts, will eventually return to their source, the void. In the course of his evolution, the thinking being reaches a stage where his past and present experiences allow him to perceive the futility of matter and the suffering then the importance of reality which generates felicity. He finally acknowledges his reason for living and from this moment on, he can take his destiny into his own hands and accelerate the evolving process which will allows him to reach the truth more quickly, as have done wise men before him. Meditation has always been the quicker way to go from ignorance to wisdom. But among all the various types of meditation, the meditation on emptiness (void), also called the path of kings, is the fastest. This meditation is exceptional because it takes no detour to reach the anticipated goal. According to great past and contemporary wise men, reality or truth rests in the inner void. This is what the adept of meditation on emptiness meditates on. The wise man says that someone who meditates on love finds love, someone who meditates on sound finds sound, etc., and that the one who meditates on reality finds reality. From emptiness emerges the illumination of the searcher.

Why is it impossible for a human being to find anything else than what he is looking for?

ACCOMPLISHMENT

The action of doing or achieving something.

All the grandiose projects carried out by humankind since the beginning of time slowly crumble into dust under the eyes of the new generations. The human being, this great architect of all times who incessantly projects, plans and realizes great works, each more extraordinary than the other, this great maker, witnesses helplessly the slow crumbling of his accomplishments. Would it not be more profitable to work upon projects that do not age, spoil, fall into obsolescence, disappear swept away by time, the great equalizer? The wise man's accomplishments are defined in the present moment. He does what he has to do, at the time he has to do it, no more and no less. He does not fritter his time away in lengthy future planning or projections, he meditates instead to acquire the immutable and eternal wisdom. He knows that in life he has to do what he believes needs to be done. He follows his intuition, this faint voice that comes from within. He listens closely to the voice of wisdom.

What is the nature of intuition?

ACQUISITION

The act of becoming the owner of something.

The human being is looking for what he calls happiness and security because he is constantly haunted by fear, anguish, boredom, uncertainty, avidity, etc. He is always pulled in different directions, stretched from left to right without respite. He suffers a lot. In his search for happiness he always believes that tomorrow will be better, or that everything will be better if he possesses a new thing. And when he finally owns that something, he realises almost immediately that, contrary to what he expected, this thing does not make him any happier, thus it must be something else, and so on. His quest for happiness drives him to acquire mountains of worldly goods, and he spends all his life working at more or less useful tasks in order to earn the money necessary to fulfil his need of possession without ever finding serenity. Yet, happiness is free, it is there, one only has to reach for it. The wise man closes his eyes and concentrates on the inner emptiness, which teaches him that real happiness resides in peace and that peace takes its source in the absence of desire. He reassesses his values and acknowledges that worldly acquisitions can only bring deception.

Why run after sparks when it is possible to bathe directly in the warmth of the fire?

ACTION

State of what is in movement or in transformation. The initiation of a change.

The status of the created universe; any thought or movement initiated by a being. Anything created is active thus in constant transformation, while all that is uncreated is perfectly static or passive from our point view. Actions and useless movements are the searcher's enemies. Only total inactivity can light the lamp of truth. Deep meditation on the void, in the absence of desires and thoughts, leads directly to the doorstep of the great mystery. Desire is the source of all actions and all disillusions while quiescence offers the inner peace of reality.

Why should intention be transcended before action?

ACTION/REACTION

The universal law insuring that each action yields result and produces a reaction.

One with limited spiritual awareness must believe in the law of action/reaction and train in concentrating his attention on an object without thinking. Each thought and each action produces a certain impact and in turn this impact reacts on the whole universe. After each new thought or action, the whole universe is altered; all is transformed, as infinitesimal as the transformation may be. The wise man weighs his thoughts and actions in order to create the best impact on the whole universe, on the people around him and on himself. Nothing is free in the material world, any action and thought brings back its lot of happiness or unhappiness. The only way to overcome this law is to transcend past actions and thoughts through meditation.

What happens in the universe when a grain of sand is moved from one place to another?

ADEPT

A person who embarks on the path to the truth. A being who believes that something better than the material world exists and wishes to reach it.

An adept can be a person totally devoid of book knowledge. An adept does not need a school degree to enter the path. The knowledge seeked is well above our worldly illusory knowledge. It is important for the searcher to find a path that suits him and to experience all knowledge acquired in books or elsewhere. The adept must never take anything for granted and must constantly reassess his position and wisdom. However, one must be cautions because although some teachings are **Great** and will lead to worldly detachment, the understanding of reality, and finally to liberation, while some are **Small** and will lead to attachment to the material world, and the acceptance of illusion; they will only bring complete confusion. The sincere adept will choose a teaching that is Great and meditate endlessly on emptiness to acquire the wisdom necessary to attain the truth.

What is the difference between knowledge acquired in books and knowledge acquired by experience?

AGGREGATE

Collection of different elements linked together.

A group of thoughts forming an active whole. Groups of thoughts meeting other groups of thoughts that form new thoughts indefinitely. No aggregate, group of thoughts or thought form is permanent. The adept must realize that his body is only an assembly of different genetic and biological elements, that his so-called consciousness is only a cluster of various genetic and intellectual data and that, in fact, the adept has no power of decision. Different aggregates, according to their individual tendency and force, regulate where to go and what to do at the right moment. The sleeper only has the impression that he runs his life. In fact, the brain receives and interprets messages from the aggregates then orders the body to accomplish some specific actions.

What is my most remarkable tendency and where is it coming from?

ALERT

The characteristic of someone who is awake, vigilant.

In the great game of the created world, the population is alert to things of this world. People are alert when they hear someone talking about victory, money, success, etc., about anything of interest to them. But when it comes to their inner self, they are sound a sleep and some even deny its existence. The more an adept is alert during his quest to control the thought process, then during his contemplation of the infinite void, the more quickly he progresses. The adept, who meditates without physical or mental effort, but with an inflexible and unassailable degree of attention, will inevitably reach his objective in the briefest of time. Everything rests on the adept's faculty to remain alert in the emptiness of his meditation. Any form of weakness of attention, any lack of interest or curiosity leads directly to failure. The wise one has tempered the steel of his attention in the fire of perseverance and his curiosity in the essence of originality. Detached from everything and yet active in all, he lives the present moment, the only one that truly exists.

Why is anyone immersed into illusion no more conscious when sleeping than when awake?

ALONE

Someone who is isolated from the presence of others.

As the saying goes, we are alone in death as we are in birth. But one should not forget that human beings are alone at all times, from morning to night, even while with friends or in the middle of a crowd. Most people are deluded by the fact that they frequently see people and make noises in the presence of others, but deep inside, they are alone. In the absence of their fellowmen, people become bored, neurasthenic, and depressive, they feel useless and sometimes they become suicidal. They have a very low tolerance level for solitude because they have no active inner life; they count solely on the external world to attain their small happiness. When alone, their thought process enters a super active phase since they have nothing to focus on (activities) that would slow it down. Then they are completely submerged into a world of thoughts. Because this does not correspond to their normal life, they become sick very quickly. On the contrary, the wise man wishes to be alone to pursue his inner research by focusing his attention on emptiness and silence. He keeps his mental balance and even improves his understanding of life by immersing himself into the solitude of silence because he is capable of stopping his thought process. By not being hampered by the thoughts that trouble his inner peace and de-harmonize him, he can acquire wisdom.

Why is solitude frightening?

ALTRUISM

Tendency to sympathize with and help others.

In most cases, actions at first sight may seem altruistic when in fact they are accomplished to help the benefactor as well as the person in need. Furthermore, very often the individual persons involved are unaware that their actions are only altruistic on a basic level: that in fact they are rather egotistical. This does not erase the fact that the action might have done something good and relieved hundreds maybe thousands of beings in need. The goal of the present exercise is not to destroy the good action, which still remains and generates its positive progeny. But one must realize that fundamentally every person performing an action expects something in return: this is the universal law. The most charitable person in the world will tell you that he receives a lot more than what he gives to others. A smile is my greatest reward. Even a smile is a form of payment. The final action of the wise man is to reach liberation for himself, who is an integral part of humankind. If he were trying to reach liberation for someone else he would fail. He is aware that his liberation reduces the negative charge weighing on the world. His participation in keeping the path open for those wishing to leave behind the sorrow of illusion to find a better world is the only altruistic action he can perform. He realizes that his own growth and understanding cannot help others. Each human being must individually progress through the night of illusion to reach the dawn of truth.

What is the reward of one giving a lung to science in order to save his neighbour's life?

ANALYTICAL MEDITATION

Concentration on a mental process without any kind of distraction.

One must not mix this type of meditation with the one practiced by the intellectual using worldly sensations in an attempt to weigh the various components and understand the object of his attention. The wise man practices analytical meditation when he has reached the stage known as quiescence, i.e. the stage where he can focus his attention on command without being influenced by mental processes. Thus the wise man in a state of perfect quiescence uses the analytical power of the mind in its natural state. In this state of perfect tranquillity, he focuses on the different facets of the mental process without experiencing any distraction. This contemplation allows him to become intuitively aware of the essence of these mental phenomena. The ultimate insight of this analysis is the realization that what is created (matter) and what is not created (emptiness) result from each other and that when he unifies them; he is carried into a state of infinite consciousness, which is the essence of everything.

Must one reject or accept the material world in order to reach the truth?

ANCHOR POINT

Something specific used as an indicator.

The human being knows that he exists in a specific environment, he locates himself in space, he assesses himself and the others with the help of thousands, maybe millions of anchor points. Without these indicators he would not exist. Let us be conscious of ourselves for a moment. Where is this part of me that thinks? I have a small pain in the belly. I feel my feet on the ground. I see a car coming toward me. I am hungry. I am thirsty. Etc. These small analyses and interpretations (anchor points) are the basis of any reasons for the human being's existence. A great part of this awareness of being in our environment is unconscious; it is often something that we learned very early in life, right after birth. For example, it took us only a couple of months to locate our feet and hands, and learn what they were and what was their use. It is the same for everything in life. All this to say that a human being relies on an incalculable number of anchor points to exist in this world. Without them his assembly of aggregates would fall apart. This is what connects him to the material world and what makes the material world so real to him. The wise man in meditation detaches himself from the anchor points which ties him to the illusion. He focuses on one point within the emptiness of his being. When he reaches the right level of concentration, the anchor points vanish and he crosses the threshold into another world, another dimension. He enters reality, within which there is no anchor point, a reality that exists alone, unique and perfectly autonomous: the world of eternal truth.

Why would someone with no more anchor point, see the world disappear?

ANIMAL

Organized life form that does not search for spiritual improvement.

A being that has not sufficiently experienced life or suffering to begin to understand that there must be something else above the material world and that it must be possible to reach happiness. Beings who do not have a glimpse of the possibility of improvement for themselves and for others. These beings should follow the law of action/reaction for their own good.

One must stare at emptiness and watch as the veil of illusion is lifted. Deep reflections demonstrate that matter can only be a source of pain. Meditation and reflection prove that matter can only exist through the desire for sensation and possession. The goal is to transcend illusion.

How can an animal also be on the path to reality?

ANNIHILATION

Total disintegration and disappearance of a being or a thing.

The annihilation probably represents a human's greatest fear. Humans are afraid of dying, of being forgotten, of not having a place in the world anymore, of being reduced to nothingness. Most ordinary people state their worry about meditation on void as this: "What?, they say, if I do not think, I will not exist anymore. I cannot stop thinking." But after trying, they find out that what thinks inside of them is not "them" since after they stop thinking for some brief moment, they realize that they still exist, that they are somewhere inside their heads observing what is happening. They are present, without thinking, and can even watch thought-images appear and disappear without feeling that their integrity is in jeopardy. They learn the difference between what is created and what is not, between what is permanent and what is not. Because in order to finally understand that what is created and uncreated is one and unified, one must first acknowledge the nature of what is created and uncreated. The wise man does not fear annihilation and it will be without regret that one day he will abandon ALL that has any value for other human beings. He will abandon all to discover . . . no one knows what, but certainly not annihilation, rather a new form of consciousness.

What is left to the wise man after extinguishing the light of the "I"?

APPARITION

The act of something becoming perceptible by the senses.

Dreams, visions and apparitions are phenomena that many human beings take very seriously. They are believed to have a significance of their own, to contain messages of happiness or sorrow. Other people are convinced that they are revelations from superior beings, even from their god. The wise man is not fooled by images or sensations he experiences during his awakened, sleeping or meditating states. He knows that anything that can be felt or experienced in this world is part of the great illusion and has no reality whatsoever. The wise man does not waste time on what he sees or experiences, his concentration is on the void and nothing else. Emptiness is devoid of sensations since it is nothingness, thus no message is emitted and the body sensor mechanisms detect nothing. If nothing is picked up, there are no stimuli to trigger the analysis and interpretation process. The wise man meditates in quiescence. When an image appears in the sky of his meditation, he looks at it without even identifying it, without analyzing it, he is only the observer of an event occurring outside his range of analysis and about which he does not want to know anything. Only sudden illuminations are of some importance to the wise man and he knows that as soon as he realizes that he just had one, his analysis process has already contaminated the essence of the truth that seemed so pure and perfect. The truth, which was one, is now subjected to the influence of duality.

Does the mirror keep a memory of those gazing at it?

APPLICATION

The action of implementing the practice of knowledge.

In the dualistic world where large schools of knowledge abound, very often teachers forget that theoretical knowledge is an incomplete knowledge. Thus they form students for years by filling their heads with the history of those who acquired, by practice, the knowledge they wrote about in books. Often the credibility of those graduates rests only on a pile of papers proving their book knowledge of one profession or another. The adept will not make the error of the "false intellectual wise man" whose illusory wisdom was only a make-believe image transmitted by the thought process. To reach the ultimate truth, the true wise man researches, analyzes and meditates on each element of knowledge he encounters in books or with persons he communicates with. This is the only way that true wisdom can grow and finally bloom into fireworks of enlightenment. The sincere searcher is an investigator who leaves no question without an answer, and who, when he obtains an answer, puts it under the microscope of meditation to extract the essence of truth from it. The wise man uses his knowledge in order to reach the truth.

What is the difference between real and illusory wisdom?

ASPECT

Angle by which a person, a situation or a thing is perceived.

Human beings in general accept what they see, hear, taste, learn, etc. at first sight, without looking any further. They believe what they see and experience without asking any questions. But for someone in search of truth and attempting to tear the veil of illusion in order to face reality, it is very important to recognize things of the material world for what they are instead of for what they appear to be. The wise man lays his attention on water and acknowledges its state and composition, and then he focuses on an ice cube. This exercise allows him to become aware of the different aspects of a single thing. The same principle applies to all matter forming the universe. The wise man in deep meditation becomes intuitively aware that the illusion of our world is one of the many aspects of reality. When the wise man takes time to spiritually analyze the world surrounding him, he very quickly discovers that matter, as solid as it may seem, is in fact only an assembly of molecules, atoms and particles more or less linked together, and that it is one's point of view which lets one perceive solid as such. The wise man realizes that what people believe to be solid and real is in fact illusory and unreal. Matter is in constant transformation and deterioration; it does not endure. Matter emerges from nothingness and returns to it after a more or less extended period of time. But emptiness (void) is quite the opposite since it is stable, inalterable, infinite, and eternal. It does not come from anywhere and does not go anywhere.

When comparing matter and void, which is the most real?

ASPIRATION

Attraction that creates a will to obtain and possess.

Aspiration is the motor of the material world since sensations on which human activity is based produce only aspirations, desires. People desire to have what they judge good and wish to avoid what they consider bad, but they process both extremes with the same emotion. The adept setting foot on the path leading to the truth will see through his meditations that all his aspirations vanish without a trace because silence purifies all. The adept will be prudent since it is frequent for beginners to mistake their aspirations for faith if their concentration is not sufficiently powerful. They wish to reach the goal, they long for the state of quiescence, they aspire to . . . Beware: the wise man does no let his aspirations take control, he simply meditates, and in this state all aspirations are transcended. Surrounded by silence, the wise man closes all doors to sensations, without which there can be no aspirations or desires. In order to long for something, there must be an object of desire; without this object, calm emerges. Meditation transcends all illusory world aspirations.

Does reality aspire to illusion?

ATTACHMENT

A close union with a thing, being or state.

Meditation on nothingness has only one danger for its adept: the attachment to illusory phenomena experienced during meditation, and which he can interpret as realities. If he does so, he departs from the path and returns to illusory beliefs. Yet, it is easy to verify if a phenomenon is real, one only has to wait a while, because everything created is impermanent and has a tendency to disappear or to change, only truth is immutable and unalterable. One must not believe that quiescence is the final state. One must not believe that a revelation is the final illumination. One must not believe that mental imagery is real. Everything is illusory, only nothingness (emptiness) has passed the test of permanence. The wise one remains neutral during his meditation, he is only a passive observer influenced by nothing, everything comes and goes without altering his state of mind. Only neutral observation can lead to the anticipated objective. In the last moment prior to divine illumination, the observer must shed his consciousness and drop his cloak of existence in order to immerse himself into unity. He has reached the great and infinite light, where creation and non-creation become one. Everything returns to the source.

Is it possible to grasp the moment when a thought becomes matter?

ATTENTION

Consciousness more or less distracted. The degree of consciousness controlled by the will.

The adept realizes that his degree of consciousness is one of the keys allowing him to more or less open the door of total awakening. The observer will not attempt to suppress the thought process but rather will ignore it. If his attention is sufficiently concentrated, thoughts will be less and less important. The adept must maintain the integrity of his attention by not letting anything distract him. Totally conscious, relaxed and without any desire, he faces emptiness and observes. He must develop a power of attention absolutely unbreakable in order to reach his ultimate objective. This is the reason why silence is so important in meditation; any distraction lowers the attention level and takes precedence over the attempted result.

What is the major enemy of quiescence?

ATTRACTION

A pleasant feeling that prompts the desire to possess a person or a thing.

Here is an important criterion of the life of people walking with their eyes closed to reality. Whatever they see, whether a nice girls or a nice car, they want it. They do not realize that the more they possess the more they will lose. The ignorant spends his life repeating the same scenario: "I want this magnificent automobile, I am sure it will bring me happiness", then "Oh yes, I need this big house, I will be the envy of the neighbourhood", and so on endlessly. Then his nice car does not deliver the anticipated happiness, it is getting old so he starts longing for another one. His friend bought a bigger house than his, thus he ends up being the envying one. Then one day he realizes that all possessions bring only deception and unhappiness and that real happiness does not reside with worldly possessions. The wise man does not desire any worldly goods and that is why he is the one having all.

What is the cause of the obsession to possess?

AWAKENED

Someone who is not sleeping and who is alert to his environment.

One who knows full well that liberation exists and can be attained. The observer who can see thoughts forming and dissolving in his head, as birds sailing in the sky, without distracting his mental concentration. An awakened person knows that he has reached an important step for anyone trying to attain liberation. Soon even spectres caused by thoughts in formation and dissolution will disappear, and will leave only the perfect void of the mind at peace. This state is preliminary to liberation, the ultimate goal to reach.

What causes a thought to appear?

AWAKENING

The fact of coming out of unconsciousness.

It can be very difficult for anyone believing that he is the centre of the universe and the only possessor of truth to discover that it is not so. One of the first signs of the superior consciousness awakening is when a person begins to realize that absolute truth does not exist in this world and that logic rather than being universal is in fact individual. Thus that each and every human being's point of view is relatively correct. As consciousness expands, it becomes more and more obvious that each human being is right in his own material context. The adept realizes then that he lives in a dualistic universe where there are millions of more or less right and wrong answers to all possible questions. This discovery generates doubts about the reality of the created world. The adept embarks upon his quest for absolute truth, which through meditation will lead him to the ultimate answer and unlimited acknowledgement of everything that exists. A time will come when, wiser, he will understand that the created universe is in perfect balance and that what is created and uncreated form a unique whole. The wise man's acceptation is limitless because he no longer sees any differences between human beings. Meditation transcends the difference.

What is a dualistic truth?

AWAKENING PATH

The spiritual journey that each individual has to go on to reach reality.

Anyone who feels the hunger to know more about his being and the world only has to look around him to discover that he just set foot on the awakening path. All of a sudden, he will find a score of literature on the subject, teaching schools and isolated beings walking the path leading to the light of the infinite truth. This is a long and often arduous road, which represents the greatest challenge to a human being. At the end of the path, the adept will be confronted with the ultimate goal of the universe. He will always find answers to his questions, whether in a book, from an acquaintance or in his meditations. One only has to ask a question, do the necessary actions to obtain the answer and the answer will inevitably come: this is a universal law. In the beginning the adept will try to find what his personal road will be, how he will reach the objective. The goal is the same for all, but the paths leading to it are countless. And that is because, if the assemblies of aggregates that form human beings are all different, the mind is the same for all. The adept will search, study and meditate in order to find his own path.

Why does meditation lead to the truth?

AWARENESS

The action of being attentive to a person, a situation or a thing.

The adept disciplines himself to become constantly aware in his environment. First of all, his aim is never to do one thing while thinking about another, then to be continuously conscious, always in a position to state, "I am present". The adept, conscious of being present, mediates. In this state his mind is a spectator listening to everything happening and watching the world through the searcher's physical eyes without analyzing anything. The adept (observer) attends to the progress of his life and to the world's tribulations. He is able to detach himself from the world while feeling totally integrated into it. The observer watches the show of aggregates managing the human machine. He realizes the unreality of creation and the reality of this immutable observer who is conscious and watches without resting, without ever analyzing or defining anything. The one watching is not the one thinking, and the one thinking is not the observer. The one watching is the observer who in reality is consciousness, eternal, infinite and omniscient.

Why is the void identifying itself to the dreams it created?

B

BAD

The negative side of the good/bad duality. Any action not following the present trends and beliefs of a dualistic society.

Any thought or action that does not promote the realization of truth. Bad, as its counterpart good, cannot exist alone. Bad without good does not exist since in order to assess what is bad and what is good one must compare it to its opposite. The wise man realizes that bad is related to the duality of which it is part and as soon as silence takes precedence, duality disappears and is replaced by unity. An action or a thought is only bad for the searcher if it impedes progress on the road to enlightenment.

Why is one responsible for the love he receives?

BECOME (TO)

To go from one state to another by identifying with it.

The material world exists because the uncreated mind is identifying with created things, the mind believes to be matter. It is trapped by emotions and feelings of the created world. This is the reason why the dualistic world in which we live exists as it is and why we are what we are, sparks of uncreated consciousness that have become feelings interpreted by an imaginary analysis mechanism called the brain. We forgot our origin and our prime state. We are orphans lost in an illusory world. Meditation allows to separate reality from illusion and unveil our true uncreated nature. We are like distracted scientists who have become the subject of the experiment. When the silence takes over and thoughts stop throwing make-believe powder in the eyes of the observer, the observer sees the material world for what it is, a projection on the screen of absolute emptiness. Meditation reveals that the observer is the creator of the observed and that they ultimately form one single being. The wise man sets aside emotions and intellectual interpretations, opens his wings of light and rises above illusion.

Why would the one mind incomplete without its creation?

BEHAVIOUR

The way a being acts, as seen by someone else.

For humankind in general, behaviour is used to demonstrate something particular, to make a statement, by either shocking, attracting the attention of or puzzling the immediate social environment. The human being, sleeping the sleep of ignorance, totally identifies to his behaviour. The wise one knows that the behaviour of all, as well as his, is generated by the interaction of various aggregates forming a being. In a world where one's behaviour influences that of another, it is important for the wise man to initiate positive actions which will generate in time their own progeny of good actions. The wise man knows that it is easier to influence the world through example rather than with words. This is why his behaviour is humble and his objective lofty. He abandons his arrogance and gives his wisdom, gathered from deep meditations, the opportunity to prevail. Realizing how unimportant other people's opinion is regarding his behaviour, the wise man continues to progress on the path leading to his personal objective without taking it into account. His only concern is to reach his goal and to leave a sufficient amount of clues in his wake for others to follow his tracks and discover the path leading to the great liberation, the one that opens the door to eternity.

What is the result of greatness of pride and smallness of wisdom?

BENEFITS

The results that a person can enjoy.

Whatever the reasons why someone practices meditation, he will immediately gain positive results. Meditation induces a deep relaxation of the whole being, both at the physical and mental level. Stress and anxiety that are omnipresent in our modern times are significantly reduced. The cardiac rhythm is slowed down to allow the heart to take a small and well-deserved rest. Respiration is also slowed down to give a chance to the lungs to recuperate. Generally speaking, meditation seems to promote the immune system and allows it to better defend the body against disease. Furthermore, meditation changes the vision of the world of any sincere adept. It permits him to become detached from the material world, which in turn allows him to live while giving less importance to material things. He will be more tolerant toward himself, his close ones and the others, including society as a whole. An important part of human sorrow comes from the fact that human beings are totally confused because they try to pay attention to too many things at the same time. The practice of meditation gives the adept the opportunity to become unified by concentrating on one single thing at a time for a short period of time. Meditation puts a mocking smile on the lips of anyone who turns his gaze inside, since he realizes that there is nothing really serious in this world. And if the adept so wishes, he can extend the experience to reach illumination, and the all-explaining truth.

Why is it preferable to look for the answer to a question at its source?

BENEVOLENCE

A feeling that encourages one to desire good for others.

Benevolence is a well-known feeling to searchers who, understanding human nature, cannot abstain from compassion for their situation. The more a person progresses on the path to truth, the more his empathy increases for all that exists in the universe, and especially for human beings who are persisting so tenaciously in creating their own problems and sorrow. The adept realizes that all the sorrow in the world come from the need to possess illusory things. People only have one reason to want to hurt others, and that is their desire to possess what others have. When the adept transcends this need, his level of benevolence toward his neighbours climbs sharply. The wise man desires nothing, wishes only good to all without exception. He realizes that the greatest service he can render to humankind is to share his experience, which allowed him to eliminate all forms of material ambition. No more illusory ambitions and the doors of peace open wide. The wise man bathes in the light of quiescence, what else could he wish for?

What is the difference between benevolence and attachment?

BEYOND

Superior to a state known to be normal.

People who live their existence satisfied with what they extract from their physical sensations, cannot even imagine that states superior to theirs can exist. This is why the fish that does not believe that other beings can live in an environment other than liquid, remains a fish. On the other hand, the adept is convinced that there are conditions of beingness superior to the human being, just waiting to be conquered. This is why his quest is focussed on objectives that have nothing to do with the material world. He is not looking for anything that could attach him even more to the vainglory brought by the sensuous state. He reaches beyond nature, trying to surpass identification; he wants to knock through the background canvas of his limited world to finally contemplate the unlimited space of reality. In meditation, he realizes this new superior state of beingness. He works at his own transformation in order to acquire the necessary characteristics for his survival in this new environment, as once long ago some fish had to mutate to be able to leave their water element and walk on the earth. The wise man knows that one day in the future he will not be exactly what we recognize as a human being, but something more. A being who will have transcended identification, personality and who, enabled by a superior level of consciousness, will realize the universe's instantaneity and the beginning of a new series of evolutionary experiences.

Why are humans pretentious when they state that they are the final product of evolution?

BLOCK

An obsession preventing a being from progressing.

The first step on the path of truth consists in reaching the inner silence. In order to reach his goal, the adept must first practice the elimination of thoughts as soon as they appear. Some adepts do not succeed in going any farther than this stage simply because they develop a mental block. They become obsessed with this task and they cannot see beyond it, do not foresee any solution to the problem. They are prisoners of a vicious circle where the more they try to eliminate thoughts the more their efforts participate to the creation of even more thoughts. This is a state of total block, a trap in which the adept can stagnate and run in circles indefinitely. Thus all adepts must understand, before developing a block, that the elimination of thoughts will never allow them to reach quiescence. However, they will also recognize that the exercise is necessary for them to experience and understand the nature and behaviour of thoughts. As soon as the adept feels the slightest rise of an obsession, he will meditate on the inseparable union of the eliminator (himself) and the eliminated (thoughts) to understand that the solution is to let thoughts go their own way while the observer observes in total indifference. Without effort, the adept will reach total indifference about the illusory phenomena.

Why is the answer an integral part of the question?

BODY

A biological assembly, which forms a living being.

The body is composed of genetic aggregates (modified by interactions) passed on by all his ancestors. The oldest genes are less pure and have less influence on the actual biological machine formation because they are diluted. We must realize that aggregates that exists in a person's genealogy have interacted with one another to form new and transformed aggregates, which serve as a base for the present body. They determine the original characteristics of a being. This type of aggregates also acts upon the brain and orders it to accomplish some tasks judged necessary or essential. One of these aggregates will often cause a dominant intellectual aggregate to back off until its task is completed before letting the dominant aggregate take its place again at the command station. When you are hungry, for example, an intellectual aggregate may delay nourishment for some time but not for long. It is the same with sex, body temperature, natural functions, etc. The brain interprets the dominant aggregate's sensation, whether it is intellectual or biological, and executes the necessary actions to relieve it. Biological aggregates dominate intellectual aggregates when it comes to body survival and well-being. It is possible to discipline these less sophisticated aggregates, although it is totally impossible to eliminate them because some of their functions are essential to the body's survival. The wise man maintains a life style that keeps his body in a good state, in order to fulfill the needs related to his spiritual research. It is not recommended to be too hard or too gentle on the body: a fair balance will assist spiritual equilibrium.

What would the physical machine become without the mind?

BONDAGE

The condition of being entirely dominated.

A human being thinks that he is free to think and do whatever he likes. Yet, without knowing it, he is a prisoner of his state. He is captive of, and bonded to, his sensations and interpretations of the material world. When he looks, he has to explain what he sees, when he hears he must comment on the sounds he perceives, and when he feels something he is driven to give it an explanation. He does not tolerate the unknown or the unexplained; anything not identified represents a danger, a threat. He is forced to classify everything in his great mental book. He has no choice since, as soon as something unknown to him occurs, he feels in danger, and insecurity sets in. Security will only come back after the unknown has been analysed and interpreted as presenting no danger. Thus the human is a slave of matter since matter forces him to acknowledge it, to give it a name and file it among other known things. Each sensation is related to a specific thing. The whole universe's existence is based on the interpretation we make of it. To the wise man in meditation with all perception doors closed, the material world disappears and the infinite emptiness of the uncreated is revealed. This is a world where nothing is interpreted because there is nothing to be interpreted. The wise man is liberated from slavery when he opens his eyes on the void of truth and recognizes reality.

Does a bird have the same appearance for everyone?

BOREDOM

Despondency due to a great sadness.

People are bored when they do not have what they desire. They are sad as soon as they feel the lack of something or a void. In fact, they are bored because they do not do well what they are doing. They try to complete a task while thinking about something else they believe to be more interesting or pleasant than what they are currently doing. They miss a loved one because while this person is away they are not doing what they should be doing. They dream about the presence of the other. The wise man does not get bored because he performs all he does from the humblest task to the most glorious one, consciously. He focuses on each movement or word and he moves or speaks as perfectly as he can, while being as present as possible. For him, each action is all-important. When he drinks a glass of water, he drinks a glass of water, he thinks of nothing else. When he communicates with someone, he listens with all his senses then answers back using all his wisdom and consciousness. He does not relive a past experience and does not prepare an answer while the other is still speaking. When he walks, he walks, when he meditates, he meditates.

The wise man does what he is doing, no more, no less. He is PRESENT in space and time. He knows that someone who does not live the present moment does not live at all. As long as the wise man is aware of being present he meditates. He carries on his work of research and contemplation.

Why is it a mistake to see the material world disappear?

BRAIN

Electro-biological mechanism that performs the analysis of perceived sensations.

The brain is only a machine that serves as a biological support for the intellectual aggregates, which form someone's personality. This mechanism can analyze and interpret sensations, then set the body in action. In other words, the brain is the central command used by aggregates to act upon their physical environment. A slightly curious being quickly understands this. After a moment of inner attention he notices that the swirling thoughts in his head are constantly confronting one another, and all of a sudden one takes over. He thinks he just took a decision. The unenlightened human being is certain that he is the sole master of his life, his decisions and actions. The aggregates without a brain and a body cannot produce actions-reactions in the created universe. The wise one knows that the body and brain are driven to meditate by the most evolved aggregates, which form his overall illusory being. He also knows that the brain and aggregates are an integral part of the illusory world and that they will disappear, absorbed by the initiating nothingness, leaving only a spark of truth.

Who is the king of idiots?

BREATHING

The act that consists of inspiring air into the lungs, then to expire it.

The rhythm and depth of breathing reflect a person's mental state. Each emotion, thought or feeling is accompanied by a particular breathing. Anger not only produces an inflamed state of mind, but also a harsh and difficult breathing. On the other hand, breathing can influence one's mood. This is quite easy to verify, just wait for a moment or a situation that makes you impatient, excited or aggressive, become aware of this fact, then take deep breaths. After a few minutes you will feel the calm invade you. The adept who has trouble finding calm will use his breathing to reach that state. He focuses on it, then breathes naturally without forcing the intake or the outtake. The wise man's breathing in deep meditation is practically imperceptible because thoughts (the makers of emotions) have ceased to appear and disappear and no more affect the observer. Your breathing pattern is the mirror of your state of mind.

How can one control the wind as he controls his breath?

C

CAPABILITY

The possibility to do something.

All human beings should be equal on the pretence that all have the same capabilities. People cry about discrimination and injustice when they believe they are not treated with justice. These manifestations are the irrefutable proof that most human beings are sincerely convinced that they are different and unequal, because other wise their actions would be useless. Each individual believes he is the centre of the universe, the best, and all others are either equal or inferior to him. It is impossible for him, and for that matter for everyone, to recognize someone more evolved than they are. The wise man watches the world show from the top of his mountain of silence where he analyzes and studies the mechanics of illusion and enjoys the illumination of eternal reality. His vision of the world is clear; he understands that as long as a being lives according to duality parameters, there can only be inequality, injustice, discrimination, etc., that all can only be sorrow. The ignorant interprets the world with capacities limited by the veil of illusion. When the wise one looks upon the world beyond duality, he sees only emptiness (reality) and when he focuses on the dualistic world he sees only illusion (unreality). But he realizes that one is the reflection of the other.

Where are one hundred blind persons going when led by one of their own?

CAUSE

The action that triggers a reaction.

Most people do not believe that the actions they take are the source of their happiness or sorrow. They abdicate their responsibility and do not realize that they are the prime cause of what they were in the past, are today and will be in the future. Each human being is the master of his own destiny; no one can penetrate the realm of the individual thought. The one taking the final decision is always the cause of the reaction. The wise man acknowledges his responsibilities toward himself and toward the universe. He is aware of being his own master and to be the one who makes the final decisions. He does not yield to the influence of anything or anyone. In deep meditation he comes in contact with the universal consciousness and realizes then that he is the cause of everything, even the cause of creation itself. The large is in the small as the small is in the large, the individual mind is in the universal mind and vice versa, the observer is at the origin of creation's emergence and immersion into the great infinite reality. The universe is a thought.

What would be the definition of a good cause?

CELL

A place of small dimension where someone is isolated and kept prisoner.

A human being is imprisoned in his body, which like a prison cell prevents him from exploring his true nature and that of everything surrounding him. He is also a prisoner of his feelings to which, although they send him an erroneous vision of the world, he hangs on as cell bars, by accepting illusion for reality. Yet, his cell has a door, which opens up to freedom.

Silence is the way allowing him to leave the isolation of the emotional self and penetrate into reality where everything is now. He would only have to extend his hand to grasp the key to this door that is meditation and use it to free himself. But, as long as the fire of passion flares in his veins, he will look at the world from his cell, regretting yesterday and waiting for tomorrow to accomplish no more than today. The wise man in deep meditation breaks down the wall of his emotions and realizes that reality in not what his senses would lead him to believe. He walks free of illusory attachment and faces directly the light of eternal truth.

Why do humans build their own prison?

CENTRE

Central point of a given space.

The centre is the awareness (attention) that focuses on a point inside the head. The fact of intensely focusing one's attention on a particular point reduces distractions produced by thoughts emerging from nothingness. After a certain period of meditation, the focused point tends to disappear and leave only the point of consciousness focused on itself. The observer is then conscious of his existence as well as of that of an infinite emptiness surrounding him and of which he knows he is a part. The centre is reached. From this state, the consciousness has a circular vision of the limitless emptiness of nothingness. This emptiness is even more impressive than what we contemplate when we raise our head to the sky on a clear night. The inner emptiness is devoid of any characteristics. The consciousness point is suspended in the absolute emptiness without thought process or any possibility to act; its only quality is observation, of the uncreated, of what is without duality and instability. The observer contemplates reality as it is. This state can be more or less perfect according to the number and importance of the distractions affecting concentration's harmony. The wise man's goal is to achieve a perfect quiescence, an unalterable centre point. From inner peace emerge revelations, the light of truth.

Why is it that each human being believes he is the centre of the universe?

CENTRE PATH

The road that leads to liberation without the help of extremes.

On the one hand, someone obsessed with illusion bears an insatiable desire for created things. On the other hand, the trap of an insatiable desire for uncreated things snares someone with too strong a desire to reach liberation. Both these beings suffer from the same problem, extremism. Anyone with too strong a desire is a prisoner of this desire, whether it is for a thing, an idea, a dream or anything else. The prison is not the object of the desire, the desire itself is. Seen differently, at the other extreme of someone who desires all that is material may be someone obsessed with possessing nothing. He has no unhealthy desire to have anything of his own. This is another aspect of extremism. The adept who understands the process of the search for truth and liberation from the illusion travels between the extremes of have and have not. He progresses on a tight rope in perfect balance, neutral. He observes his goal at the other end of the rope. His quest is a balancing act between two worlds, which form one single unit.

How could the mental picture the infinity of unity?

CHARGE

The amount of reactions that have not yet occurred produced by present and past thoughts and actions.

The mass of people who ignore the universal laws do not know that each and everyone of their thoughts and actions cause a transformation of their immediate and far-off environment. Thus, when a person performs an action, this action influences his close circle of relations, which in turn influences his social environment. And this goes on indefinitely. The original action, as a stone thrown to the sky, returns to its source bearing good or bad effects. If the thought or action was bad, the return is negative, if it was good, the reaction is positive. The result of what a person thinks or does can take a more or less extended period of time before surfacing, but it is certain that the reaction will occur at some point. Thus, the charge of a person is more or less important and more or less positive or negative. This charge greatly influences the life style of a particular individual. The wise man takes care not to initiate negative thoughts or actions since he knows that by doing so he harms others and himself. Furthermore, in meditation he acknowledges that all other individuals who form the world are also part of himself in the great and eternal void. The wise one understands that only those who do not know what they are doing can do things to harm others. They do not understand that they hurt themselves in the process.

Why will a thief pay for his crime even if he is not caught?

CHARITY

An action with an objective to help others.

Any form of charity serves as a positive energy accumulator, meaning that any action that has good as its goal will shed beneficent feedback on this particular individual and his surroundings. Charity is one of the poles of our dualistic universe. It is a part of its positive side. Thousands, maybe millions of people devote their time to helping their neighbours improve their lot, to live more comfortably or to be a little less miserable. And these, in turn, accumulate a positive energy charge that has beneficial effects on the whole humanity, a counterweight to the negative actions of others. A universe that would be only positive (good) or only negative (bad) would fall apart, **duality** itself keeps it together. The wise one understands and appreciates the importance of any form of charity toward others, but he realizes that this virtue is also part of the duality, thus an illusion. For him, the greatest act of charity to the world is to ensure that the path leading to the liberation from the yoke of matter is always obviously present for those with the desire to go from the sorrow of illusion to the peace and calm of reality. This allows the forever elimination of illusory injustice and unhappiness that were affecting them. The wise man has realized that only meditation can cure the disease of ignorance. When the patient opens his eyes, he sees the importance of worldly things melting in the sun of reality.

What is the purification effect of the void?

CHASTITY

A behaviour devoid of sexual activities.

A small sentence «Sex is leading the world», highlights a great truth in human behaviour. But sex is good, it is a very good thing, it is even an essential behaviour for the survival of the race. Generally speaking, human beings have little to say, since when glands give the orders, humans execute. The so-called modern nations can make a game, an attraction, a product, etc. out of sex, but it will always remain that reproduction is the original essence of two beings physically getting close to each other. In order to survive, humanity must reproduce itself and to do so people must copulate. The wise man is preoccupied when he sees a people ceasing or nearly ceasing to reproduce itself as it is now the case in industrialized countries, where they succeeded in finding a way to keep the pleasure of the action while denying the reproduction. The wise one recognizes sex for what it is and can accept or refuse to practice it at will. But he also knows that it is not constructive to inhibit a primary impulse and that this energy can only be used for other purposes after the primal urge has been transcended. The wise man alone can determine if it is preferable to continue or to cease sexual practice. The act in itself is positive as long as it does not become detrimental to the search for truth.

Why would a complete people attempt global suicide?

COLLECTIVE PAST

Everything that happened in the universe, including the present moment.

All elements and aggregates that form the present. The whole universe assembly of thoughts and actions forming the present. The universal actual trends are the result of all that is past. The universe is a machine that continuously amplifies and complexities itself. The wise one realizes that he is also the result of the collective past, in addition of his own cumulated past. He acknowledges that his liberation in the present will impact on the whole universe and that the future will be that much better and less confused. The adept knows that he owes his capacity to see the path of truth and to work toward his liberation to the research, reflection and meditation of his ancestors. The past is responsible for all present sadness and happiness.

How can one change the past?

COMMITMENT

The action to compel oneself to honour an agreement involving one or several persons.

Most agreements do not carry much weight for human beings. They agree one day to one thing and disagree the next. But this is normal, since it is practically impossible to make an agreement endure in a world where everything changes constantly. The cause of an agreement never stops changing. When the reason for an agreement is modified to the point where it does not exist anymore, there is no point in honouring it. For example, two individuals promise to live together on the premise that they love each other today and will continue to do so as long as they live. If both partners are not ready and conscious that they will have to renew their affinity to one another every day from now on, the agreement will soon be broken. A commitment can only last in our world if adjusts to the changes that obligatorily alter the initial reasons for the commitment. The wise man sets a foot in the illusory world and the other in reality. From this vantage point he observes the absence of durability or permanence of all that exists in the material world. Drawing strength from this observation, he commits himself to incessantly work toward an ever-deeper understanding of the illusory mechanisms and to meditate on the permanence and immutability of reality. The closer the wise man comes to the truth, thus reality, the more he is capable of honouring his commitment toward himself and humanity. His transformation goes from a finite environment to the infinite one.

What is the goal of any commitment?

COMMUNICATION

The action of exchanging information.

Communication can be divided into three distinct levels. A) Anyone blinded by illusion does not really practice communication. When the wise one observes them, he becomes aware that they do not listen to each other since they talk simultaneously. They do not communicate; they use one another as a sounding board for their own words. In fact they talk to themselves. If we could stop them for a moment to ask them what the other has just said, they would be surprised to realize that they do not know. Of course, they only had ears for their own discourse. B) The adept awakened to the universal law recognizes the basic principles of communication: 1. a desire to send a message, 2. the emission of the message, 3. the reception of the message by another party, and 4. the understanding of the message by the other party. Without these four factors there is no communication. This is why the adept listens, understands the message received in order to form his own answer and starts another cycle of communication the other way. The assembly of these cycles from one person to another represents communication. C. Then, there is the great and ultimate communication that can be reached through meditation. The wise one closes the door on the illusory world and contemplates the emptiness of reality. In fact he places himself in a receptive state and when the nature of the observer becomes sufficiently similar to reality, communication is established at a superior level. The liberated wise man has reached the highest level of communication imaginable, he has demolished the wall between reality and illusion. He is now the transmitter and the receiver.

How can thoughts make anyone deaf?

COMPARISON

The evaluation of one thing by looking for similarities or differences with another.

A human being would not survive long if he was suddenly deprived of his capacity to compare one thing with another. This is what allows him to recognize what is dangerous from what is not, what is tall or small, nice or ugly, green or red, good or bad, hard or soft, high or low, edible or poisonous, etc. Life is entirely based upon this primary capacity to analyze, which allows thinking beings to sort things. People also recognize what they judge real and unreal. For them, when they can touch, smell, see or hear something, they consider it real. But they do not realize that they can smell, touch, taste, bite, and eat these illusory things only because they too are part of the illusion. When a wise man looks upon the world and compares things, he soon realizes their impermanence. Nothing lasts. But when he establishes the inner silence and contemplates emptiness, he is confronted with something that never changes, and which he acknowledges as real because of its permanence. It is by comparing reality with creation that the wise man realizes that the latter is illusion.

Why can't comparison exist in reality?

COMPASSION

A desire to share other people's problems and sufferings.

Meditation on nothingness, and focussing on emptiness allow the adept to perceive the world as it is. During a revelation he is submerged in bliss, and in a moment of such intensity he touches, with his mind, the reality of what does and does not exist. He acknowledges the illusory world and the ultimate reality of eternal nothingness. He knows that humankind is a reality that ignores itself. When he tries to find the difference between himself and any other individual, he finds none. He only finds that he is humankind and humankind is he. He feels like an almost imperceptible point of light shining in the night of humankind's ignorance. When he sets his eyes upon humankind he sympathizes with it, acknowledging that it never stops running around trying to catch its tail. The role of any individual is to awaken himself to reality and, once this objective is fulfilled, to leave the path open and to assist anyone who opens his eyes on a world that does not satisfy him anymore.

Why is it that human beings believe they are alien to reality?

COMPOSED

All that includes more than one element. All that is material.

The material world is composed of multiplicities. No one should doubt that multiplicity is the source of all of humanity's problems. The wise man searches for the source of confusion by contemplating the void within him. Element by element, the observer goes back to the source of all things, where nothing exists but the light of reality.

What happens to the stream water when it flows away from its source?

COMPREHENSION

To have a clear idea of the composition and operation of a thing.

It is impossible, for someone who does not practice meditation, to fully understand the essence of the First Principle, of the created and uncreated. This is impossible because the illusory comprehension process, using analysis as a clarifying tool, is a dualistic phenomenon that cannot make an exact duplicate of what is impossible to express with words and pictures. Even a scholar who spent his life in books studying the greatest masters' researches and realizations cannot grasp what he did not experience himself outside of the illusion. Only the practice of meditation allows to reach the sublime confrontation with the First Principle. Realization can only come from the state of reality. The essence of truth is inaccessible to the material world speculations. Meditation is the discipline that leads directly to the ultimate reality. When nothing is done, nothing gets done.

How can one touch nothingness with the tip of one's fingers?

CONCENTRATION

The focus of attention on a physical or mental point.

Concentration allows the observer to focus his attention and to eliminate every distraction. The control of the mental process is essential to reach quiescence, which is the first step on the road to liberation. The adept, after focusing on a point inside his head, often experiences difficulty keeping mental emptiness. He is distracted by thoughts that keep coming and going. When that happens, he can become conscious of his breathing while keeping his concentration on the focused point. This helps stabilize the attention by creating a second anchor point. During the day, the adept must try to remain present during each and everyone of his actions and to become aware of his breathing every time he feels his attention wandering; he will instantly feel his concentration tightening. But this is not a breathing exercise, the adept must not alter his normal respiratory rhythm or volume.

The process is only to become conscious of the respiratory mechanism.

Why is it so difficult to concentrate on a single thing?

CONCENTRATION ON AN OBJECT

Concentration of the attention on an object placed in front of the observer.

The adept can use an object placed in front of him to discipline his mind not to be distracted by the thought process. This technique allows him to reach the level of concentration required in order for the essence of truth to appear. In the silence acquired by concentration, the observer becomes aware of the truth. Procedure: With his body in a comfortable position, but not conducive to sleep, the adept focuses on an object which he previously placed at about 1m to 1.5m in front of him. It is preferable to use a simple object such as a small ball, rock or piece of wood. A complex object could induce the observer to define its nature, which is to be avoided. The adept focuses on the object, without ocular tension, and does not let himself be distracted by anything else. Very quickly, he will be isolated and totally alone with the object of his concentration. It is important for the adept not to become the object. The adept must be present in his head at all times while focusing on the concentration point. He will chase any parasite thought attempting to invade his concentration. After a while the object will disappear and leave only pure consciousness resting in the total silence of divine essence. Slowly, the mechanisms of the great cosmic machine will become more comprehensible for the one who, without ever getting tired, focuses his attention on the inner silence.

Why is emptiness the essence of human beings?

CONCENTRATION ON EMPTINESS

The attention that focuses on the internal emptiness.

To reach the state of mental rest required for illumination or in order to become aware of reality, the adept has at his disposal several attention concentration disciplines. One of them is the concentration on emptiness. This void exists within each human being, but most of the time it is not perceived because of distractions generated by the outside world and thoughts process. Procedure: With his body in a comfortable position, but not conducive to sleep, the adept focuses his attention on a point in his head, disregarding anything else. He does not think, does not analyze, does not meditate, he is just there focused on the fictive inner point. The adept eliminates all parasite thoughts one after the other as they come up. If he is distracted and dragged along by a train of thoughts, as soon as he realizes it, he will slowly, without irritation or fatigue bring his attention back to the initial concentration. After a while, the adept will be able to ignore the thoughts, to let them do their illusory dance and remain focused on his concentration point. He will slowly develop the art of absolute silence, where the mind assumes its natural state, invulnerable to the distractions of the thought process. In this state, awareness, and finally the ultimate truth, will come to the surface.

Is silence the result of all the noise in the universe?

CONCENTRATION ON THE BREATHING

To concentrate the attention on inhaling and exhaling.

Breathing can be used as a tool to discipline the thought process and allow the adept to reach a level of concentration required for him to become aware first of some universe fundamental truths and then of the ultimate truth on which the creation rests. Procedure: With his body in a comfortable position, but not conducive to sleep, the adept becomes slowly conscious of his breathing rhythm. He acknowledges the inhalation and the exhalation without attempting in any way to modify the natural progress of this vital function. Then he begins counting one complete breathing after another disregarding anything else. He is present in his head and his other point of concentration is his breathing. He does not let any thought destroy his concentration. He ignores them. If the adept is distracted by a parasite thought or if he forgets to count, he will bring back his attention, slowly and without irritation, to his breathing and will start counting again from zero. The adept must not let himself be invaded by his breathing; he must remain present in his head throughout the exercise. After a while, it will be possible for the adept to stop the breathing exercise and to only keep his presence in his head. The absolute silence is the mind's natural state. When the mind is no longer distracted by the illusions of the created world, it comes in direct contact with its source and then the adept becomes aware of the truth.

Is emptiness the result of all that exists in the universe?

CONCEPTION

The formation of a thought or idea. The capacity to imagine.

It is impossible to conceive anything else than the mind. Everything we look at, everything we see, imagine or think comes from the mind and nowhere else. The whole created universe and what it contains is part of the mind and cannot be separated from it. Everything that exists emerges from the mind and the mind is perfectly empty. Here we are confronted with the deepest paradox ever imagined by humankind. If all that exists is mind, thus nothing else than mind exists. Even the wise man's goal has no reality since realization is a dualistic concept, it does not exist. What will the wise one find at the end of his quest? He will encounter reality for what it is and he will acknowledge it only at the moment of immersion. Only experience makes it possible to grasp the essence of reality. It is impossible for the individual mind to confront the infinite mind (First Principle) while retaining its individuality. Let us recall the fact that the individual consciousness is only illusion as is the rest of the created world, thus it emerges from the First Principle where it will return. The wise man acknowledges the material world and the uncreated world for what they are and, as an acrobat on a steel wire, balances his act of faith with his willpower. Only an ignorant can deny the presence of a mind superior to the one centred in all human beings.

How long will it take for a wise one to open the mind of a silly person to reality?

CONFUSION

The state of what is perplexed, impossible to define. The normal mental state of humankind.

No one knows what is really good or bad. Everyone has his own logic, his own solutions to problems. Consensus is practically impossible and when it occurs it never lasts for very long. Everyone is king of his little kingdom and ignores his social as well as natural environment. When one states that something is black, thousands rise to say that it is white, and the rest pretend that it is rather grey. Understanding and harmony is impossible in a dualistic universe since it is continuously in transformation, nothing is stable. Nothing can really be true when everything balances between positive and negative. Confusion covers this world as clouds on a rainy day. The thought process is the prime factor of confusion, thus the adept must bypass this avalanche of sensations by developing an unbreakable power of concentration. Then he can rise above confusion and visit the stable and permanent void within.

Why isn't logic universal?

CONQUEROR

Someone who does not hesitate to fight to acquire what he wants.

The conqueror is the one who does not rely on anyone to fulfill his goal and who, without hesitation, declares war on what he wants to defeat. This being realizes that masters, gods and saviours are only crutches invented by those unable to look truth in the face. The conqueror with a valiant heart knows that he can only rely on himself since no one else will walk the road for him. At truth's door, a being is entirely alone and therefore the fate of the entire universe rests on his shoulders. The paths and maps of ancient illuminated beings, although some are almost unreadable, are the only valuable tools the awakened being can use in his conquest. No form of grace or salvation, any sacrifice, self-denial or virtue can lead the searcher to the ultimate goal. Only individual efforts and perseverance in focusing the attention on nothingness can bear the fruits of infinite light. The conqueror does not think of himself as weak, defenceless or limited. On the contrary, he knows that he is the creator of the universe, the king of the world and the dictator of his own beingness. He is conscious of the futility of trying to conquer the world while not being able to control oneself. The wise man is attacking his most important enemy, HIMSELF. He analyzes it, dissects it, and criticizes each component to finally understand that it is only an illusory concept. The great conqueror slowly enlarges his dominion until one day it extends from the shore of illusion to the end of reality.

Why is it that the winner of a battle, instead of freeing himself from an enemy, attaches himself to a victory?

CONQUEST

The domination of a state, a being or a thing.

The adept during his long journey toward the light of truth must conquer four levels of knowledge and wisdom that will allow him to locate himself on the path. First he will reach the state of quiescence. This is the state where the adept realizes the inner silence, pure and unaltered by the never-ending flow of thoughts appearing and disappearing in the sky of mental emptiness. Quiescence is considered as the foundation upon which the adept can build his castle of reality. The adept will then learn how to grow from the experiences occurring on the path. After considering some of them as negative to his evolution, the adept realizes that anything appearing or disappearing on the path is part of the created, of the illusion, of all, thus nothing is real and truly negative or positive. From then on, he can stop focussing uselessly on these illusory phenomena and carry on his quest in a state of total indifference. After a while, he learns how to differentiate various experiences, recognize his degree of fervour and identify the stage he has reached on the path. Finally, he will learn to recognize that his accomplishments have allowed him to continue working uselessly toward a goal already attained.

Must the wise one abandon his mean of transportation once the destination is reached?

CONSCIOUSNESS

The acknowledgement of one's own existence.

The human being realizes that he is a living entity. However to be totally conscious of himself in the created world he must be able to become conscious of his surroundings. During his whole life, he tries to remain what he thinks he is, and he resists and often rejects changes, whether inside of him or outside. He is afraid to lose his identity. He fears "non-beingness". Yet, he can only be conscious in the actual moment, thus he is only conscious of what he is immediately, now, and not of what he was yesterday or will be tomorrow. He wants to believe that he does not really change, that he is always the same. In fact, he is always the same in eternal transformation. The consciousness line is immaterial and eternal. Only recall mechanisms are illusory and impermanent. The human being is in constant transformation whether he wants it or not. The aggregates that form him continually change and always make him a renewed being, always conscious of being in the present. Each child is conscious of what he is and does not want to change and each adult is aware of what he is and does not want to change either. In spite of this, they are both different from one moment to the next. The wise man looks upon experiences happening and realizes the futility of identity.

Is the wise man looking at the river, conscious of being as well the river watching a wise man on its shore?

CONSCIOUSNESS IN TIME

Consciousness of the world at different moments in the life of a being.

The illusory consciousness of a human being cannot be the same from one moment to the next. A human being changes from one minute to the next, from one day to the next. He acquires new knowledge. He lives new experiences. His whole personality (illusory consciousness) is altered. A twenty year-old person will not have at 50 the same consciousness and vision of the world as he has now. Yet this being will continue stating, "I see things this way and this is the truth", and "This is how I understand the world and I am right". The adept becomes aware that his perception of the world constantly changes, thus he cannot trust it. He knows that what he believes and understands today will be seen and understood differently tomorrow. The consciousness (attention) of the wise man in deep meditation never changes, it is always the same and cannot be modified, it is EMPTY of what could destroy its unity. Even truths emerging from this void stay pure for only a moment before being altered by the duality of the illusory world. The wise one believes only in absolute emptiness.

What is the difference between illusory consciousness and real consciousness?

CONTEMPLATION

The intense observation of some thing without intellectual analysis.

Within the world of ignorance, people usually admire artistic beauty, whether it is musical or visual. They are enraptured with the originality, depth, harmony, refinement of what they see, hear, taste, etc. Once in a while, one of them raises his eyes toward the sky and contemplates the infinite magnitude of the cosmic universe. On those occasions, he comes very close to the essence of creation. The wise man, after appeasing his thought process, contemplates, with the unique and omnidirectional eye of his mind, the foundation of his very existence. He remains in contemplation; since the more he moves away from matter the closer he gets to reality. Then suddenly, he sees no more emptiness (void), and no more matter, they have merged and reveal the true face of the universe. Then he realizes that there is no void that there is no matter, there is no creation or non-creation. There is only the essence of the consciousness of the whole. He just tore veil that kept the truth hidden from the searcher's eyes.

What is the secret of contemplation?

CONTENTMENT

Realization of the opportunity offered by life to the one who wishes to improve.

Someone who searches for the truth must make good of the opportunity that corporal life offers him to achieve his goal. The wise man does not waste one moment in futile illusory actions. He lives every day of his life as if it were the last and hurries toward liberation.

What is the difference between yesterday and tomorrow?

CONTROL

The fact of directing, commanding, managing or mastering.

Willpower allows the adept to analyze himself. The observer is in control when his mind is in a state of quiescence and the thought process has stopped: the individual mind is now one with the First Principle. The difference is abolished. From this state emerges the volition that invents beings and materializes them while being them. Volition is all beings as genus is all species and void is everything. As the adept becomes conscious of this volition, this intelligence through his quiescence, he recognizes that he is the eternal created and non-created. The wise one becomes ONE as soon as he abolishes the difference between illusion and reality. Without control there is no possible liberation.

How is it possible to control the thought process?

CONVERGENCE

The fact of working toward the same goal.

The universe is filled with an infinite number of beings, all believing that they are the centre of the world, and who are all different from one another when they are observed from an illusory point of view. They are all aspiring for the same and unique sensation, happiness. Any action performed by a living being is intended, in a large sense, to bring him happiness. Human beings in general turn to material things to find happiness. Most of them believe that happiness is proportional to the number of things one owns. Others who understand that possessions only bring more or less temporary pleasure that quickly turns into sorrow, look for their happiness beyond the created matter, in the kingdom of reality. The goal is the same for all, but the path to reach it is different for everyone. We are all going to the same place by a different road. There are as many methods to achieve real happiness, as there are beings in the universe. But the objective never changes and it is called REAL HAPPINESS. Do not mistake it for the illusory happiness that has no real consistence or duration. The wise man knows that meditation is the royal path to reach quiescence, and finally the absolute knowledge (real happiness). Meditation has always been acknowledged as the shortcut leading directly to the eternal light. Meditation is a neutral zone where all beliefs are accepted, because meditation is not the goal but the tool allowing anyone to get closer to what he thinks is the Supreme Being. Meditation has nothing to do with religion;

it is only a discipline helping to control the brain. When the adept no longer suffers from the confusion caused by the crazy dance of his thoughts, he takes a moment to rest in the inner peace, after which he can look beyond his own fantasies. All beings converge toward the same and unique unity.

Why is the fool attempting to bite the wind?

CORPORAL DISTRACTION

Various discomforts sustained by the body of someone who attempts to keep it still.

Meditation can only be practised if the adept can concentrate without being distracted on the inner emptiness. Even in a comfortable and appropriate position, the body often refuses to keep still and destroys all efforts to reach mental silence. The adept, who suffers from a mild case of corporal distractions, can attempt to take several deep and complete breaths before beginning his meditation. This is often sufficient to calm the machine long enough to allow the closing of the doors on the world. People whose body suffers from a chronic case of fidgeting can try to perform some mild physical exercises just before beginning their session of meditation. These exercises must be mild, one should not tire or wind the body, since this would only make things worse. These exercises will encourage the body to remain calm and to rest for some time. If these two solutions do not solve the corporal distractions problem, one must consider the attention factor. The adept does not apply sufficient energy to his concentration on the mental focus point. Therefore, he must reinforce his attention so it becomes able to ignore those superficial distractions. Care must be taken not to cause corporal or mental tensions. The reinforcement of the energy devoted to the attention is a question of WILL alone, nothing else.

What are the limits of the individual will?

CREATION

The action of giving existence to something drawn from the void.

Creation at its very beginning is composed of one unique thought that emerges from the MIND. This unique thought incorporates two opposite poles (positive/negative duality). Thus, at the dawn of creation there is the formation of this original and unique thought composed of one positive unit and one negative unit (sub-thoughts) which come into contact at the instant 0 + 1 (big bang) of the creation. The dreamlike (illusory) impact is phenomenal. The eternal game of action/reaction has just started, one new thought is generated that causes the production of another thought which joins other thoughts producing groups of thoughts (aggregates) at an unimaginable speed, and so on, until thoughts organize themselves and produce dust, celestial bodies with all their mechanics and entities, the material world as we know it. We must be careful though, because the unique thought which forms the whole creation of yesterday and today has reality as its essence, therefore, the material world that we know is reality under a disguise of illusion. Reality is here; only we are not able to see it. Creation is illusion and all beings part of it cannot know that something else exists for two main reasons: first, since all beings are immersed in the illusion, it is impossible for them to see anything else than illusion. Second, as long as they do not possess the necessary mental capacities, coupled with a long experience of matter which enables to analyze and realize that the latter is illusion and cannot be representative of reality, they remain locked in the valley of tears. The human being is an illusion imprisoned in another illusion. In meditation the illusion raises the veil of illusion and looks reality in the face.

How is it possible that matter that we can measure and touch is illusory, thus nonexistent?

CURIOSITY

The desire to acquire new knowledge.

Curiosity is the motor of apprenticeship and the key to the development of intelligence in human beings. Without it, without this appetite to learn and experience new phenomena, without this pleasure to juggle with new concepts and new visions, humankind would not evolve and would stagnate in a status quo without any way out. It is curiosity that allows human beings to challenge their environment and to force the door of reality. A person can be endowed with all the physical and intellectual attributes required to become a genius in the material or spiritual domain, but if he does not have the motor (curiosity) of his intellectual development, he will only be another ignorant under the sun until he develops this essential faculty. Curiosity is a characteristic that can be developed and cultivated. When the adept feels the desire to learn more about the spiritual nature of his being and the world surrounding him, he must seize the opportunity and work to grow and develop this new tendency which, if treated right, will become an inexhaustible thirst for knowledge that will lead him to the objective of his quest. Poor people are not those without money, a being is really poor when he is deprived of curiosity which would allow him to put his being and his world into question. This is the characteristic that gives the wise man the chance to question his nature, to study his environment and the world, to analyze his behaviour and finally to contemplate the inner void, this master above all others who, with the tip of a finger, slightly raises the veil of illusion.

What is the main activity of someone without curiosity?

D

DEATH

Absence of visible life in this dimension of the material world.

Change of aspect of a same intellectually unimaginable phenomenon. Death is another demonstration of duality in our world where life is good and death is bad. In fact death is only a modification of the human consciousness, one moment it possesses a body and the next it no longer does. For a being liberated from duality, death does not exist. A being dies every day when he sleeps and yet every morning wakes up very much alive. It is the same scenario at the end of one's life. Dreams experienced in the course of the night are mainly based on events of the previous day; the same applies during the sleeping period encountered at the end of a life where the individual will experience dreams based on his previous life. But whether dead or alive the sleeper is subjected to the created world dualities, among which the possession of a body, the dualistic cycle of life and death. No one can escape this cycle except the enlightened ones.

What does the rich do with all his wealth when he dies?

DECISION

The act of judging or taking action unilaterally.

I am my own master when it comes to making a decision. I do not let anyone or anything influence me. People in general are certain that they control their destiny, that they decide everything in connection with their lives. What really happens? When the wise one focuses on his own decisional process, he discovers that he decides nothing. Everything is decided for him. His consciousness is in fact only his mind identifying with the assembly of physical and intellectual aggregates, which form his being. After intense observation and meditation, the wise man realizes that the decisional process is entirely controlled by physical and intellectual tendencies (aggregates). But it is easy to be fooled into believing that one must personally analyze different factors (aggregates) in order to reach a decision, this is just an illusion. In fact, aggregates of different capacity struggle among themselves and the most powerful prevail; the mind only acknowledges the final decision-making, it has no active part in it. It is the same with actions. Several factors fight together and the winning assembly orders the body to act this or that way. The wise man in meditation clearly sees that his own decisional mechanisms work without his having any part in it. As an observer, he is mind, pure, uncreated and immaterial. Mind is the source of thought, mind is not thought.

Who is subjected to the consequences of decisions?

DEEP VIEW

The capacity to see beyond what is considered real.

Ordinary people are satisfied with their perceptions to define the world in which they live. They do not search beyond what they see and feel. Yet if they would only stop for a moment, they could discover that what they thought was one thing is in fact quite another. The wise one does not reject the material world; he only considers it illusory and unreal. This is why he uses it to his personal benefit without letting himself get caught in the illusory game. The wise man practices the deep view, meaning that he does not accept at face value what he sees, smells, touches or tastes, he goes further, he dissects his sensations to understand what they really are under their illusory make-up. For example, when he looks at a tree, he does not only see a trunk, branches and leaves, he becomes aware that the tree, just like him, is an assembly of aggregates which took a particular shape. The tree is not unique; it is but a link in a long chain of trees. He realizes that what he sees is the interpretation of what his visual mechanism senses, and that it is not reality. In fact, a tree, a person, and everything material is only a grouping of atomic particles glued together by a magnetic field. And when he meditates on the nature of an atom, then that of an atom particle and of particle substructures, he comes to the point where he realizes that energy is thought, as our physicists are tempted to believe. The wise man acknowledges that he and all other living beings of the universe are creators of the material world.

Why must one understand nothingness to transcend the world?

DELIVERANCE

Someone's liberation from a situation or suffering of which he believes to be a prisoner.

The human being, who feverishly looks for deliverance from his work, wife, poverty, old age, sickness, prison, etc., will one day realize that liberation from it all really does exist. But no efforts, glory, honour, virtue, nor prayers can release him from his illusion. His prison is inside his head and the bars are his thoughts that never stop emerging and immersing in eternal emptiness. Even the wise one will not find deliverance in quiescence or bliss. Deliverance can only be found after ignorance has been conquered, when the human being no longer finds satisfaction in the material world. When he has burned the last material desire, the flame goes out for lack of fuel. Then, he realizes that he is not the body or the mental process, but that he can use them to find truth. From then on the wise man focuses his attention on nothingness and discovers the silence of reality, of which he is the reflection. He is on the doorstep of deliverance.

How can the prisoner's dream open his prison door?

DESCRIPTION

To expose in details, verbally or in writing, characteristics related to a person, a situation or a thing.

Everything must be described, identified and catalogued in a dualistic world. Human beings have to describe what composes the material world in order to make normal and known what is not. A description is the result of comparing one thing to another. For example, an apple is an apple because of its shape, taste, texture, colour, etc., which are similar or different from other. Whether it is by comparing similarities or differences, this is what human do with everything new in his life. For the wise man, description is only possible in the dualistic world of creation, since as soon as he enters the world of reality, only unity reigns as sole master. And in a world without duality, comparison is impossible, thus nothing can really be identified, described or recognized for what it is. Everything must be realised to be known. Consequently, the wise man cannot describe with any certainty what he has experienced in deep meditation. Since such an experience cannot be compared to anything else, the wise one tries to give an idea of what he experiences by using illusory images and feelings. He is comparing apples with oranges and he knows it, but he has no other way to explain what he has experienced. As a result, no one should accept as absolute truth the words, which attempt to describe spiritual experiences. The only way, for an adept, to investigate the words taught to him is to experiment them personally in deep meditation.

How could one explain that creation is the expression of void?

DESIRE

Attraction to a person, an object or any other thing.

The will to possess illusory people and things and to keep them in a static state by fear of change and of the unknown. The wise man knows how to recognize signs of desire and quickly transcends them by concentrating his attention on emptiness, the only stable data in the created universe. Desire produces attachment to the thing or being desired. In the absence of desire, the ever-blinding light of truth bathes the observer.

What should desire the one who wants to know the truth?

DESIRE-REJECT

Both extremes of the scale used to evaluate what is sought after and refused.

Some people spend their lives longing for what they do not have and refusing what they possess. For them, everything can be summarized by «I want» and «I do not want», and these two positions serve to show their attachment to worldly things. For that matter, the desire for one thing and the rejection of another produce the same result on human beings. When someone desires something, he confesses that it will bring him something, therefore he is somewhat submitted to it. When this same person rejects something, he is then demonstrating that this thing bothers him; therefore that it has a certain hold on him. The wise man who realizes that all materiel objects are illusion, stops desiring or rejecting things. This is how he practices indifference for worldly things and enjoys a freedom that no person ignorant of this fact can experience. Anyone who recognizes the created world for the reflection of reality that it is, turns away from material endeavours and searches for reality and permanence. The wise one, liberated from attachment to the created world, enjoys a perfect tolerance toward creation because he understands its precariousness and unreality. In deep meditation, all unreal structures pertaining to the world in transformation fade away before the light of reality.

Why are reject and desire harmful to the evolution?

DESTINY

Events about one's life that can be modified at will.

Human beings in general usually transfer onto others the responsibility of what happens to them. The ignorant goes as far as to believe that he bears no responsibility whatsoever for what occurs in his life. He thinks everything is caused by some external source. It is true that someone refusing to take control over his own actions and life finds himself under the influence of others taking decisions in his stead. But in fact he is submitting to the consequence of his own decision and in the end he is still responsible for what happens to him. A human being is submitted to only one source of influence in the course of his physical existence: the product of each of his actions. When the wise man in meditation realizes that creation is a unity of which he is an integral part, and in turn finds creation integrally in himself, he becomes aware that he is not only responsible for his own schemes, but also for all actions undertaken in the universe. Humankind is one and shapes the universe in its own image. It continuously creates the world. No one is damned; nobody bears the consequences of a curse on humankind. We all bear the weight of our own actions, whether good or bad. A human being does not have to take on any challenge other than the one set by his own actions.

How can one be king of his destiny?

DESTRUCTION

Modification of a being, thing or state until it is annihilated.

It is practically impossible to totally destroy something in our world. Only transformation is possible. A form can be changed but the essence of creation is unalterable. The ignorant is terrified when he imagines his annihilation due to a confrontation with the Supreme Being (reality) while practising meditation on nothingness. He announces the destruction of the "I", the total destruction of his being and soul. Just knowing that he has to control the stream of his thoughts makes him sick, because he thinks that without thoughts he will no longer have emotions and that without emotions he would not be. All these erroneous interpretations are dualistic, thus falsified by the distorted view of a being who does not possess the long vision or has not experienced some moments of revelation in deep meditation. A person who meditates slowly progresses in his quest for truth toward the ultimate confrontation with the creator of everything, and has absolutely no fear of losing anything during or at the end of the search. He knows exactly what he is and acknowledges that any confrontation with the First Principle could only allow his individual mind to meet its divine essence. He knows that he is not thoughts and emotions but rather absolute light and wisdom. The wise man sees illumination as the birth of a superior being and the beginning of a new and fantastic adventure to the end of the unknown.

How can destruction generate construction?

DEVELOPMENT

The action to grow, to increase in size, to become more important.

Living beings develop physically and mentally. Food is used for body growth and maintenance, and life experiences, readings, studies, researches, analysis, reflections, meditations, etc. feed the being's intellect. The physical and intellectual entities are composed of aggregate groups of the same type battling for the domination of the physical being. The group of aggregates dominating the machine can be of a biological or intellectual nature according to the moment. All biological functions (physical aggregates) have priority over the mental functions (intellectual aggregates). This statement can easily be demonstrated: it is practically impossible to control the biological group of aggregates managing breathing for example, we can discipline it but certainly not stop it altogether, and it is the same for hunger, bowel movements, etc. All these dominate the intellectual aggregates when their needs are not satisfied, but as soon as they are satisfied they step back and leave the stage to the intellectual aggregates. The latter, as the others, are entities with needs they wish to fulfil, but contrary to the physical aggregates, they can grow, become more important, take more (intellectual) space, become more powerful. The more powerful one of these becomes, the more it is in a position to command the body, this unique tool through which positive or negative aggregates with the capacity to dominate can express themselves in the material world. The wise man takes advantage of moments during which the intellectual group of aggregates with a tendency toward spirituality is dominant to give it as much new data as possible. Any new information related to spirituality will contribute to the growth of this group of aggregates, giving it more power and the possibility to remain longer in a position to dominate the biological machine. The wise man, through his researches, analysis and particularly his meditations, increases the power of this group of aggregates so much so that it will eventually dominate the body permanently until the wise one is illuminated.

How can neutral observation bring wisdom?

DIFFERENCE

The characteristic or characteristics that distinguish one thing from another.

The difference is what stops people from realizing the similarity between the created and the uncreated. The dualistic world never stops comparing and establishing what makes the difference between one thing and another. However the difference only exists in our interpretation of the world. The adept who wishes to achieve the non-difference, thus inner peace, and to understand the world, must discipline his thoughts, take possession of his thought process and analyze what he really is, beyond the differences. The purpose of concentrating on an object or a mental point until one is perfectly concentrated is to control the thought process because without this control there is only confusion. As soon as the thought process is under control, quiescence takes hold and it becomes possible to analyze the difference. The wise one realizes that the created world has no reality; differences exist only if one's sight is not sufficiently piercing to distinguish reality behind the veil of illusion. The more difference crumbles, the more powerful sight becomes.

Why concentrate one's attention on a single thing or point?

DIFFERENT

The characteristic of a being who has no similarities with another.

The behaviour of the mass of human beings fluctuates under the influence of the latest trend. As the tides are submitted to the gravitational force of the moon, human beings are slaves to their emotions and interpretations of the world. In America anyone who lives in solitude is seen as a strange being, very different from others. Solitude is known as unhealthy and harmful to the human being's mental stability. People immersed in illusion are avid for feelings the crowd generates. As long as they receive a sufficient amount of external impulses people are not afraid to stop thinking (to stop being), they feel revitalized. The wise man recognizes creation as an illusion in which reality is only sustained by the cerebral interpretation of feelings gathered by various corporal sensors. Thus he realizes that all actions undertaken by those not aware of reality are illusory and useless to the pursuit of his ultimate goal. He is different because he is looking for solitude, silence and peace. He is different because he does not respond to external stimuli. His behaviour differs on all counts from that of humanity at large. He does not feed off dualistic illusions that only pass by to vanish without a trace. The purpose of everyone of his action in this world is to allow him more time for his search, analysis and meditation, which will eventually open the door onto reality.

Why is solitude detrimental to anyone immersed in illusion?

DISAPPEARANCE

The action of not being visually perceived and of being out of existence.

The ignorant drowned in the ocean of illusion believes that only matter exists. For him reality is what he can experience through his various senses. On the other hand, the adept who has realized that a reality superior to matter exists can sometimes push his discrimination too far. Anyone attempting, via meditation, to annihilate matter, to make it disappear in order to prompt the appearance of void is in error. Anyone who believes that creation is something exterior or foreign from the eternal void is mistaken. Anyone who tries to separate the created from the uncreated is mistaken. Any attempt to divide the unity of the universe is a mistake. The wise man acknowledges the nature of creation's illusion and its source, the infinite emptiness of reality. He also realizes that the created together with the uncreated, form an indissociable unit that contains everything. The wise man looks at the created world as a facet of truth and at void as another facet of truth, both being merged and forming reality. As soon as he deprives the created world of his attention, it disappears. The wise one knows that he has reached the ultimate objective when he sees the infinite in the created as well as in the uncreated.

If creation is immaterial, why does hitting your fingers with a hammer hurt so much?

DISCIPLINE

To train one's mind in order to see reality as it really is.

Discipline is the key to the searcher's progression toward his goal. Anyone who does not possess the necessary will to commit to a self imposed rigorous mental discipline will never reach his objective. The wise man sets attainable objectives which he reaches at his own pace while he perseveres in his search for liberation. Discipline and perseverance are among the indispensable qualities needed to succeed in the spiritual adventure.

What is the difference between a winner and a loser?

DISILLUSION

The fact of not believing in one's dreams anymore.

Illusion makes the world go round. When a person does not have enough of it he creates some more. People seem not to tire of experiencing deception and disillusion, yet nothing in this world ever ends otherwise, every dream taking root in duality ends by disintegrating, disappearing or simply collapsing unto itself. After many years of hard work, the worker attached to illusory things sees them disappear into dust, until there is nothing left of the material effort, and even the initiator vanishes without a trace. Disillusion is the major tool of evolution. After countless disillusions, a person inevitably starts asking questions about the possibility of a better world, then about the reality of the created world. This is the beginning of the long ascent from illusion to reality. From the darkness of the material world, the adept strives to reach the light of truth. The wise man has left disillusion behind long ago since all his efforts and meditation are strictly dedicated to the research of a reality. The void has always been and will always be. When the wise one's mind rests in its natural state, it contemplates the infinite void, the ultimate truth.

How can disillusion wake up the ignorant?

DISPATCH

The characteristic of something done with speed and zeal.

The inhabitants of the illusory world work with dispatch to build their houses of cards that are only awaiting the slightest breeze to collapse and bring them pain and sorrow. The adept wants to build his temple with indestructible and eternal material. He is not fooled by worldly knowledge and practices meditation with zeal. Meditation is the unique source of real wisdom, the one coming from the inside. If your house is built of void, nothing can shake it. The wise man researches and studies with diligence all sources of knowledge related to the field of spirituality. But knowing that this knowledge is only temporary and illusory and that real truth rests in the infinite emptiness, he builds his home with indestructible illuminations drawn directly from the creative essence. In meditation he contemplates the infinite light of void, allows eternal wisdom to impregnate him and acknowledges the reality of everything.

Why must one reach reality with dispatch?

DISSIPATION

The action to destroy by wasting.

The ignorant, during his dissipation period, runs in all directions, spends his vital energy in crazy adventures bringing only sorrow. He is like an autumn leaf floating around on the northern wind, wandering around without goal, not even looking to where his course will end. Sensations covered with emotions, and interpretations dressed in passions control him as a puppet hanging from his strings. He totters, staggers, and eventually falls consumed. The strings of his emotions have just broken. From this heap of ashes rises a phoenix, miser of movement taking advantage of the remaining time, of each moment, to finally contemplate beyond the mirror of moving things. The time of wisdom has come. The wise man calmly focuses on the inner emptiness from where first emerge flashes of truth, then the intense and blinding light of reality. The infantile stage is over, the being is promoted to adult rank.

Why is it that one running is stopped while one stopped is running?

DISTANCE

Subjective space which separates one thing from another.

The false interpretation that causes one to believe that things in the material world are far away from one another. Illusory spatial measure of illusory time spent between departure and arrival. One must not be fooled by material world measures. Nothing exists, nothing can be measured, in reality everything IS. The wise man closes his eyes and realizes the proximity of all things since he can touch the other end of the universe with his fingertips. The material world is a dream.

What is the distance between departure and arrival?

DISTINCTION

A characteristic that differentiates a being, a thing or a situation from another.

It is important for the human being to differentiate things. On one hand, anything that is not him, or part of him, is strange and potentially dangerous. He must weigh and analyze what distinguishes him from the others in order to recognize who he is. Without comparison points (without distinctions), the human being could not become conscious of himself as an individual. His interpretation of differences sets him apart from others. On the other hand, what he interprets as non-different or similar allows him to realize that he belongs to a group rather than another. The wise man in meditation transcends all illusory distinctions and realizes that all beings in the universe are intimately linked to one another. When finally all differences vanish into the inner emptiness, he recognizes that any difference is the fruit of illusion and erroneous interpretation of creation. When silence dissolves the veil of illusion, the wise one becomes aware that the universe is a unique entity with spasms believing to be individualities. In deep meditation, the wise man, stripped of his shell of illusions, returns to the essence of unity.

What is the measure of desire?

DISTRACTION

The diversion of attention due to an outside factor.

Distraction is certainly the greatest enemy of the adept in meditation. He is looking for silence, emptiness, hence absence of thoughts. In meditation, his mind totally relaxed, he is balanced between the action of thinking and not thinking, meaning that he is intensely focused on an inner target and that he remains in that state of observation without letting anything affect him. He is neutral before nothingness. He must not press it will come to him gently and quietly. He must not force things one way or another; instead he intensifies his concentration, does not forcefully reject thoughts, he lets them come and go without affecting him. Force is harmful in meditation, because the use of force is an action that generates thought forms, in other words because it is an action that produces a reaction. The adept in meditation does not act or react to anything, he only observes without letting himself be distracted by thoughts fighting among each other to emerge at the surface of consciousness. He is totally calm and relaxed, and at the same time, he is filled with wonder and does not try to understand. The adept does not think of the past, present or future, nor that he is meditating, he does not see emptiness as something. He does not interpret anything in any way. The spark of consciousness that subsists in meditation is called the observer because its function is only to observe.

What is the state of the mind at rest?

DISUNITY

The action of dissociating things and beings habitually together.

Disunity is certainly the major reason for all great sorrows striking humankind. Humans suffer when separated from something or someone of whom they are fond. The human's great theatre play consists in acquiring and possessing as many things as possible and then to try to keep them as they are. The more a person is deeply buried into the illusory morass, the more energy he preserve to possess and conserve. His life is entirely controlled by these illusory compulsions. It is obvious to the wise man that these people are doomed to experience great sorrows since he knows that nothing materiel ever stays unchanged. He sees everything appear, change and disappear. Thus he sympathizes with the ignorant beings when they do not succeed in obtaining what they desire or when they lose persons or objects to which they were attached. But the wise one rests in peace since he desires nothing of this world, he contemplates the void, never changing, stable and immutable for all times. He contemplates reality and tries to tell those ready to listen, that there already is a well-defined road leading to serenity.

Why must one die to things in order to be born to truth?

DO (TO)

To execute an action in order to produce a result.

The ignorant does everything without knowing why he executes this action instead of another. He is not concerned by the potential impact of his actions on others or on himself. He does not acknowledge that his actions can have consequences. This is why he is tossed about and around, as a rag in the wind, by the impact or the reaction of his various actions. He is always asking himself, "Why is this and that happening to me?", whether it is good or bad. He is a very confused and irrational person. The adept however follows the law of action-reaction. He does what he feels like doing when he wants to do it, making sure that he does not harm anyone in any way. His actions do not generate any negative results and do not increase his negative charge, furthermore, his meditation work makes him progress on the awakening path. Meditation gives the searcher the opportunity to withdraw from the material world, thus reducing his illusory needs. Less material needs equal more peace, more calm and more serenity. The wise one, having realized that he decides nothing, that he is only a spark of consciousness identified to the aggregates that form his being, does what he has to do and nothing else. The wise man always says, "I will do what I have to do when the time comes to do it", and he lives each moment in perfect consciousness. He is not concerned by the result of his actions since they have only one objective, the awakening of humanity. His main goal is to lighten the universe's negative charge by becoming free and by keeping the path open for other awakened beings ready to embark upon the path leading to reality.

Who really decides the execution of an action?

DOGMATISM

The characteristic of an incontestable act of fate.

The searcher is never totally immune from disillusion and illusion. Through his experience he reaches extreme heights of understanding about the universe and if he does not concentrate sufficiently on transcending all this new and powerful knowledge, there is a danger that he may be trapped by dogmatism. Many an adept have mistakenly believed that their realizations and understanding were complete and infallible. They had then fallen into a trap. Because of a lack of concentration on the spiritual nature of the research, they considered only its illusory and egocentric side. From then on, as they refuse any new experience and knowledge, their progression comes to an abrupt stop. The adept with this problem must face the fact that immutable truth and infallible knowledge cannot exist in our material world where all is in constant transformation. The immutable, the infallible, the perfect, the infinite can only be experienced beyond the realm of matter within the domain of reality resting on the infinite void alone. The wise man knows that nothing can be entirely true as long as the veil of illusion covers the eyes of the searcher.

What must be the only act of fate of an adept?

DOMINATING AGGREGATE

An assembly of thoughts that dominate the brain.

The aggregates that form what is called a person's personality or character are constantly changing. Their transformation is caused by interactions among them or with what comes from outside. At all times, the dominating aggregate must fight to keep its dominance over the brain in order to pursue its particular objective. Any change of idea leads to believe that a replacement, or at least a more or less important modification of the aggregate managing the events, has occurred. For example, someone is on his way to the gymnasium to perform his weekly exercises. On his way there he meets a friend who invites him for a drink instead. A confrontation immediately arises between the aggregate that likes physical exercises and takes seriously the health state of the body in which it lives and the other aggregate that hates physical effort and does not believe that the state of health of the machine it inhabits is important. This is a very simplistic example, but this is how it goes for everything that a person has to decide at every moment of his life. The dominating aggregate is the one that reigns on the machine via the brain it controls. No aggregate, dominating or not, is a unique entity. An aggregate is composed of several other aggregates, which also comprise other aggregates. All these aggregates more or less influence the dominating aggregate of the moment. The wise man visits a place where aggregates are not allowed: quiescence. But in order to do so, his dominating aggregate must wish it.

What is the difference between a dominating aggregate and a non-dominating one?

DOMINATION

Total control over persons, situations or things.

The adepts works without rest at the domination of his sensations, tendencies, instincts, thoughts, etc. He can perform this task from one direction or another. He can start by disciplining his sensations, tendencies, etc., in order to reach the domination of his thoughts and analysis process, to finally rest in quiescence. Or he can start directly by disciplining his thoughts and analysis process and reach quiescence by transcending everything else. This is the most direct known approach to peace leading to illumination. The short cut between the world of sensations and that of emptiness (void) is silence. The silence path is the one with fewer dangers for the searcher because all he experiences is automatically transcended and used as energy to feed an ever-deeper concentration on the state of creation and non-creation. Silence is a close relative to void which is reality.

Why must the adept first dominate before accepting everything?

DOOR

An opening to elsewhere.

The awakening door remains closed to those who have not yet reached a level of disillusion high enough for them to desire something else, a different life, better than the present one, another world, better than the current one, happiness that is real, that would be permanent, a stop to the suffering, etc. Those who do not understand that possessions do not bear real happiness, continue their march on the difficult road controlled by emotions. Emotions bring little joy and great sorrow. It is important for one who has stepped through the awakening door, walking the path to reality, on his way to truth and happiness, to persevere in his quest and not to let worldly sensations invade and dominate him. Emotions offer a lot of strong feelings but very little joy and no peace. The ignorant beings are slaved to emotions. The adept's dominant aggregates, that allowed him to step on the awakening path, must be encouraged and fed in order to remain dominant. Otherwise, without proper sustenance they will weaken and other, less evolved aggregates, will take the lead and prompt the body to succumb to illusory world offerings, and the search will be delayed for an unknown period of time. Spirituality, like anything else in this created world, has to be nourished in order to grow.

What is spirituality's nourishment?

DOUBT

Uncertainty about a thing, a fact or a declaration.

The hesitation to believe in the reality of void. The hesitation to believe that the material world is only suffering. The hesitation to take the road to illumination. Doubt intrudes into the heart of the strongest and must be fought off at each instant since faith in silence is the key to the real universe. Doubt must roll off the wise man's faith without leaving any harmful traces. The observer knows that one cannot reach liberation through studies and analysis but by experimenting and living various steps along the royal path. In doubt, the adept follows the path of silence.

How can one measure the solidity of emptiness?

DREAM

Wild mental projection occurring during sleep.

Dreams are images produced by a mental process and derived from daily situations, although they do not possess any physical reality and pertain to the immaterial and impalpable realms. However, it is impossible to state that dreams are totally independent of the situations from which they sprout. It is the same for the material life of human beings in the waking state, which is nothing else but a dream projected on the screen of void during the sleeping period or, in other words, ignorance of truth. Human beings immersed in the ocean of every day illusions are only conscious of the sensations and knowledge coming from their physical and intellectual experiences in their sensual universe. They are not awakened to (aware of) the fact that their material knowledge is unreal, and that the illusory experiences' egotistical tendency conceals the ultimate truth to the ignorant being's eyes. The illusory dream perpetuates itself, and the mass of ignoring humans bathes in it, not aware of the path leading to the awakening state and to the great liberation. The wise man realizes that dreams, as everything else existing in the dualistic universe, have no existence of their own outside the mind. In the silence of meditation, he rests his spiritual attention on an idea, a concept or a phenomenon and realizes that everything which exists outside of him or within him, the created and the uncreated, are inseparable from each other and that they can be transmuted into a universal moment (instantaneity). All spiritual or material phenomena are one with all.

What was the dream's dream last night?

DROWSINESS

The uncontrollable tendency to doze, to lose consciousness.

Drowsiness is a preliminary step to sleep, thus the last stage toward a loss of consciousness for the person experiencing it. The main cause of this prelude to sleep is physical as well as mental fatigue. The adept meditating for long periods of time is likely to feel some physical and mental fatigue; the result is a state of drowsiness and loss of concentration. There are many ways to remedy this effect, for example, the adept can open his eyes if he meditates with his eyes closed, then stare at a point as far away as possible while maintaining his mental concentration. He will close his eyes whenever he feels refreshed. It is also possible to eliminate drowsiness by focusing part of one's attention on one's breathing and counting it without altering the rhythm. The adept counts his breathing without altering his major concentration point. This exercise relaxes and rests both the body and the mind. Fatigue can also be caused by too great a corporal tension; if it is the case, the adept must, while keeping his initial concentration, relax his body step by step by reviewing it with part of his attention, always maintaining the state of mental silence. An even better way is for each and everyone to develop their own method to cope with physical and mental fatigue resulting from meditation. You certainly are the only person to know the real cause of your drowsiness.

How is it that a thinking person is in reality sleeping?

DUALITY

Characteristic of what possesses two aspects.

The concept of opposition, such as positive and negative, good and bad. The duality depends solely upon the thought process and is in relation to an illusory situation in the material world. One with average spiritual awareness must acknowledge the duality of the created and the non-created and practice concentrating on the First Principle, illusion and consciousness. The wise man knows that duality holds the illusory world together. Without the two opposite poles of duality, the material world would not exist. One must acknowledge that duality is illusory and thus negative to the searcher's progress. In the silence of deep meditation, the observer witnesses the fusion of the universe's duality into a unique and indivisible whole. The wise man acknowledges that what is considered bad is only the inverted image of good and that both come from the same source.

How can good and bad emanate from the same source?

DURATION

A given period between two events.

The duration of a meditation period cannot be ordered by anyone but the practising person himself. He alone can decide when to start and when to terminate this exercise. The adept who practices meditation follows some parameters allowing him to know when to meditate and for how long. 1. He meditates when he desires to for a reason or another. 2. He meditates in a peaceful place of his choice. 3. He meditates during periods of the day when his state of wakefulness is at its highest level. These moments change from one person to the next. 4. He meditates only when his stomach is empty. 5. He immediately stops meditating when he feels mental or physical fatigue, unless he specifically works on these types of fatigue. 6. He never strains his focus, attention or meditation. 7. He meditates for as long as he believes that meditation is giving him something. Meditation cannot be forced, meditation cannot be ordered, meditation is the most intimate thing that each one of us practices in his inner silence. A meditation session can last only a few seconds, several minutes, hours and sometimes days, but the true meditating adept is the one who finds silence. Without silence there is no meditation.

How can we measure the value of a meditation?

E

EASINESS

The characteristic of what is done effortlessly and with ease.

Anyone who attempts to force things, to accelerate the concentration process in order to reach silence or quiescence more rapidly can only fail and be disappointed. Meditation is an art that is practised slowly, without effort, in peace and with easiness. Silence must be conquered through patience, not effort. Any effort or constraint will be absent from the whole meditation process, whether during preparation or execution. Concentration is easily and effortlessly attained. The adept settles his attention on an inner point and maintains this mental concentration without being distracted by endlessly appearing and disappearing thoughts. Easiness of execution also concerns the body: if the adept feels any corporal uneasiness, he immediately stops his session to solve the problem or waits until the next session to resume. Concentration is reached and maintained without effort, tensing or any other unpleasant sensations or fatigue. The adept comes out of his meditation refreshed, rested, in peace, happy with himself and the world. As soon as he comes out of meditation, he plans his next session. The wise man in deep meditation is as calm as a sleeping baby and as watchful as a child watching his favourite TV program. The wise man's mind is at rest in its natural state.

What does the wise man observe in deep meditation?

EDUCATION

Methods and tools used for human beings' training.

Education is absolutely not necessary and is even detrimental to those who are just beginning to realize the futility of the material world. The more important illusory education is, the more real the material world seems to be. The more educated a human being is, the less capable he is to stop and listen to the inner intuitive messages. Education is a sensation amplifier that deepens the ignorant being's sleep. The adept keeps as far away as possible from any form of education whose goal is to solidify the belief in matter. He concentrates instead on researches, reflections and meditations that will raise him above the beliefs of the sleeping mass of beings. All human beings will one day realize that the material world leads only to pain and that experimenting reality is the path to follow in order to cure oneself of misfortune. Meanwhile the wise man meditates in silence.

What is the purpose of education?

EFFECT

The result of a cause or the consequence of an action.

Each action undertaken by beings in the universe has an effect, each one of them have repercussions on the whole and on the cause. Whatever the action, either positive or negative, whether it impacts something or someone close or far away, its effect will take the road back and alter the point of origin, the cause. Everything in the universe is a consequence; even new actions are effects of old actions. Nothing in all the creation is unique and autonomous, everything depends, ensues from, everything is the result of something else. The wise man in meditation discovers the reason for the universe's endurance:

it endures solely because of reactions, effects. When the time comes when all actions will have exhausted their reactions and when the ultimate action will not be taken, then and only then will the universe vanish as mist in the morning sun. Then, will «exist» only the transparency of the eternal reality, until the emergence of a new thought.

What would happen if the last living being were to take the last action in the creation?

EGO

Presence acknowledged as the conscious entity inhabiting a body.

The ego is what people believe they are. I am I, I am ego. For the wise one, the ego is the assembly of intellectual aggregates passing from one body to another. It inhabits a body from birth to death. During the period between death and rebirth, the ego is passive because it has no means of acting upon the external world, it requires a body to do that. This is the ego that has a never-ending desire to do all things possible and imaginable and that gives the impression of consciousness. It is the clown doing his tricks and funny faces for the audience. The belief that the ego is conscious and permanent generates an individual (an individuality, thinking that it is separated from all). This erroneous interpretation is the source of attachment to worldly things that produces misery. Without ego, without me, there is no one to say I like or I dislike. The word ego gives birth to the notion of isolation from the rest of the universe. After innumerable lives, the ego realizes its mistake and collaborates in its own destruction by participating to the quest for truth where all returns to the source.

What is left when the ego has vanished?

ELATION

A great joy which arises following the realisation of a beneficial fact.

The joy and felicity represented by elation are usually felt in relation with religious events and never last for long. Elation is a sensation that occurs instantly contrary to happiness which one acquires slowly through continuous efforts to reach peace and serenity. This emotion, since it is one, brings the need to share one's joy with others, to shout to the world one's elation and the reason of this sudden joyfulness. When the wise man in deep meditation realizes that all living beings of the creation will find the road back to their origin and will return to the light of reality from where sorrow is absent, he experiences elation. He rejoices to know that suffering and sorrow is not eternal and that as soon as people will become capable of ignoring the illusion, they will embark on the quickest path to return to their fundamental nature. He would like to cry out from the roof of the world that no one should despair anymore, that there is hope, that pain and sorrow are only temporary and that they cease their destructive deeds as soon as one relinquishes illusory desires.

What does a wise man think when he feels a good emotion?

EMERGENCE OF THOUGHTS

The sudden appearance of thoughts in the mind.

An ordinary person's mind is constantly full of thoughts and if it were otherwise he would think he is sick or crazy. "The thoughts? But, they come from me, he will tell you, I think therefore I am. I am my thoughts and my thoughts are me." The wise man first realizes through meditation, that what he believed himself to be is in fact an assembly of aggregates of thoughts of all kinds. These thoughts are first our intellectual baggage which includes our biological trends resulting from our gene pool, then all the information we gathered in the course of all our existences as material beings, plus all other information we appropriated through our present life's education, at home, in school and in the society. All these thoughts congregate in various trend groups competing with one another in order to control the body, this machine that allows them to act upon the external world. Thoughts that fill a human being's head emerge from these aggregates fighting for dominance. Thus people say, "Ah yes! I want to do this" or "I do not want to do this", etc. This is why the wise one who has succeeded in suspending the drive of his aggregates, realizes that in fact he is an immaterial and eternal mind and not these intellectual aggregates, which, as everything else, are part of the illusion and have no permanence.

When the wise man's head is empty, where are his thoughts?

EMOTION

The affective reaction to a false interpretation of an experience.

On the one hand, we realize that the material and illusory interpretation of the universe is false. On the other hand, a false interpretation of this interpretation leads directly to insanity. A parent collapses in tears at the accidental death of his child while he is unmoved when thousands of children die a couple of thousand kilometres away from his home. What happened here? The emotional response comes first from the belief that the illusory world is real and second from making a difference between the death of our own child and that of a stranger. For the wise one there is no difference; he knows that death is only a transitory state and that the body is nothing but a temporary machine. The entity does not die but carries on its course under another aspect. He also acknowledges that the death of a child, as sad as it may be, whether that child is yours or a pure stranger, is always the death of a child in the universe. He sees only the normal eternal pursuit of events of this world where illusions appear and disappear as thought impulsions dictate. The adept acknowledges that emotion is only another way of showing the influence of matter over us. The need to possess and the fear to lose.

What effect has the death of a human being on the universe?

EMOTIONAL RELATIVITY

Perception of events influenced by individual interpretations.

Everything is relative and we all interpret our experiences according to our own values and through our understanding. The overall experiences of an individual act as a magnifier through which he looks at the world and interprets what he sees and experiences. What is good for one may be bad for another and vice versa. For example: Someone lends a certain amount of money to a friend who does not reimburse the money when the time comes. The lender thinks that his friend is ungrateful, or that he is trying to steal his hard-earned money. The friend, on the other hand, could be thinking that the lender did not need the money if he was able to lend it in the first place concluding that he can keep the money without the lender ever noticing. Both have their own version and comprehension of the facts, each one rationalizes in his own way. The purpose of this example is not to demonstrate what is good or bad but how each antagonist could individually interpret the situation. They both think that they are right. This is the basic situation with everything in the material world. Logic is absolutely not universal since each person has his own. The wise one meditates in order to eliminate false emotions, false interpretations of experiences encountered in the illusory universe. He wishes to cease analyzing and comparing, as he knows that a comparison is always false since it is, like the compared thing, a misinterpretation on an illusory experience. By comparing false with false one obtains a wrong answer. The wise man in deep meditation goes beyond comparison and analysis and confronts reality in its global truth. He goes where analysis does not exist anymore, only confrontation.

Is humankind sane?

EMPATHY

The faculty to intuitively feel the state of mind of other beings.

People in general are so distracted, or maybe totally dazed, by sensations generated by the illusion that it is practically impossible for them to share the state of mind of their fellow men, to sympathize with them. Empathy is a rare staple in this material world where the main rule seems to be "me, myself and I". For humans, for the most primitive of animals, individual survival has precedence over everything else. But the wise man at the end of his quest realizes the truth beyond life and death, beyond the world in transformation and sorrow. He has reached the state where he recognizes that mind and matter, the created and the uncreated as well as all dualities, are but a single unit. He experiences the infinite illumination of the ultimate truth. In the course of this spiritual awareness he feels an irresistible empathy with humankind, which remains a prisoner of its ignorance, and an intense desire to participate in its awakening, then in its quest for truth and real happiness. The wise man has just crossed the frontier between human evolution and superhuman evolution. He enters the domain of higher evolution, which goal is unknown to all, even to the greatest wise ones, because it is totally elusive to an individual mind.

Why is egocentricity inversely proportional to evolution?

END OF BREATH

The instant at the end of expiration just before one begins breathing in.

Among searchers of truth of all times, this instant has always been known as exceptional and often sacred. This is the moment during which any living being can experiment the inner silence. During that moment, the thought process is suspended. It stops its activities. Thus anyone who takes in a long breath then slowly breathes out can at the end of this cycle taste, for a few seconds, mental calm and peace that the practice of meditation brings. The wise man states that someone who is conscious in that precise moment associates himself with the truth. Meditation is the observation of the absence of thoughts. At the end of breath, the conscious observer contemplates the infinite emptiness of reality inside his head. The beginner uses this simple technique to experiment the inner silence and to realize that even in the absence of thoughts, he is still conscious; he still exists. He acknowledges then that he is something else than thoughts, and that his natural state is a unique, infinite and eternal mind. The wise man stretches this moment of reality into infinity.

Why is the mind a prisoner of illusory things?

ENEMY

A person, a situation or a thing opposing another.

Ignorance is certainly the worst enemy of human beings since it generates the thought process that makes emotional machines out of them. The thought process does not take reality into account in its interpretation of sensations. When someone lives in ignorance, i.e. when he does not know that reality is absolute emptiness (void) and that truth is unique, he lets the thought process weigh, analyze and compare the sensations he receives from his perception centres (vision, touch, taste, etc.). The thought process can only produce a false answer, because it is based on false data. Complexity is illusory; unity is reality. Truth rests on the absence of analysis; truth is observation without identification. When you think that you hold the truth about something and that this truth is complex, i.e. it involves more than one element, this truth is an illusion, it can be valuable in the material world, but it is not permanent. The wise man tries to reach a natural state of mind, where consciousness bathes in eternal silence and peace. He does not take into account his illusory analysis and accepts only what is unique and permanent, the void. He is aware that any other identification, interpretation, etc. can only be temporary and changing. He acknowledges that all that composes the material world can only change and be transformed and that his biggest enemy is ignorance.

What is someone sleeping with his enemy guilty of?

ENTITY

The constituents of an independent unity.

Such as the millions of sun rays shining on the world, of which not one can exist without its source, the sun, each entity or individual in the creation is only the prolongation of the universal mind, the immutable unity. No entity or group of entities can survive separated from each other or from their source. Just imagine for a moment the disappearance of comparison points and landmarks used by a human being to locate himself in his personal universe. He would immediately lose his means of identification. Human beings only exist as long as they can compare themselves to the external world. The entity interprets the world in his own way and imagines himself as an individual separated from the rest of creation. In fact, life phenomena give a relative existence to the personality a human being dresses in. And personality creates the illusion of separation and independence from the rest of the world, as well as the sense of permanence. The wise man in deep meditation, in this space where creation does not exist, loses all notion of individuality while staying aware. He sees how easy it is for a human being to mistake a consequence for a cause. Creation is in fact the development of thought and is devoid of reality, it is only appearance and illusion.

How should a wise one react after hitting his thumb with a hammer?

ENVY

The unhealthy desire to enjoy other people's possession.

The ignorant envies everybody around him. He believes that others obtain things more easily than he does. He even imagines that they did not have to make efforts in the past to gain what they own today. He looks at what he covets and hates those who possess it without taking into account the hard work they had to perform in order to acquire it. These kinds of thoughts lead to the rationalization of robbery. He does not realize that there is nothing free in this world, and that everything has to be paid one way or another. Any action produces a reaction. Moreover, the ignorant is eaten away by envy because he does not have the energy or the courage to get up from his seat and make the necessary efforts to gain the object of his desire. The absence of envy is a characteristic of the wise man. He has understood that in the created world, one has to act in order to get; that without action there is no result. The wise man works a lot harder toward his liberation than toward accumulating illusory worldly goods. In meditation, when duality is quiet and when the silence of unity invades the searcher's consciousness, the only objectives of value that deserve action are those enabling to open the door of reality a little wider.

Is the body only a spiritual development tool?

ERROR

The action of the intellect perceiving what is true as false and vice versa.

The adept will meet several obstacles on his way and will make many mistakes. One of the most common errors comes about when the adept develops too great an affinity for a particular discipline. When he discovers that he is too interested in analyzing his thoughts or the thought process, in reflecting upon analysis or simply in the quiescence state, he has just uncovered an important mistake. When the searcher becomes attached to anyone of his practices, progression is no longer possible. Focus is limited to this close horizon and the great vision and objective lose their reality. This is a total stop and the adept stagnates in a state of confusion in which he imagines that he has reached his goal. The primary source of this problem is egotism. The adept abandons his altruistic vision to centre his attention on his little realization and himself, and suddenly forgets his ultimate objective. The adept must be very vigilant and always ensure that his vision and mental projections are focused on the real goal and that they keep their altruistic aspect. As soon as he notices some traces of egocentricity, he must immediately concentrate on the unity of all that exists and the part he plays in it. The adept must recognize that he is but a minute part of an incomprehensible project and that all research work must lead to his liberation, which will place the universe closer to the final liberation. The adept must meditate on the ego as an illusion.

What does the illumination of one being in the black of infinite ignorance represent?

ESCAPE

The action to flee a situation or a place.

Meditation is a refuge for anyone questioning the world and its existence. This is a mean to confront the created and uncreated universe. Anyone practising meditation will be at one point confronted with the great-unveiled mysteries of the world. The adept uses meditation to escape the illusory world, to attack ignorance, conquer unconsciousness and look reality in the face without weakness. Meditation represents the greatest challenge a human being can undertake. Through meditation the adept will face his greatest enemy, himself, then the whole universe in all its nudity and impartiality, and finally he will try to measure up to the absolute and infinite void of reality. Meditation is an art of transformation that allows those who practise it sincerely to become tearless and valiant knights capable of defending their aspirations against the erosive attacks of matter. Meditation cannot be used as a shield of insincerity; it is rather the defence wall of truth, the road of wakefulness leading the searcher at the foot of the altar where worldly emotions are immolated.

Why is meditation the antidote of illusion?

ETERNITY

A period without beginning or end. A period impossible to conceive in terms of time.

The absence of markers indicating the beginning, the duration and the end of a period. Eternity is an integral part of the First Principle or the uncreated. Eternity is only possible in the total absence of mental or physical movements. Perfect passivity is not measurable. The adept has glimpses of eternity in deep meditation in which time is absent, leaving instead a consciousness without temporal markers. Duality disappears and the eternal void illuminates reality. Individual mind is as eternal as the First Principle where it takes its source. This is the reason why the adept can experience temporary eternity (a feeling of eternity) before being completely awakened to eternity by the great illumination.

Why is time relative?

EVOLUTION

Slow but continuous transformation of a situation or being.

Spiritual evolution has nothing to do with technology or sociology. The material world does not really evolve as a whole; it stagnates in the eternal re-enactment of old mistakes and follies. As for technology, it does not evolve either since it is nothing else than the illusory invention of machines ever complicating the world and confusing humans. The material world exists in order to give individuals the opportunity to embark upon the evolutionary path. Evolution is strictly a mental process by which the adept will be transformed from his state of illusion into a being embracing the reality of the whole created and non-created universe. The illusion becomes disillusion, ignorance comprehension, sleep wakefulness and the unreal reality. The creation is composed of a positive and a negative pole and illusion is located somewhere in between.

How is mankind evolving?

EXCESS

That which goes beyond the limit of reason.

The adept looking for spiritual knowledge must avoid excesses, whether in his nourishment or abstinence, his activity or inactivity, his thoughts or meditations. By avoiding excesses, he can see the world from a brand new point of view. If he does not accept or reject the presence of the material world or the void, he can consider them as a single (void-matter) unit. If he stops considering for real what surrounds him and unreal the rest, he can join these two extremes into a single unit. The wise man knows that if he considers something to be "existing" he errs in excess, and if he considers another thing to be "inexistent" he errs at the other end of the spectrum. Excesses are to be avoided because they separate and oppose, they identify everything in existence as positive or negative, good or bad. Excess is the major characteristic of the material world's duality. The wise man, by transcending the excesses of the illusory world, meditates on the universe's unity where nothing is good or bad, positive of negative, existing or inexistent. He realizes the unity of what is created and uncreated. He discovers truth.

Does unity's indivisibility reflect the material world's duality?

EXCLUSION

The action to reject and not accept a person, a situation or a thing.

When someone realizes that he has done something wrong and is sorry about it, he would often say, "I shall never do that again". In other cases, the reaction would be, "I will never accept such a situation, I do not recognize his authority". The expressions "never" or "forever" are common among ignorant beings who do not realize the impermanence of all that exists in the world they inhabit. The wise man does not exclude or reject anything, he accepts every one and every situation or thing in this world without labelling it as good or bad. He knows that everything has a beginning and an end that nothing lasts for very long, that everything disappears after a while. For him, all that is impermanent can only be illusion and he sees it only as something to transcend. In meditation, evil and good become joined to form an indissociable whole. Thus the wise man does not see things in terms of bad or good; he sees only assemblies of more or less negative or positive aggregates fighting for the supremacy of the body they inhabit, which they can use after their victory to further their own agenda. Without positive and negative poles, the world as we know it could not exist. The wise one does not exclude, nor accept, he only observes without analysis. Peace rises from silence and non-interference.

When someone wants to eliminate evil, is he attempting to destroy the created world?

EXISTENCE

The fact of recognizing one's reality.

A human being realizes his existence when he notices the existence of his environment. He becomes conscious when his mental mechanism (brain) begins to interpret the interaction of his various aggregates with those forming his environment. Thus, beings acknowledge their existence from sensations they perceive. The existence and its counterpart non-existence are also only illusions and cannot in any case be applied to the definition or to the research of reality. Reality transcends everything that exists and is expressed in the material world. The wise man does not delay his search trying to define or establish the characteristics of existence or non-existence. He knows that it is possible to reach the absolute reality but that it is impossible to describe it with words. He uses every minute of his existence to try to realize the truth. Existence is every searcher's opportunity to accelerate his progression. But one must remember that the object of the search is absolutely inexpressible in this world. One can only experience it.

What is the role of thought in the existence?

EXPERIENCE

The occurrence of something different that will bring a greater understanding.

Someone's life is based on the experience of new facts through which he learns to successfully face the multiple environments in which he lives. Even the most conservative person has to go through new experiences. In our universe, nothing repeats itself exactly the same, everything changes and is transformed from one moment to the next. Although everything may seem the same to one deprived of insight, anyone who takes the time to stop and look deeper into things will realize that it is quite the opposite and that each instant in life is a new experience. Thus, consciously or not, a human being learns, evolves and is transformed. The wise one is deeply conscious that he is developing, that he is an experimental pool. This is why he ceaselessly provokes new physical, intellectual or spiritual experiences that will allow him to better understand and realize the why of things around him. He knows that the world is the best teacher from which human beings are learning to become entities with their eyes open on something else than confusing sensations coming from the great illusion. After tasting the inner silence, he accepts inside of him what is real, eternal, indivisible and invincible: the VOID. In the infinite silence where he rests without notion of past or future, in the present moment he awaits immutably the appearance of instantaneity.

What makes an experience positive instead of negative?

EXPRESS WAY

The fastest road to reach a destination.

Most travellers progress first at a turtle pace on the path leading to the ultimate destination. Then they discover less busy roads with fewer turns. Later, some find secret short cuts allowing them to save even more time. But all of them, at the end of the journey, will find what they are looking for and nothing else. Someone who sees matter as his ultimate purpose will find matter. Someone who meditates on sound will find sound. Another who concentrates his attention on love will find love. Someone who disciplines his body will find body control. Finally, someone who meditates on reality will find reality. The wise man refrains from meditating on anything other than the infinite void, which is the essence of reality. He meditates on the void, because he has discovered that it is the only "thing" which is not part of the illusion. Void is unalterable, immutable, unique and permanent, all these are characteristics of reality. Then, after having observed it for long enough, he realizes that truth radiates from void.

The wise one takes the expressway to reach his destination as fast as possible. In the silence of contemplation on void, suddenly the intuitive light blinds the wise man in ecstasy.

Why is it that paths leading to the truth are so different from one another?

EXPRESSION

The action of communicating someone's feeling.

The adept must continually remain conscious of his various means of expression. They are: physical actions, mental actions (thoughts) and words. These are the different means managing the present and future of a being, they build a happy or unhappy future. All actions positively or negatively react on the source according to their initial charge. The body is controlled by a multitude of aggregate assemblies ceaselessly fighting among them to take over the brain that they control to act on the material world. All of these aggregates are more or less positive and negative and depending on which group is influencing the brain, the human being will accomplish actions, which may be positive or negative. For example, when a person regrets an action or a gesture, it is simply because the aggregate that regrets is different from, and certainly better than, the one that was controlling the brain when this action was performed. When a better aggregate is in command, the human being will accomplish good actions; a bad aggregate will push the body to perform negative actions or tasks. This is why it is very important for the adept to remain conscious of his being at all times. This is an efficient way to keep a positive group of aggregates in control and to ensure a happy future. The future is made of yesterday's and today's action results (reactions). A positive action generates a positive reaction and a negative action a negative one. The wise man accomplishes today actions that he will be proud of tomorrow.

If the aggregates are controlling the body, who am I?

EXTERNAL SELF-ANALYSIS

Decomposition, comparison and evaluation of what makes something, a being, a tendency, an idea, etc.

This type of analysis is performed at the beginning of the wakening stage, when the being becomes able to face the fact that he is not perfect, that others exist that can be right and he wrong, that everything happening to him is not anybody else's fault or responsibility but his own. This is a great moment on the road to awakening. As soon as becomes critical toward one of his contemporaries, he must reverse the situation and ask himself the following questions: What about me? Am I not the same as this person I just criticized? How am I different? In similar circumstances, would I have acted differently? Etc. Another very important point: the adept must accept his responsibility in life and understand that what is happening to him is the consequence of his own actions. He must acknowledge the action/reaction law. This understanding is essential since it is impossible for someone not able to take responsibility for his own life to take responsibility for his own evolution.

Who takes the decisions that affect me?

EXTRAORDINARY LOVE

Unlimited affinity for the whole created and uncreated universe.

The understanding that anything existing is one and indivisible. The type of love and compassion that one awakened to reality can feel toward the material world. This love is eternal. The searcher must reach the realization that ALL is ONE and ONE is ALL. He must be able to differentiate between a love blinded by illusion that is nothing else than a desire of possession, and an eternal, transparent and totally altruistic love taking roots in the unity of the whole.

Why must one love his enemy?

EXTREME

One opposed to another. The farthest possible position from the middle.

Extremes are not recommended either for the physical, intellectual or spiritual routine of a being. The adept does not let himself lean to the left or to the right; he tries to maintain the balance between various trends. A teaching favouring physical, intellectual or spiritual privations or their opposite can only be a side step on the path to the truth. One recognizes a teaching leading directly to reality by its simplicity, by the lack of disciplinary rules. As the teaching about meditation on nothingness recommends, one must only live in harmony with his body, his human and material environments and meditate on nothingness in order to reach reality. In the inner silence, all of the answers surface and shine their purity upon the observer. One meditating on an extreme will find this extreme and one meditating on reality will find reality. Any meditation leads to the goal intended nowhere else. The adept must not let any extreme distract him from the middle path leading directly to the truth.

Why would an extremist be rushing on the road to ruin?

EXTREMIST

Someone who pushes the practice of a belief beyond reasonable limits.

Anyone embarking on the practice of some discipline without first having sufficiently studied and understood the basics and purpose of the belief runs the risk of falling into extremes. Such an adept takes the chance of wrongly interpreting his experiences and losing sight of his ultimate goal. Someone erring in extremes has deviated from the shortest path to truth. In fact he has taken a long detour and lengthened his road. The wise man always remembers that the objective to be reached is not material, that it is not a part of the created world. This awareness is his lighthouse keeping him from the pursuit of emotional and false extremist impulses. As soon as he feels the material world calling, whether it is a physical or intellectual need, he knows that it is part of the illusion and processes it as such. The wise man walks the centre path, where no extremes exist. That is why he eats, but not too much, he works, but not too much, he lives in solitude, but not too much and he meditates. He is looking for the great physical, mental and spiritual balance that opens the searcher's eyes to the blinding void of eternal illumination.

What would result from too much meditation?

EXTROSPECTION

The action of experiencing what is outside.

When the mind rests in its natural state, in introspection, there is absolutely no notion of matter and personality, all is silence and calm, rests in perfect equilibrium. It is only when the thoughts appear in the brain and use various senses to experience and interpret energy exchanges (gives them shapes and names) that the material world starts to exist. It is this extrospection that invents the world in which we live. When introspection prevails over extrospection, everything vanishes and the eternal great silence reappears. When the adept focuses on nothingness, the material world vanishes, soon followed by the personality. Confronted with nothingness, the universe disappears. After a while in the quiescence silence, the wise man experiences reality as it is. The mind in its inalterable, eternal pure state immersed in itself.

What does the mind gain from its material experience?

F

FAILURE

The inability to achieve a project or a venture.

Failure seems to be the cause of deep sorrow for human beings who suffer from the disease of ignorance. People who experience some kind of failure only see the negative side of the event, the part that qualifies them as incapable and incompetent. They wanted something, worked to obtain it and did not succeed. The adept seizes a failure (in a material endeavour) with both hands and dissects it into its simplest components in order to understand their nature. Then he uses each of these elements as a correction tool for his future actions. He accepts his failure as a lesson that will allow him to succeed on the second try. In his search for truth or reality, the wise man uses meditation as a craft to help him cross the great river of illusion. He recognizes that at this level a failure and its constituent elements are illusory and unreal. By perceiving the failure for what it is, he reinforces his concentration on the void and sees these phantoms of the material world vanish. Failure cannot touch anyone juggling with reality.

Without failure, would it be possible to evolve?

FAITH

The fervent and total belief in something, a being, an idea or a dogma.

The first act of faith of the wakening being is to realize that there is another truth, a reality different from the one he experiences every day. Experience and analysis will prove to him the existence of the law of action/reaction, the fact that his actions, good or bad, influence his present and future, and that these actions will eventually affect him with their positive or negative charge. He will also acknowledge reincarnation, this essential evolution tool with its life and death cycle, as two different consciousness states of the same being. Then he will come to believe that mankind's misfortune is directly related to the duality managing the material world and the humans' illusory need to possess. He will also realize that happiness comes directly from the degree of comprehension of the created universe and the elimination of desires confining human beings in a state of perpetual pain. The intuition that the answer to all rests on the understanding of the mental process and its mastery takes shape in his mind. Finally, his faith turns toward meditation, the tool that will allow him to experience quiescence and offer him the possibility to free himself from the illusory world, and finally let him experience the eternal joy of truth. The adept must not let any weakness weaken his determination to dominate his mental machine and unveil reality.

Why is faith so powerful?

FEEDING

The action to give the body the fuel it needs to operate.

Feeding is the foundation of the biological operation of the human being. When someone does not take enough food, he becomes sick and may die from it. When a person takes too much food he gets sick and may die from it too. This is certainly an indication pointing toward moderation. Some believe that in order to practice meditation one needs to be a vegetarian; this is totally false. Vegetarianism cannot be commanded. It is a method of nourishment that a person may adopt for personal reasons when he deems it necessary. Others imagine that one must fast. This is another falsity. Meditation does not rest on feeding methods or customs but on a person's mental skills and determination. Meditation is favoured by a healthy and balanced diet. Meditation will yield better results when it is practised on a stomach that has completed its digestion cycle. Meditation in turn promotes a balanced life based on the inner self-exploration reflecting the outside world. The adept is free to eat as he wishes and according to his tastes and needs. His duty is to feed himself in order for his body to give the best possible performance for as long as possible. The longer the body will be operational, the longer the adept's quest for truth will last.

How long must one digest spiritual food before understanding?

FIRST PRINCIPLE

The cause of everything existing and non existing.

Principle essentially unitary (simplicity) from which derives the multitude (multiplicity). The unmodified and unalterable primordial state. The unique cause of the material and immaterial world. Void, immaculate and indescribable. The universal source of energy resulting in the various aspects of the divine manifestation. The container and initiator of all that has been, is and will be in all eternity. Even if the First Principle may seem to be divided into a multitude of individual minds, it is an indivisible unit, just as the thousands of individual rays heating the farthest corners of the world do not alter the unity of the sun.

What is a sun without rays?

FLEXIBILITY

The characteristic of a person who easily adapts to the world.

Human beings believe that they are the rulers of the world. However they are only people who do not understand the nature of creation. They have no flexibility when it comes to events and therefore have a lot of difficulties adapting to them. They try to control and manage everything. They can hardly tolerate that others think differently than they do. While fighting the essence of the world, they become the slaves of illusory machines. While refusing to stop for one moment to understand the nature of their environment, they destroy their habitat. The wise one looks upon the world and understands that everything contained in the universe and all that is illusorily or otherwise accomplished in the context of creation is part of the evolution adventure. While listening to the message of nature and pricking up one's ear to inner silence, he acknowledges his destiny, develops his action plan and works to open his eyes ever wider to the reality of what surrounds him. He slides and skirts around situations of life smoothly and gracefully. Nothing is complicated to one who recognizes the essence of illusion as the eternal emptiness of reality.

In what does the wise one differ from the rest of humanity?

FLUCTUATION

A movement that comes and goes.

Everything in our material world fluctuates and is modified from one moment to the next. Nothing was ever stable, nothing is stable and nothing will ever be stable in a universe governed by duality. The same applies to meditation when a beginner lacks practice and discipline. Before the adept becomes competent in the art of meditation, his efforts may sometimes seem useless. One day he obtains good results, at least he his happy with them, the next he cannot achieve anything right, silence evades him, thoughts fill his mind, the body refuses to remain quiet, it seems like nothing can be done, the attempt is a failure. The adept will accept, especially at the beginning, the fluctuation of the results of his efforts. Perseverance, will and time will defeat the illusory thoughts and calm the body; then silence, stable and immutable will take place to remain, and the adept will be able to taste it without being distracted. The adept will not lose heart; he will instead use his small failures as tools to help him reach his goal.

What is the nature of apprenticeship?

FORCE

An action applied with effort.

When the adept wishes to increase the intensity of his concentration in order to improve his state of quiescence, he must avoid applying force to his concentration. The attention intensity must be increased by raising the concentration; without effort or tension. The adept immediately realizes that he is applying force when he feels a physical or mental tension. Force is always followed by a more or less perceptible physical or mental action. We already know that an action generates a reaction that produces another one, etc. Thus, when used in meditation, instead of favouring thought control, force increases its activity. The adept receives a new shower of thoughts that attack his concentration. Meditation must be the ultimate relaxation; there should be no distraction, irritation or disturbance on either the mental or physical level. Any force used in meditation destroys the harmony and equilibrium and the material world emerges from the void scoffing at the faulty observer.

Does silence contain all of the universe's noises?

FORGIVENESS

The action of forgetting an offence and abandoning any desire for revenge.

Forgiveness is so important in the development of human beings that it could be used as a standard of measure of his evolution. <u>The more easily can someone sincerely forgive, the more that individual is evolved</u>. The capacity to forgive is proportional to the ability of the offended party to understand the reason behind the offending person's action. The capacity to understand one's behaviour or that of someone else is based on one's knowledge of human nature (assembly of physical and intellectual aggregates) and one's comprehension of the concepts of reality and illusion. When a person who has been hurt by another refuses to forgive, he worsens the situation because hate, desire for revenge, etc., are negative energies that destroy the one who uses them in an attempt to balance things according to his primitive point of view. Forgiveness allows to continuously clean the slate of negative links which have a tendency to bind the adept to the material world. It is also a way to ensure that he directs all his energy toward evolution and not vengeance. The wise one forgives instantly any fault, because he knows the unreality of the author and has no desire to waste his energy in vain pursuits.

What is the product of vengeance?

FORM

Interpretation in space of sensorial messages received by the brain.

Forms are part of the universal dream in which we are all immersed. They are, as everything else, illusory. The human body coming to life, maturing, aging and deing can illustrate the constant transformation of forms, but this applies to anything in the material world. The wise man does not forget the impermanence of his corporal envelope and that of the environment.

Of the old one or the infant, who has more time to reach liberation?

FOUR GREAT TRUTHS

The basic truths stated by the Buddha Gautama after he reached liberation.

1) Every life form in the created world is irremediably linked to suffering and sorrow. 2) The only cause of suffering and sorrow is the desire to possess. 3) It is possible to stop the suffering and sorrow by eliminating the desire to possess. 4) The practice of the art of meditation allows the cessation of suffering and sorrow by eliminating the desire to possess. These are four of the most important truths revealed to humans since the beginning of time. Those who have heard and understood the first three points and have practised meditation with sincerity have reached inhuman levels of liberation and happiness. These four truths could have changed the face of the world if more people heard and understood them. However, one must rejoice that such a lighthouse exists to indicate the way to those searching for truth in the night of illusion. The wise man who contemplates

the light of reality, has no more ties with the physical world: he is free from the limitations of suffering and sorrow.

Why can some people hear and understand while others cannot?

FRIENDSHIP

Affinity between two beings who are not necessarily related by family, race or sex.

Friendship, for most people, is a means to make allies who can become useful at some points in the future. A friendship that does not include the possibility of taking advantage of the other, is usually a relationship that does not last very long. Even very altruistic people take advantage of their friends up to a certain point, often without even knowing it. The simple fact to like to be with someone is in a way an advantage. The wise man tries to keep friendships alive as altruistically as possible, but as long as he is not completely liberated, he will be submitted to the same worldly laws as anyone else. However, one recognizes the wise one by the fact that he keeps friendships alive while staying impartial toward all living beings. The wise man knows that all living beings of the universe form one single unity, thus he considers them all equitably. When he communicates with one of them, he knows that he communicates with the whole.

Why does the word altruism represent impossibility in our world?

FRUIT

The result of an accomplished task.

When the wise man finally benefits from the thousands of hours of arduous discipline and work and can experience faint glimpses of truth, it is said that he is finally tasting the fruit of his efforts. The fruit of contemplation is thus a glimpse of what the mind really is when not distracted by the thought process, a moment of truth. During these short moments, the wise man is overwhelmed by intense peace and happiness generated by the intuitive knowledge of belonging to the first source of the universe and by the awareness of the instantaneity of all things. The wise one is no longer an ordinary human being but an awakened human, a divine being in perfect harmony with the absolute truth. The wise man's periodical illumination is the beginning of still another quest during which he will have to prolong these moments of illumination and learn to experience them at will. The ultimate goal is to reach a state of total and permanent union with the truth and participate even more actively in the great evolving adventure of creation. By looking into the depths of the universe the observer's eyes open and catch the light of reality.

What fruit does the universe reap from a wise man's liberation?

FUNCTION

The accomplishment of one's duty. The fulfilment of one's role in a specific environment.

After deep meditations and careful considerations, the wise one comes to the conclusion that the mind's first function is to create concepts. He also realizes that this is the first function of the individual mind as well as that of the infinite mind. It is impossible to specify the real reason why, or the process by which, the mind generates thoughts, but as soon as the wise man closes his eyes he sees them emerging from nothingness and going back to it indefinitely. The universe is thus the First Principle's great conceptual realization. As for the individual mind, it conceives and realizes its little illusory world every day until it is ready to return to its creator. The material world is the First Principle's dream and has no more reality (for it) than the dream of anyone sleeping. If the material world is a dream, we can state that the dream dreams, since we also can conceive and create things. This thought opens to another interesting reflection. The mind's function, at this point in our evolution and comprehension, is to express and evolve, and, in order to do so, it generates the world in which we live. Everything perceptible has its source in reality's nothingness, in the First Principle's essence.

How can perfection generate imperfection?

FUTURE

The result of all present and past actions.

Future is the present moment that has not yet arrived. The wise one does not initiate any action today that he will not be proud of tomorrow. One's present actions are the foundation of one's future. Since it is impossible to change the past, the searcher understands that everything rests on the present moment and that only his present actions will regulate the future. The universal law of action/reaction is inevitable.

On what depends future happiness if present unhappiness has its source in the past?

G

GLIMPSE

A quick perception modifying understanding without analysis.

A brief look on truth in the course of an illumination must not be interpreted as the final realization. The adept will not be fooled into believing that he has reached the goal before he has followed every step required for his purification from illusion. He will continuously be watchful in order to avoid the error that could bring his search to an end. Someone mistaken into believing that he has reached his goal, cannot progress anymore because he has stopped searching. If the wise one has the smallest doubt, he carries on with his meditation; he knows that the void cannot lie, cannot induce in error and that his contemplation will eventually open the door to reality. The glimpses of reality witnessed by the wise man on his journey are signs indicating that he is on the right path. The instant of illumination provides him with an insight of what awaits him at the end of his quest. The wise man preciously keeps inside each one of these luminous instant to reassure him in his search and allow him to better understand the great universal machine.

What is the source of illumination?

GLUTTONY

Excessive avidity for food.

Some adepts do not take enough nourishment to sustain their body, while others gulp enormous quantities of food exceeding by far their body's needs. The glutton usually eats food to compensate for his emotional problems and quickly becomes the slave of his eating habits. There comes a time when he can think of nothing but food. The person not eating enough is also obsessed with his desire for food and neither can think of anything else. Furthermore, this one may be jeopardizing his health. Both cases are extremes, thus counterproductive on the path to reality. This is why the wise one is content with sufficient nourishment to keep his machine healthy and operational, no more. He realizes the importance of health since without it, it would be more difficult for him to carry on his search. For him the body is a tool allowing him to progress toward his goal. The wise man does not entertain any food taboos; he is only frugal. Balance and moderation are his key words.

Does a salad contain less life than meat?

GOAL

The objective someone wants to achieve.

When one listens to what is said about meditation, we realize that there are as many and different goals as there are adepts. Some people are looking for calm and relaxation and others are attempting to develop supranormal powers (travel in time, produce energy at will, control people around them, float in the air, etc.). All these objectives are part of the illusion and will not lead directly to the ultimate goal of meditation. They are secondary practices that will give secondary results. A person in search of power demonstrates his attachment to the material world, his faith in the reality of what is created. Someone who develops powers before he acquires wisdom risks becoming attached to those powers and being slowed down in his progress toward perfection. It is preferable to find wisdom first instead of playing with powers if powers are one's goal. But let us not forget that one is searching for what he is ready to find and understand. The adept needs much wisdom and will in order not to succumb to the lure of power. Meditation's ultimate goal is the perfection and illumination of the one who meditates. The practising person works to become fully awake to created and uncreated things, to develop into a fully enlightened and energized being possessing total and perfect control over matter. At this point he is wise enough not to let himself be blinded by the powers at his disposal. The wise man prefers to leave things as they are in their divine perfection, thus powers are practically useless to him in the realization of his objective.

Why jump in the river when it is possible to cross the bridge?

GOOD

Positive side of the good/bad duality. Any action observing the present trends and beliefs of a dualistic society.

Any thought or action favouring the realization of truth. Good, as its counterpart bad, cannot exist alone. Good without bad does not exist because, for example, in order to assess if a situation is good, one must compare it with a bad situation. The wise man realizes that good is relative to the duality of which it is part and that as soon as silence takes precedence, duality disappears and is replaced by unity. An action or a thought is only good for the searcher if it favours progress on the road to enlightenment.

Is the victim of a beating responsible for his injuries?

GOOD-BAD

Both extremes of the scale balancing between beneficial and malefic.

All well-intentioned people would like to live in a universe where evil would not exist. They say that is would be marvellous to live in a world where everyone would be good and without malice. However, it is obvious that this scenario is impossible in a world based on duality. Everything in this created universe has its counterpart, this is an inescapable fact, and good, like everything else, has its opposite, bad. The wise one sees good and bad as the two extremes of an emotion. Thus, for him, these two opposed notions are false interpretations of the illusory world. Through meditation, the wise man tries to transcend his positive and negative emotions in the hope to reach a perfect state of neutrality. A state of tolerance where good and bad do not exist. In deep meditation, the wise man constantly faces what he calls reality, the state of emptiness containing and knowing everything, which is eternal, immutable and in perfect neutrality.

Why does God possess an infinite tolerance?

GREAT DIFFERENCE (THE)

The main distinction between people's status.

Of all times, the question: What is the difference between a being considered ignorant, because immersed into illusion, and a being said to be liberated, in other words free of all attachments to worldly things? Is there a hierarchy in evolution? Is a wise man superior to an ignorant? The wise one of yesterday and today proclaims that all of us are liberated beings, and that we are all an integral part of the universe's perfection. He even states that nothing distinguishes ignorance from liberation. Therefore, why search for the truth? What is the great difference? It rests in the interpretation of feelings perceived by the body's various sensors. The ignorant confuses two states, he sees reality in illusion and illusion in reality while the liberated one sees illusion in illusion and reality in reality. The ignorant does not know that he is ignorant while the liberated one knows that he is liberated. Illusion dominates the ignorant while illusion does not affect the liberated one. The ignorant bathes into illusion and sorrow, the liberated one is immersed into the blinding light of truth and bliss.

How can the liberated one be sure of his liberation?

GREAT PURIFICATOR

The silence that crushes all desires.

The silence of deep meditation is called the great purificator because it is capable of eliminating any desire to possess. The silence cures sick intellect and forgives the ignorant being's sins. Any negative or positive charge attached to a being loses its capacity to operate since there is nothing to act upon anymore. A person without desire is totally unalterable and unaffected by matter. Nothing based on duality can work in an environment of unity. Anyone in deep meditation realizes that in this state, bad and as well as good no longer exist. In the perfect silence where the analysis and thought process are out of commission, the observer alone remains, as a spark of consciousness looking upon the progress of creation. This "entity" is not material nor a part of the dualistic world; creation has absolutely no influence on it. Before the silence of deep meditation, all passions vanish; all desires disappear. The positive and the negative merge to become what they always were and will always be: the universal unity, the essence of everything. The wise one looks upon the world and contemplates the void without seeing any difference. The created and uncreated are one for the inner observer.

Why should anything be purified?

GREAT TEACHING

The communication of true information from one person to another.

Teaching is great when it recognizes that only one truth exists but that we all must find our own way to reach it. Those who practise a great teaching state that no one can impose his vision of the universe onto others. The searcher recognizes a serious teaching when it advises him not to accept anything as truth but to verify every information passed on to him, and then to constantly doubt and search for proof of new precepts or principles taught to him. A great teaching does not attempt to dominate the adept, to force him to change his way of life or to ruin him financially. Those who preach a great teaching understand that all beings willingly embark upon the path of truth when they are personally ready to do so, that they change their lifestyle only when they realize the importance of doing so and that they practice their chosen discipline in order to reach their chose goal. A great teaching states that those with ears to hear, hear and those with eyes to see, see. Furthermore, it recognizes that all beings move the same destination and that only the road differs from one person to the next. The adept in search of truth chooses a great teaching.

Why are there millions of different path to reach one single truth?

GUIDE

A source of knowledge used to advise and direct someone toward a goal.

The adept in search of the right path often tries to find along the way a guide who will be able to advise and direct him in his quest. A guide may be a person with obvious wisdom, or simply documents containing information about the search to undertake or continue, about the destination of the state to reach, etc. Under circumstances must the adept count on the knowledge or work his guide to reach his personal objective. The guide must never be seen as a master responsible for the adept's results. A guide can advise, share his own experiences, help the adept avoid some traps on the path, but his wisdom or knowledge cannot replace the adept's own experiences. The adept is his own master and the maker of his own rules, he is the ultimate one to decide the validity of his research and the methods he uses to it. He must understand that he has to be the one to walk the path leading to the truth. Each aspirant must be subjected to the results of his own activities, whether positive of negative. Each individual is entirely responsible for his own actions, words and thoughts. The adept is thus his own light and his own refuge. The truth cannot be reached by proxy.

What is the price of the final illumination?

H

HALLUCINATION

The perception of images having no reality.

Hallucination in meditation has two causes, the first one is purely mechanical and comes from the fact that the adept focuses on his physical eyes, which are stimulated into transmitting false information to the brain, which in turn interprets this information in way that makes the adept perceives the false results. The second cause is a manifestation of the aggregates constituting the adept's intellect: they are in fact thoughts. If the adept does not perfectly control his thought process, he can experience all kinds of hallucinations that have no more reality than a dream. In meditation he will be suspicious of what he sees, feels or hears. He will be capable to recognize what is real from what is not, by identifying as an illusion and misconception all that is constantly in transformation, all that is in motion. The truth is perfect stillness. The wise man in meditation focuses on a point in his cranium before entering a state of perfect indifference toward thoughts and their products. He experiences the immutable and eternal emptiness, the void. Anything else must display the same characteristic as void in order for him to accept it as real.

What happens to the wise man when the last thought vanishes?

HAPPINESS

A state of joy and pleasure.

Among the sleeping population, sleepwalking through the world, the notion of happiness consists in an assembly of acquisitions of various natures. The ignorant believes that he will reach happiness if he gets married, if he buys a particular make of car, if he obtains a promotion or a paid holiday, if he buys a house or a company, if he has a child, etc. This list is far from exhaustive. But to this day, except for some wise people looking for happiness elsewhere, no one has claimed after the fact, for very long anyway, that he had found the happiness he was looking for. After a while, they see their small happiness vanish as an ice cube in a sun ray, replaced by another thirst, another hunger for some other pleasure, which, according to them, will finally bring them happiness. In this way history is perpetuated since the beginning of time. The wise one acknowledges the impermanence of things of this world and tries to find happiness in what is stable and durable. After a long search, he discovers that the only stable and unalterable thing that he can experience is the emptiness (void) he observes within himself after appeasing his thought process. This void gives him an inner peace impossible to achieve in the material world. There, surrounded by nothingness, he observes, without thinking, without analyzing, relaxed and focussed on emptiness. After a while, he perceives some glimpses of revelation. When he has reached a state of perfect quiescence, he can contact his own source or reality, in other words, the First Principle. And when the wise man has acquired the absolute truth, he knows limitless happiness. At this stage no illusory notions can affect him; he has transcended creation.

Who distributes shares of happiness to humankind?

HAPPINESS-SORROW

Both extremities of the scale used to evaluate the well-being of human beings.

The human being is stands somewhere on this scale of physical and intellectual well-being. He believes that he is happy one day then unhappy the next according to the present moment and the progress of events which affect him directly. In general, people say they rather be happy than sad. But what about the great evolution machine of which we are an integral part? When the wise man analyzes the people considering themselves as happy (illusory happiness), he discovers that they do not favour change in their state. Thus they are less motivated to act with the objective to learn and progress to a better state. They evolve slowly. When he observes unhappy people, he notices that, unlike the others, they try by all means to improve their situation and learn new things in order to reach a more acceptable level of happiness. These individuals evolve rapidly. Then the wise one notices that happiness, like sorrow, is illusory, thus temporary. Some great wise men from the past said that sorrow must be accepted as a great master capable of indicating the path to reality.

What is the main cause of disillusion?

HATE

The emotion that pushes a being to wish harm for another and take pleasure in his misfortune.

One who hates someone else is often incapable of forgiving himself for mistakes he considers has committed. It is practically impossible to forgive others when one cannot forgive oneself. The wise one attentively analyzes hate because it is a very destructive emotion. He realizes that a person who hates another does more harm to himself than to the target of his hate. He witnesses the mechanisms of the action-reaction law. Someone who wishes misfortune to another cannot be happy because all his negative projections automatically come back to him with their charge of sorrow. This person deteriorates, becomes practically inhuman and often very sick. The wise man does not hate anyone, and he could not find any basis for such an emotion, since he understands that all beings constituting his world are like him, only assemblies of illusory aggregates, not knowing what they are doing. In meditation the wise man sees only shadows fighting and leaving no trace on the infinite screen of void.

What are the components of hate?

HINDRANCE

Anything that slows the adept's awakening.

Desire, malice, idleness, pride, doubt, etc., are some of the factors which slow down one's progression toward liberation. Hindrances, as everything else composing the material world, are also part of the great mystery. Autocriticism is the essential tool in the detection of anything that can impede one's progress toward wisdom and liberation. The searcher continuously analyzes and compares himself with models he wants to emulate. Purity can only come after all hindrances caused by desire have been transcended.

Between beauty and ugliness, which one is a hindrance on the path?

HONESTY

The characteristic of one whose respect for others matches his respect for himself.

In a dualistic world, in order to maintain the balance between good and evil, there are as many honest people as there are dishonest people. It is also possible to say that everyone possesses a more or less elevated level of honesty and dishonesty. No one is totally honest or dishonest in the created world. The more a person is submitted to matter, the more is he centred on his own well-being and the less is he interested about other people. The more a person becomes aware of the futility of worldly things and of the reality of the union of creation's elements into an unalterable whole, the more honest he becomes toward himself and others. A person looking for improvement discovers the universal law of action-reaction and realizes that every one of his actions positively or negatively influences his own being, his immediate surroundings and ultimately the whole universe. The wise man, conscious of creation's indivisibility, transcends hypocrisy and his inclination to deceive others in order to enjoy profits. His only goal is to be as honest as possible with himself and others, in the hope that one day everyone will walk the accelerated path leading to the liberation of all suffering.

What would become of creation if all living beings were suddenly to become good?

HUMAN BEING

An animal that has human characteristics, in other words Man.

The human being is recognized as the most evolved animal known in our universe. Man has the ability to grasp, understand and even create abstract ideas, that's why he can imagine physical, intellectual and spiritual states of beingness superior to his own. Man seems to be the only animal with the faculty to recognize his spiritual and physical nature. He possesses a curiosity that has always pushed him to analyze and understand his world and the body in which he lives. The adept starting a serious quest is aware of the importance of his body as a necessary tool in his search to find truth. Without the body, it is impossible to act upon the physical world and without the brain, it is impossible to think or analyze anything. The adept uses the life he was given to find again the natural state of his ultimate being. A human being is a machine created to discover truth, understand the why and how of what appears to him as a universal tragedy. A human being is a stepping-stone to reach a new level of evolution.

What is the difference between a human being and an animal?

HUMANITY

The assembly of men and women who form the superior animal race dominating the earth.

The unit of billions of First Principle manifestations. This unit shares the same illusion and hallucination because every individual in it is a projection of the same universal mind (First Principle). The adept acknowledges that there is a cosmic consciousness and that each creature of the universe draws from it. Creation is one and indivisible and one must acknowledge that members of this creation form a whole. The observer looks at his neighbour and sees his mirror image.

Why is humanity in constant transformation?

HUMILITY

The feeling of modesty and absence of pride and arrogance.

Human beings in general are not very prone to be modest. They try to impress each other in some way. Appearance is the game master in a dualistic world. Humility in the contemporary illusory world is certainly not a characteristic very useful to an individual's survival. A humble or unobtrusive person does not have much chance to succeed in our society of make-believe and illusions, where appearances make the man. The wise man can humble since he does not yearn for worldly success. Those who have nothing to gain or lose do not have to impress others. The wise man's humility points to the impermanence of worldly things and to the importance of using any event as an awakening tool. The wise man freely reaches out to anyone without distinction and quite openly uses his failures to pursue his search of truth. But he knows that humility, like pride, only has reality in the illusion.

What is the difference between a victory and a failure?

I

IDENTIFICATION

The action of becoming identical.

Human being says that he is unique, he is convinced to be what he thinks he is. Is this also true about the wise one who studies the composition of consciousness? The wise man understands that a human being is composed of biological and intellectual aggregates that manage all that is happening in the course of one's life. Who is I, who is this consciousness convinced that he decides, does, accepts and refuses things? After reaching the state of the inner silence and succeeding in appeasing all thoughts, tendencies and the other characteristics which form an illusory being, the wise man sees what is left, and that is a very small spark of consciousness lost in the void. He realizes that this spark is in fact the "I", revealed beneath his fantasies and free from all illusions. This "I" does not possess any volition or capacity to do; it is there and observes; that is why it is called the observer. But it is also the essence of all that exists, identifying itself to the physical and intellectual aggregates composing the human entity. Thus, the "I" is this spiritual entity (spark of consciousness), real and eternal and identified to the aggregates of a specific being in the material world. After realizing this, one is free from illusion.

Why search in the light for something that was lost in the dark?

IGNORANCE

The fact of not knowing and to live as an ignoramus.

Thought process that produces the belief that the material world is real. The material world is ignorance. The wise man destroys ignorance by going back to its source, by self-analysis and meditation on the inner void. The wise man weighs the ignorance against the standard of emptiness. The power of the void sweeps away the last bits of illusion to leave only the blinding light of reality. Ignorance disappears when confronted with truth.

What could a king be delivered from?

IGNORANT BEING

A person who is unaware of some things.

The ignorant is someone who does not know that attachment to matter is the unique source of suffering for human beings. He is this being who unrelentingly believes in the reality of the impermanent. Only after countless painful experiences can he become aware of the unreality of the creation. The ignorant and all other beings of the universe are on the same path leading from ignorance to wisdom. No one can escape creation's destiny which is to proceed from total submission to matter, to its domination and finally to the realization of its natural state. The ignorant is slowly and painfully coming out from under the yoke of emotions originating from the erroneous interpretation of life. But as soon as he begins to see the truth, he takes the proper actions to accelerate and further his understanding of himself and the world in which he lives. Once he is awake, the adept discovers meditation that allows him to progress more quickly on the path leading to the realization of his being. In the emptiness of deep meditation, he becomes aware that all beings of the universe are one and inseparable and that only their perception of the world keeps them apart. In the silence, the unity of the creation is an irrefutable truth.

Why are human beings considered imperfect?

ILLNESS

A disturbance of organs or functions managing the body.

Illness is considered a great sorrow, particularly if it is serious. People who suffer try by all means available to discover the cause of the problem and the possible cure. Some define illness as a punishment from their god for their wrong actions, while others think it is only a question of luck. The wise one knows that illness depends on a collection of past factors that can be rooted in his heredity, his own past actions or simply in coincidence. But mainly he sees illness as an opportunity to realize the impermanence of the corporal machine and the fact that there is no time to waste in order to reach the objective of the spiritual research. Beyond the illness inhabiting his body, he sees the disease that gnaws at the universe: impermanence. Wisdom is always the same whether it follows a negative or positive experience. In deep meditation the wise man uses his illness as a tool to evolve and understand. He acknowledges that illness, as any created things, has a beginning and an end.

Why is illness often an incentive for someone to become religious?

ILLUMINATION

Blinding revelation on the nature of reality.

Illuminations are common on the road leading to liberation. They are steps the adept has to go through in the course of his search for realization. The final liberation will be the illumination of illuminations. In the absolute silence of in-depth meditation emerges the light of reality. The adept meditating on any subject will find what he is looking for, but that will not necessarily be the truth. The ultimate truth is based on nothing and resides in emptiness. Meditation must be done on emptiness, the most simplified form of meditation. As the wise man gets closer to the truth, things become more and more simple. The further an ignorant is from reality, the more complicated his world becomes. Beware: The adept must not mistake a partial illumination for the ultimate one. Anything emerging from the void will disappear in the void. The truth is ONE.

Why is everything in our world becoming more and more complex?

ILLUSION

Erroneous perception and interpretation of real phenomena.

All things contained in the material world are illusions. Projections of the collective consciousness forming the material universe are also illusions, as well as anything the ignorant considers real and solid. No one should be fooled by the marvellous illusions or promises of the impermanent world. One should rather experiment with eternal permanence, unity and the ever-blinding light of truth.

What does it feel to touch reality with the tip of one's finger?

ILLUSORY

The characteristic of something unreal that does not last.

All that is material and managed by the mental process is illusory and impermanent. The material or illusory world is but one facet by which the First Principle is expressed. The void can express itself without becoming impure, as the numerous colours coming from it do not affect space. The illusion is transparent for one possessing the in-depth vision given by meditation on emptiness. The illusion disappears when the observer realizes where it comes from.

What is a thought made of?

IMMATERIALITY

The characteristic of what is not composed of matter; the uncreated.

When the wise one finds truth, he intuitively realizes that even the ultimate duality of what is created (material world) and uncreated (void) are in fact an inseparable unity. He seizes the essence of the immateriality of all things but he cannot intellectually describe his experience. The wise man has understood that emptiness is matter and matter is emptiness, that all is nothing and nothing is all. He has discovered that reality is neither this nor that, but both. It is impossible to state that parts of the mind are independent from one another; they are various material manifestations of an indivisible whole. What would happen if we eliminated one of the components used to produce light, such as the electricity, the bulb, the heat, the filament, etc.? The light would automatically disappear. Thus light and its constituents form an indivisible whole, as the different aspects of the mind and intellect are the inseparable rays of the eternal light. This discovery is however only another step on the path leading to the First Principle, where the wise man will become totally immersed in the primordial essence and achieve infinite consciousness.

Can anyone totally absorbed in the material world ever find truth?

IMMOBILITY

The state of what does not move nor undertake any action.

For most people in our society, immobility is practically impossible. They move incessantly, their heads overflow with totally anarchic worlds of thoughts on which they have absolutely no control. Furthermore, their bodies walk, run, dance, twitch, itch, etc. unceasingly. They are unconsciousness personified; they flee from confusion just to find more confusion. The adept in meditation realizes that he must remain mentally immobile. Meditation is defined as the observation of emptiness, without analysis, reflection, or interpretation, inside a body in perfect physical balance as relaxed as a baby a sleep. As soon as the slightest mental action occurs, meditation is broken off. The adept must remain bodily and mentally immobile without any volition or consciousness other than observation. He observes as if he were an independent entity, detached from everything, he is simply there observing. The more immobility copies the nature of reality the closer it gets to the truth.

Does the realization of immobility represent a movement?

IMPARTIALITY

The quality of someone who does not take sides, someone neutral.

Knowing that everything is prejudiced in this world, the wise one tries to remain neutral, to avoid theories or opinions for or against anything material. He follows the central path, the one that leans as little as possible toward the negative or positive pole. He walks in balance on the wall between the positive and negative worlds. He does not try to refute the world or to lose himself in it. He is the observer using the ultimate tool of neutrality, the meditation on nothingness. He focuses on the inner emptiness, without thinking, without analyzing and totally relaxed. He holds on to his consciousness and assists, filled with wonder, to the unfolding of the great tragedy. He does not accept or refuse, understand or question, believe or doubt; he is only an observer without opinion, an image sensor. Then he realizes that he is the mirror of what exists and the source of the image he perceives. He is progressing in balance on a tight rope pulled between the abyss and nothingness.

What is the value of an image traced on the canvas of emptiness?

IMPERFECTION

That which is missing some elements to be complete.

Someone looking at the material world and only seeing imperfection does not understand how the universe operates. The ignorant believes that everything, including himself, is imperfect and lacks some finishing touches. Others see the action of humans on the world as something totally unnatural as if human beings were entities foreign to nature. Some religions place human beings above all that exists and make them benevolent or evil masters of the world they manage. The wise man looks upon the world with a smile because he understands that all is in perfect balance and order, and that all is subjected to the only universal law that regulates the entire created world, action—reaction, from which nothing can escape. If in the current moment nothing falls apart, it is because everything is in equilibrium. Thus all is perfect in the immediate moment. Furthermore the wise one knows that only the present moment really exists in the illusory world. He also understands that if human beings harm the environment in which they live, eventually they will have to pay the price, whether by disappearing or mutating in order to survive. The wise man understands that all beings do what they have to do at the time they do it and that everything tends toward equilibrium.

Can the infinite and perfect void produce something imperfect?

IMPERMANENT

The quality of what does not last.

All that a human being wants to cling to in this world is impermanent. Despite this, he wants to believe that things last. He thinks that he loves forever, gets married forever and will live forever despite various proofs that nothing persists, that everything wears out, deteriorates, ages, then finally disappears. A human being does not want to accept, simply because this would demonstrate how fugitive is his identification, his self. He wants to live eternally and would do anything to achieve that goal. Yet, if he could only open his eyes a little to reality he would understand that he is and always was immortal. Deep down inside the wise one observes thoughts emerging and vanishing into nothingness. The moment he opens his eyes, he cannot refrain from making the parallel with the phenomena of the world in which he lives. All that exists in the present moment disappears in the past and gives way to all that emerges and exists in the future. Nothing is ever exactly identical; all is in constant transformation. This modification altering the whole universe is perceived as wear and tear due to the passage of time. Furthermore the wise man knows that what he perceives as his being, his personality, is also temporary and that it is only a breath of identity resting on a series of ephemeral perceptions.

What is the difference between one who knows and one who does not?

IMPORTANCE

The degree of seriousness given to a person, a situation or a thing.

Human beings qualify everything, they cannot tolerate what is not precisely defined and filed. The importance attributed to a situation is practically always related to the proximity of the cause. The closer a positive or negative fact occurs to a person, the more importance is given to the impact. Sorrow in one's house is always worse than sorrow in someone else's home. On one hand, the wise man knows that the scope of sorrow is proportional to the importance it is given and that one's sorrow is often someone else's happiness. On the other hand, in deep meditation he realizes that nothing is really important since everything in the illusory world balances between importance and insignificance. No one can find real happiness in this world, however important we think it is. The wise man knows that it is only interference on the universe's screen.

When the cause of someone's sorrow brings happiness to someone else, should we rejoice with the latter or feel sorry for the former?

IMPOSTOR

A person who tells lies and takes advantage of other people's credulity to gain profit.

Whether it be to dominate a profession in the material world, or master the discipline leading to the truth, the knowledge required is first and foremost practical. Intellectual knowledge has its place but it is not essential to the success of the searcher. On the other hand, without practice failure is certain to happen. The adept will avoid impostors who profess loudly but are unaware of the power of inner silence. They may pretend to enjoy universal wisdom and all the power it may confer, if they do not practice the art of meditation, they do not deserve the confidence of the searcher. The adept will be wary of noisy people, promising other things they overlook in themselves. The wise man does not profess anything; he whispers his experience. If the adept feels a need for a master, he will choose a very silent person, very silent indeed, since the desired answer rests in the silence the searcher creates at will in his inner self.

Why does noise generate foolishness?

IMPULSE

A thought, a word or an action triggered by a sensation.

A person first becomes conscious of a sensation coming from one of his perception centres. He then interprets this sensation as negative or positive, good or bad, dangerous or securing. This interpretation will in turn generate the impulsive reaction that will be translated into a thought, a word or an action. Impulses generate reactions and desires. The wise one learns during his meditation that if there is no perception, there is no sensation, and that in the absence of sensation there is no desire. When the wise man reaches the state of quiescence, he is capable of closing all doors to external perceptions, thus eliminating impulses and desires. In this solitude, the external world ceases to influence and the wise one can contemplate the void without any more distractions. He is there suspended in emptiness, without a body, just a small spark of consciousness ready to merge into the universal light from which it will emerge as a luminous beam that will sweep the world with the truth.

Is wisdom synonymous of absence of control?

INCREDULOUS

A person who hesitates to believe and doubts everything.

People in general believe everything; they are credulous. They believe in permanent happiness, in politicians, in media publicity: they believe in anything and everything. They do not have much choice because if they want their world to keep on existing they must believe in it, they must constantly recreate it. It is only after countless acts of faith which are eventually found false, after anticipated happiness which never came through or lasted only one instant, after having believed in anything and everything and realized that nothing survives the test of time and that all disappears, only then will a credulous person become incredulous. The wise one does not believe in the material world and uses it only as a tool to progress toward his ultimate objective, his research for truth. He dissects everything, studies and experiments in order to discover his true nature that of what surrounds him. Even in meditation, he does not accept at face value anything he sees or feels, because he knows that as soon as the analyzing process takes over an experience, the pure truth is mostly removed and leaves only a comparative interpretation of the phenomenon. The wise one knows and believes that he can accept as real only what he experiences when his mental process is turned off.

Once stripped of illusion, is the universe only energy?

INDIFFERENCE

The state of a person who is insensitive to or detached from certain things.

When during contemplation a thought emerges, it triggers the "search, find and destroy" process. This process first recognizes, and simultaneously acknowledges the situation, then takes the decision to eliminate this thought in order to carry on the contemplation. All this happens at the periphery of consciousness, but it is enough to destroy the perfect harmony of deep meditation. Furthermore, any conscious action originates in a thought and all thoughts generate other thoughts, thus the cycle is endless and the adept's distraction permanent. But the wise one, with time, has developed an unalterable level of attention that automatically controls thoughts (the interrupter). This interrupter faces thoughts in formation and prevents them from reaching completion and in doing so stops the creation of other thoughts. The interrupter is an autonomous system that enters into action without the need of the "search, find and destroy" process that an undisciplined mind must use. When the wise man has reached this stage, he can practice contemplation without interruption, without distraction. In this state, there is no reaction to emerging thoughts. The indifference to the parasitic movements of the thought process is total. In perfect indifference, the wise man ignores illusion and contemplates reality.

Must one be indifferent to life to experience immortality?

INDIVIDUAL MIND

The manifestation of First Principle in human form.

That which gives life and reveals the truth when silence is established. The mind is not created therefore it is not part of the material world. The individual mind is the extension of the First Principle. What the ignorant beings call their soul. The awakened adept acknowledges that the mind inhabiting his body is an integral part of the First Principle and therefore is one with it. Since the individual mind is an extension of the First Principle, meditation allows one to reach a level of non-altered perception about the initiating source, and merge with it.

Does water remember that it used to be liquid when it becomes ice?

INDIVIDUAL PAST

Everything that all the aggregates forming a being have thought or done in the past.

The elements and aggregates forming the present of an individual. An individual must not place more importance on past actions than on present ones because these are the ones that will shape his future, where he will spend the rest of his life. One that recognizes the path of truth is not concerned by past illusory thoughts and actions; instead he works constantly toward his liberation as if his life had no tomorrow. The adept uses present consequences of the past as experiences to advance on the road to liberation. He acknowledges that happiness and sadness are only illusory and can only serve as tools in his search for reality.

How can one erase the consequences of his past?

INEVITABLE

Anything impossible to avoid, not to suffer or not to experiment.

It is inevitable that what is formed or born will sooner or later suffer dissolution or death. The material world is totally impermanent; anything appearing in it will disappear from it. Every human being without exception will experiment happiness and misfortunes in the course of their life, where nothing can really be stable or permanent. After long analysis, experiments and meditations the adept realizes that he cannot count on anything in this world because everything is constantly changing. Everything which exists today will disappear tomorrow or soon after. No manifestation has any more reality than a breeze and affects reality anymore than a white cloud would mar the blue of the sky. Anything that can be created, shaped or generated can also be destroyed, dispersed or dissipated. Thus what is not created, formed or generated transcends those characteristics. The First Principle (void) does not possess any particular characteristics, it is the essence of ALL without being all, thus it is superior to the material world. Void transcends existence.

Why is death inevitable?

INEXPLICABLE

The characteristic of what is impossible to define or understand.

The First Principle, infinite and nothingness without characteristic is inexplicable because it is uncreated. All that is mind and what comes from the mind, matter that is in reality mind, uses illusory, inexact and ill-defined words in order to try to explain the **inexplicable**. All these eternal or temporary things which are mind and matter, this finite or infinite knowledge, everything that exists on the objective and subjective plane, is totally inexplicable in words because words are very primitive and limited means of communication. However, words must be used in an attempt to share one's experiences and knowledge with others who could profit from them and discover for themselves the path to reality. The wise man considers that any knowledge other than the one arising from his inner meditations must be verified and experienced. Nothing must be accepted without verification by means of meditation. Anyone who believes that he alone is right and possesses the truth is still sleeping under the veil of illusion and ignorance. Let us remember that anything said or written in this world can only be temporary and does not represent the absolute truth. Let us meditate on worldly knowledge.

How is it possible to experiment the inexplicable truth?

INFLUENCE

The impact of a person, situation or thing on another person or his state of mind.

In the course of his meditations, the adept is subjected to the continuous influence of mental processes that never stop producing image-thoughts that seem to emerge from nowhere and disappear into nowhere. Whatever the thoughts or passions distracting him, the adept must not in any way surrender to them or let them take control; he will let them pass by without trying to eliminate, transform or direct them. If the adept only recognizes thoughts for what they are, and persists in doing so, neutralize them, keep their real identity (void) so they will not be able to build sufficient strength to become substantial. A thought that is not accepted or is rejected has no more reason to be and returns to emptiness.

A thought without reason to be does not exist. The wise man becomes an observer totally indifferent and insensible to the mental process game. Matter has no more influence over this being who bathes in perfect quiescence.

Why is a wise one subject to the influence of goodness?

INNER PRESENCE

Keeping a constant inner consciousness.

One of the objectives of an adept who practices meditation is to remain present at all times, not to let himself be invaded by what is happening outside or inside himself. When the adept loses consciousness of what is happening, the aggregates operate the body without his knowing. The more the adept's environment is agitated and noisy, the more it is difficult for him to remain an indifferent spectator of life's progress. This is why he first practices in calm places that are not too demanding. The most difficult situation is certainly to take part in a conversation while trying to be the spectator of what is said by both parties, and while being conscious in one's mind at the same time. The adept immediately feels overwhelmed by illusion and loses consciousness. The easiest situation is to walk. Then the adept can remain present and observe his body's deambulatory walk through life, which from this point of view, empty of false emotions, is homage to creation in all its splendour. As long as the adept is present in his head, he is meditating.

Who is looking out on the world from inside the adept's mind?

INSENSIBLE

The lack of reaction to some stimuli.

The adept must tirelessly try to achieve inner silence. He must become completely insensible to the appearance or disappearance of thoughts. He must reach a level of concentration that will not be altered by the endless movement of thoughts. The adept realizes that thoughts are illusory creations that can only exist in the dualistic world. With practice and intense concentration, he will succeed in remaining immutable before pleasant or unpleasant images presented to him by the mental process. He will become the neutral observer of the parade of intellectual aggregates in full action. The more he accepts this random movement of thought forms, the less capable the thoughts are to affect him. Accepting them, and letting them follow their normal course free him from any impact they might have on him. The adept's focus becomes an unlimited space of peace in direct contact with the universal mind. The wise one, immune against the effect of thoughts, looks upon the unveiled reality.

Where was the thought just before it emerged in the thinker's head?

INSEPARABLE

Anything that cannot be separated, or is impossible to keep apart.

When the adept discovers that his individual mind is in fact an integral part of the universal mind that is nothing else than the First Principle, he realizes that he is inseparable from his neighbours, from all beings and things of the world. He faces the fact that everything is inseparable and that nothing can be altered since reality is one indivisible unit. This great discovery shows him that the created and non-created fuse into a whole. Furthermore, the realization that creation is an indivisible whole allows one to catch a glimpse of the universal instantaneity. In fact, since everything is ONE, the notion of multitude does not exist anymore, interactions do not exist, movement is nil, time and space disappear, quiescence emerges and void appears. The adept realizes that his mind is not a part of creation, that it is non-created like the First Principle, from which it is derived. In this instant of intense illumination, the adept forever washes free of all false concepts he accumulated in the course of his lives of ignorance, and becomes pure, transparent and luminous. Nothing will ever be the same for him; he is now liberated.

What can a liberated person do?

INSOMNIA

Inability to sleep and get rest.

Most people who suffer from insomnia have no control on their mental process. Insomnia is usually caused by a continuous series of more or less confused thoughts on which the insomniac has absolutely no control. As soon as you ask him "What keeps you from sleeping?", he will answer "I can not stop thinking". The moment a person can discipline his thought process, even just a little, he falls asleep unless he strongly focuses on something specific. Needless to say that a meditating person never has insomnia problems and can sleep at will. The wise one realizes that the cacophony of thoughts in his head emerges from nothingness one instant to be swallowed up by it the next. Because of this fact, he focuses his attention on a specific point, relaxes and simply tries to ignore this ballet of confusing thoughts. One must not attempt to erase or destroy thoughts; one must let them pass without being distracted. Slowly they become less and less distracting, and then they totally disappear from the mental scenery of the mind focused on nothingness. Quiescence is the reward of the one who persevered in his quest for silence and discipline.

Does an insomniac dream of being awake?

INSTANTANEITY

The concept stating that everything is happening at the same place at the same time.

The moment during which the positive and negative fuse together into a unity wherein no good or bad exists. Only our interpretation of the material world leads us to imagine and measure space and time. In the First Principle's reality, everything is happening now in its unalterable unity. Only deep meditation allows the adept to grasp this paradox. The material world is only a reflection in the mirror of reality. But this reflection plays an important role in the development of the universal instantaneous evolution. Illusion exists anyway as a dream and no one can deny that. The wise man in balance between illusion and reality meditates in silence on the void.

Is the reflection also the mirror?

INSTINCT

Emotional and glandular impulses leading human beings in the battle for their animal survival.

An important part of mankind acts under the influence of its purely animal impulses. No one can reach truth by following his natural instinctive tendencies. These have to be transcended, discipline must control the machine and the will power will sublimate life. The sincere belief that something greater and better than the material world exists, together with an indomitable will to reach the goal, and a method to control the thought process are the mandatory tools the searcher must use in order to be successful. But one must not forget that it is impossible for anyone to understand what he is not ready to understand or practice what he does not believe in. In order to transcend instinct, one must first realize that instinct must be transcended before reaching another level of understanding of the world.

Why is a being who is controlled by his instincts a bad person?

INTEGRITY

The state of what is pure, virgin.

The cause of all sorrow lies in the fact that the divine essence of people, pilgrims on the way to illumination, is corrupted by thoughts. In fact, people are so polluted that they have lost their integrity, they believe they are thoughts, they identify with thoughts. Ask them what would become of them if they suddenly stopped thinking, and without exception they will give you this type of answers, "I would not exist anymore", "I would be a zombie". Nevertheless, it is very easy to verify that someone who stops thinking does not become unconscious, quite the opposite . . . Thus integrity is very important for the adept who practices meditation, which is the concentration of his attention on a mental point. He must maintain the integrity of the observer (his attention). When thoughts have calmed down and silence has taken over the adept's mind, the attention is totally focused on the concentration point. This attention (observer) will not in any case be distracted by thoughts, the observer will keep all his integrity and will remain present at all times. As soon as the adept loses control of his attention, he becomes thoughts again. Here is what can happen, "Ah yes, I forgot to close the garage door, hum, I don't know if Bob will come to the beach with me tomorrow, I sure hope that Lauren noticed me in class today", etc. Gone, the observer is completely gone. The attention (observer) must remain, totally pure, and contemplate void.

If the observer is not thoughts, what is he?

INTELLECT

The faculty to analyze, learn and know, which humankind falsely identifies as the individual mind.

What human beings understand as the intellect (what they believe to be the mind) is a complex assembly of various sensations, perceptions, reasoning, memories and consciousness (aggregates). This complex mix forms the personality of a being, which is temporary, thus has no relation with the mind since mind is first unique and eternal. The wise one is not fooled by the ignorant who views the intellect as divisible, decomposable and analyzable. He realizes that all these different characteristics only apply to the illusory world. The various facets of the intellect do not resist the analytical meditation that immediately acknowledges their empty nature, making them indissociable from the universal unit (the universal mind). The wise one, in the course of his research, has discovered that the individual mind, this observer of the intellect, is in reality the reflection of the universal mind containing all that is created in its instantaneity. The complexity of creation, once divided into its simplest expression, contains nothing but void. Only the intellect believes in the existence of a physical world. As soon as the wise man severs the communication between the reception centres and the analytical centre, the material world vanishes. Then he eliminates the thought process. THERE REMAINS ONLY VOID.

If the mind is unique and indivisible, how can it express itself in so many ways?

INTELLECTUAL ANALYSIS

Analysis based on an erroneous perception of the material world. Analysis using information perceived and interpreted in the material world.

This type of analysis allows to understand the illusory aspects of reality. This is the analysis used by everyone in order to understand what is happening in the world and in their own life. This exercise is illusory and cannot lead to the eternal truth. The adept will be wary of intellectual analysis, it can only be wrong and bring confusion since it relies on false data. One must gather his knowledge in the silence of meditation, in the absence of thoughts or any other mental process. Alone in silence the searcher acknowledges the eternal truth.

How can silence contain truth?

INTENSITY

Level of power applied on something.

The concentration of the attention on a particular inner point is the fastest method to reach emptiness, silence or the absence of thoughts. But this method will fail if it is not supported by the intensity necessary to ignore distractions. The beginner often mistakenly thinks that power is synonymous with force. Quite the opposite, power must be applied by an amplification of the attention energy, without tension, without effort, gently but with certainty. Thoughts which form the almost all of the distracting factors possess also a quantity of energy which, once unified, can often break through concentration and distract the observer. When this happens, the adept re-focuses his attention without giving any attention to the guilty thought, then amplifies the intensity applied to his concentration. There will come a time when intensity the power of the concentration will be in perfect equilibrium with the energy of the distracting thoughts. Then, in quiescence, the adept will be able to contemplate the great blackboard of reality.

Why is failure more profitable than success?

INTERFERENCE

Intervention into other people's personal affairs.

In a world where half of the population would like to dominate the other half, it is easy to realize that interference is an international as well as national, local and family hobby. Everyone would like others to do everything exactly as they would, and when some don't, they rebel, criticize and try to influence their way of doing things. They believe that they are the only ones who know the truth and the good formula. The wise man does not interfere with the affairs of others, since he knows that all have their own scale of values, that everyone understands and interprets the world his own way, according to his own experience. Furthermore, he knows that within a dualistic universe, i.e. based on opposite poles (- and +), nothing can be perfectly the same, everything is different from one moment to the next, everything is different from one being to the next. The wise one lives his life and lets others live theirs at their pace, the way they like it, without intervening. Only in moments of illumination, can he glimpse the reality of the infinite unity, where nothing changes, where all is stable and eternally true. The wise man practices total tolerance.

Why does the creator tolerate the folly of human beings?

INTERPRETATION

The explanation of what is perceived.

All type of interpretation, explanation or clarification must be excluded from meditation. The meditative state is one of contemplation, observation and total neutrality where the observer must resist any kind of analysis, and avoid explanations and rationalizations. Analysis is a dualistic function of the brain based on the two major material world parameters: the positive and negative. Any form of analysis can only be false in the absolute sense of the term since the comparisons used in this process are also the result of more or less accurate analysis. Any interpretation must be considered illusory and subject to review. The adept in meditation observes without distraction and if he becomes transparent enough to matter and identified enough to the WHOLE, he will perceive flashes of absolute truth. These are easily recognized: the adept is practically blinded by the intensity, clarity, transparency and totality of the truth he sees under a completely different angle. The reaction of the observer exposed to an absolute truth could be summarized approximately like this: "Of course, yes, this is it, how could have I thought otherwise, it is so obvious, etc." The adept can keep this state as long as he remains in quiescence, but as soon as he comes out of it, he feels this beautiful evidence crumble in the attempt of the rationalizing process to vulgarize and compare everything with what is known and accepted, and finally leave a weak memory of this intense moment of truth. At the moment of final illumination, the whole absolute truth will become permanent.

Can a subjective presence compensate for an objective absence?

INTROSPECTION

Observation of one's own inner universe. A look inside.

The attention the observer focuses on his inner emptiness after having successfully mastered the thought process. The fundamental study of the individual mind by the mind. The adept concentrates on the emptiness with the intention of realizing this: his mind, being the First Principle, is totally empty; his empty mind is thus eternal, without beginning or end; the knowledge emerging from it is infallible and unalterable; his mind not having any objective appearance cannot be influenced by illusion; all that is illusion comes from our own concepts and form all worldly things; all that is created in an absolute cycle must appear and disappear. To prove that all this is true, one must look inside and focus all his attention on his inner world.

Why look inside when there are so many exciting things happening on the outside?

INTUITION

The knowledge acquired without the use of intellectual analysis. The knowledge not coming from experience but from nothingness.

The wise one acknowledges that intuition is wisdom and gives it precedence over pure analytical knowledge. The intuitive knowledge is not tarnished by human illusory prejudices. A person who knows how to listen is used to this type of manifestation, and knows how to recognize solutions to some problems or questions emerging from nowhere and imposing on his mind. The wise man harvests the fruit of his silence, and his comprehension of the created universe grows constantly. Intuitive knowledge is not an illumination such as the one happening sometimes in deep meditation or shortly after. It is instead an inner mundane knowledge of the mechanisms of the world. The first idea is often the best one, simply because most of the time it is intuitive. The wise man in meditation cultivates his intuition to help it eventually become an illumination.

Why would intuitive knowledge be truer than analytical knowledge?

INVADING THOUGHTS

Thoughts left alone which take over consciousness.

People who do not practice any kind of thought control have their mind entirely invaded by various thoughts. When they talk, they express their thoughts as they come to them. When they think, they believe to be these appearing and disappearing thoughts. The beginner who closes his eyes in an attempt to control his thought process, with the intention to meditate, is literally invaded by hundreds of thoughts, some of which will only pass by while others will assault his attention, forcing them to identify to the thoughts. For example: The adept closes his eyes and for a few seconds silence prevails. Later on he will recognize that he existed at that point without thoughts, that in fact he is something else than thoughts since he was still conscious, at that very moment without thinking. This instant, as short as it is, allows him to experience meditation (silence without thoughts and without effort). Then, he is under attack: thoughts start to emerge. The adept observes that some thoughts go by without distracting him, but all of sudden, "I forgot to mail my mother's letter, it is not important I will mail it tomorrow morning . . . I believe that I made a good impression on Mr. So-and-so today . . . Bob forgot his keys again, he will never learn . . . , etc". This is usually how it happens, as soon as a thought a little stronger than the others appears, it takes over the attention, the consciousness. The adept is reimmersed into pure illusion, enslaved by thoughts. He has lost the natural state of his consciousness, the state not polluted by thoughts. Only tenacity and a proven method of thought control will allow the adept to vanquish this enemy in order to reach and prolong the silence of meditation.

What is the nature of human consciousness?

INVULNERABLE

A person who cannot be hurt.

Someone who is tired of being hurt by life's trials and tribulations is looking for protection. Meditation is the art of concentrating one's attention on a particular point, to deliberately control the thought process and establish a state of consciousness immune to distractions. In this state of silence the adept comes closer to the essence of all things (god) and experiences glimpses of truth. Slowly he learns to recognize the world for what it really is, an illusion and the cause of all small and great sorrows of humanity. After realizing this, the adept becomes less and less vulnerable to false interpretations of illusory sensations and practically invulnerable to worldly problems. He sees, he knows, he recognizes, he understands, and he smiles. Meditation is the road leading to the invulnerability of the one who practises sincerely. In deep meditation, the wise man, his eyes turned inside, offers no resistance to the wind of various worldly attacks. They appear on the horizon of his life, come close to him and do not find any hold. They pass and disappear without a trace. The wise man contemplates the essence of creation.

What is the main cause of man's vulnerability to the material world?

IRRELIGIOUS

A person not looking for self-improvement.

Any religious practice demonstrates the desire for something else, a better world, a greater perfection, etc. The material world does not bring enough satisfactions; the mirror is scratched. This is the early beginning of the quest for truth. This is when one acknowledges more or less consciously that he should become better with an objective to achieve. All great wise ones have admitted that the religious search is the only difference between a human being and an animal. The beginner still has many battles to win before he can drop the cape of illusory beliefs and open his eyes to the real truth, never changed, never altered, infinite and eternal. The adept finds this first and unique truth in the depth of his meditation during this short moment when thoughts stop their frantic dance and let the mind recapture its fundamental nature. The wise man looks upon the world with great compassion because he knows that all will have to suffer a long time before disregarding illusions, before transforming themselves and letting their mind grow to finally fly free.

What is the YOU taking a decision?

IRRITATION

The state of someone who is aggravated, exasperated by a person or a situation.

Most people are usually irritated when they encounter some persons or situations not corresponding to their own vision of things. Often they will discuss, argue, shout, get angry and they may even fight to convince their interlocutors of their views. They do not understand that others cannot see things differently, and then they feel very frustrated. They never take an instant to think, to analyze the others' visions. They unrelentingly believe that they are the only ones endowed with the truth; that no one else can be right according to their reasoning. Irritation will gnaw at them until they grasp the essence of the problem. The wise one says: What is the difference between two points of view? And the question contains the answer: The point of view of course. It is obvious that as long as each human being looks at the world from his own angle of vision, tolerance will be scarce in our world. But, as soon as someone a little wiser takes a minute to see the world as a whole, egotism vanishes and then appears the possibility of a universal union of all human beings who are parts of an indivisible unit. It becomes difficult to argue with oneself.

Why do human beings' points of view differ?

ISOLATION

The state of being separated from a thing, a person or an environment.

Several great wise men have discovered the truth in isolation from the world and what it represents. Above all they were trying to eliminate all sources of distraction that are harmful to the awakening and the progress on the path leading to the light. Others choose a different route, the one going through the crowd and society in which they see an almost inexhaustible source of study and comparison. Whether the adept decides to tread one route or the other, he will very quickly realize that, in meditation, isolation is total the moment he closes his eyes, his windows on the material world. Meditation is practised in total isolation, where one can only rely on oneself and alone walk the path. Whether the traveller lives on top of a mountain which dominates the world, or in the heart of a noisy and smoke-filled city, the real cause of distraction comes from the thought process which incessantly pollutes the purity of the inner void. The battle occurs in isolation and silence between the observer and the observed. When finally one merges into the other, the goal has been reached.

What is the nature of distraction?

J

JUSTICE

The impartial evaluation of each other's merits.

Human beings who do not know the universal laws are looking for justice in the judgment of men. They try to gain acknowledgement for rights and merits resting on the erroneous understanding of the world and its values, by an assessment system also taking roots in errors of interpretation, false emotions, prejudices and biases. Real justice cannot exist in a dualistic world where everyone interprets it according to his own understanding based on his personal experience of life. The justice of one is the injustice of the other. Justice in the material world, as everything else that composes it, is only illusion and fantasy. The wise man is guided by the only real law; the single universal law managing the whole created world without fail. The law of action-reaction impregnated into the essence of the universe. This law guarantees that any positive or negative action will produce a positive or negative reaction that will first influence the initiator, then his immediate surroundings and finally the whole creation. Anyone who sows negative will harvest negative and anyone who plants positive will reap positive. The return of a reaction sometimes takes long, but there is the assurance that any thought or action always has an impact and that eventually that reaction will come back to its source. Thus, the wise man makes sure to generate positive thoughts and actions that will take him toward an ever-higher summit of bliss.

Who decides the destiny of each human being in the universe?

K

KNOWER

The possessor of a practical knowledge.

If it were possible to know and understand the First Principle (nothingness) from our world, the creator principle would exist here and the dualistic world would be real. The First Principle would not be alone but would be part of an ultimate duality which would comprise on one side the known thing (First Principle) and on the other side the knower, the observer who executes the analysis (comparison) required for intellectual comprehension. The great truth is that the First Principle and the knower are one and the same; they are indistinguishably one. Thus in order to reach the ultimate knowledge, the illumination; the observer must become the First Principle, the essence of all. After partial illumination, a glimpse of absolute truth, the adept realizes that the revelation and the real truth which was so real a moment ago vanishes very rapidly shortly after coming out of meditation. This is due to the thought process doing its job of dualistically analyzing new data. When the analysis is concluded, the absolute truth is transformed into illusory knowledge retaining practically no reality. The adept keeps a faint memory of what real truth is and wishes to experiment this state again. In his meditation, the wise man at first partially experiences the light of truth, then if he so desires he can immerse himself into the vast ocean of reality. Is it possible to return from it? No one knows.

If the observer and the observed are indistinguishably one; who is the creator?

KNOWLEDGE

Learning acquired through physical sensations, analysis and interpretations.

Material knowledge is illusory and impermanent; it is in constant transformation. What we believed to be true yesterday is false or different today. All knowledge acquired in this lower world must be considered temporary and must constantly be reassessed. The adept knows that the only way to acquire real knowledge is by intuition. Intuitive knowledge does not come from analysis or interpretation; it seems to appear from nowhere, from silence. An intuitive solution is the right one. The wise one is not blinded by worldly knowledge and concentrates his efforts on his search for reality and permanence. Illusory knowledge is the creator of confusion and sorrow.

How can material knowledge be detrimental to the searcher of truth?

KNOWLEDGE OF SELF

Knowing and understanding the different components of the human being.

In order for anyone to undertake the long apprenticeship for the knowledge of self, one must first acknowledge that there is something to learn and understand why he should do it. People who are totally blinded by the illusion see themselves as perfect and everybody else as imperfect; they are always right and others always wrong; the world for them is a very small place totally centred on them. These people see no point in self-analysis. But the sincere adept who has realized that the world goes beyond the tip of his nose and that what surrounds him is certainly not all that there is, is a likely candidate for the path leading to the truth via the knowledge of self. He starts by comparing, as impartially as he can, the differences between his thoughts, words and actions and those of others, then he goes on to the intellectual introspection. It is usually at this stage that he finds out about the path leading to the truth. There starts the real search of self. Among other things, he discovers the components (aggregates) of his physical, mental and spiritual self, their mechanisms, links, etc. The adept climbs back the great chain of life allowing him to find his real place in the universe by piercing through the mask of reality.

Why should the adept ask himself, "What am I not"?

L

LAW

Control system by which we can preserve virtue and eliminate vice in the dualistic world.

As long as mankind is hooked on illusion, it will use terms such as moral and immoral, good and bad, divine and diabolical, etc. The wise one knows that all beings are part of the same and unique whole. One must understand that anything that affects one member of this community, either in a good or bad way, affects the overall group. The adept realizes that he does not want to be hurt and that this is what would happen if he hurts others. Furthermore, the universal law of action/reaction ensures that each action will produce good or bad results according to the original projection. Any action or thought always comes back to its source with its positive or negative charge. Everything affects everything in the universe; we are ONE in ALL an ALL in ONE.

What is a killer's probable fate?

LIBERATED

A being delivered from his servitude.

One who has transcended the illusion, who rises above the mirage of matter to look the naked reality in the face. The quality of one who has transcended space, time and matter. Someone not influenced by sensations. Meditation is the only known tool that can lead to the liberation of the created being. The adept concentrates on the internal void without letting worldly thoughts disturb him, and with patience becomes conscious of the unity of everything that surrounds him. Only an indomitable mind discipline can open the door to reality.

Why must perfection be perfectly empty?

LIBERATION

The fact of being delivered from an enslavement.

The cessation of all desires related to the material world. The realization of the reality of void. The permanent awakening to light and truth. The sincere searcher's ultimate goal. The reason for the existence of the path leading to the light. The searcher must maintain his fate in the existence of a non-confusing reality (without duality) and in the possibility to reach it through meditation on emptiness. Faith, meditation and perseverance are the major vehicles used for the great voyage toward eternal reality. The observer must make sure not to interpret what he sees or experiments, or identify with any sensation (sensations are not real). Only the infinite, inalterable and permanent great light is important.

What can be the sensation of a rider galloping between reality and illusion?

LIFE

A string of happy and unhappy experiences happening to individuals and leading to disillusion.

It is only after a vast life experience that the wise one realizes that the great game is nothing but disillusion. Nothing in life leads to real and permanent happiness; anything gained one day will be lost the next. In the world of dualities any loss is a tragedy. The adept must reject none of his good or bad experiences, and good or bad actions. He will realize that everything is part of the great evolutionary machine that allows him to experiment good and bad before understanding that something that transcends life must exist. The traveller must understand his desire for possessions before he can embark on the path to enlightenment.

Why is it that life eventually takes back everything it gives?

LIGHT

A source that illuminates things.

The light illuminates the observer since the beginning of time. The light of the mind is the one endowed with the real knowledge. The light of truth is inalterable and eternal. The eternal light illuminates everything, the past, present and future; nothing is hidden from it. The divine light illuminates the eternal present moment that the wise man finds in his inner self. The light that blinds without shining allows the observer to experiment the instantaneity of creation. The power of the light revelation transcends the searcher and transforms him into a luminous being holding the divine truth. The wise one does not hesitate to look truth in the face and be blinded forever. The one who sees beyond can choose his dwelling habitats. The wise one with a piercing sight realizes that illusion and reality are the two faces of the same coin. The light dissipates the shadows of illusion and allows to see the pure and transparent emptiness of reality.

Is it possible to find the reflection of the light of truth?

LIMITED INTELLIGENCE

Faculty to know and understand based on the analysis of the material world.

The limited intelligence is restrained to the illusory analysis and understanding of the ever changing created world. One must never accept analysis results or conclusions achieved by the thought process. One must continuously keep in mind that all that data is erroneous since it comes from the tainted environment of the thought process. The limited intelligence takes only duality into account and duality is illusion. The only valuable knowledge is acquired in the silence of meditation by means of the unlimited intelligence. Only the intuitive intelligence is real because it is not the product of the thought process. The searcher will discipline his thoughts in order to communicate directly with the infinite and pure intelligence.

What is the product of thoughts meeting thoughts?

LIVE (TO)

To possess life and to behave in it in certain ways.

Among living beings, some live for others, in order to please or hurt them. Their only interest is the impact of their actions onto others, making forget them the effect of their actions on themselves. Others live only for their organic glands; they respond and react to every biological impulse they feel. They do not realize that they are beings capable of dominating their lower instincts. Still others live only for their emotions, which are in fact only erroneous intellectual interpretations of what is happening in their life. They do not understand that they are not the thoughts which run around in their head and that they can stop their crazy race at will with the appropriate tool: meditation. Finally, there are those who live only for these three reasons, they are very unhappy people. The wise man looks upon all beings of the universe as an extension of himself, he does not listen to the impulse of his glands and he stops the frantic dance of thoughts unceasingly appearing and disappearing on his mental screen. The silence teaches the wise man that he is something else besides an assembly of glands and emotions. He transcends his illusory impulses into constructive energy which he uses to progress on his way to liberation. The wise one in deep meditation floats in the emptiness of his inter-temporal space.

What level of activity can be called life?

LOVE

An affinity more or less developed between two human beings.

Love may be divided between two major levels: ordinary love which is a physical or intellectual attraction between two human beings, and extraordinary love which is the infinite love for all beings created and the entire creation itself. Ordinary love only leads to suffering and pain. This love is limited to things in transformation, thus it can only change and become something different from what we believed it was originally. On the contrary, extraordinary love is infinite and eternal; it is stable and permanent since it is rooted in the total giving of oneself to others in the absence of desire. The universe is ONE and INDIVISIBLE.

Why is it that ordinary love will necessarily lead to deception?

M

MARKERS

That on which one relies to determine his position, what he is and what he does in a specific environment.

A human being is what he is because of markers; without them he would only be consciousness. He determines, locates and interprets those landmarks by analyzing sensations transmitted to him by his sensors (hearing, sight, smell, touch, taste, etc.). Without them he would be practically nothing, he would not be created, since thoughts are responsible for the world, as we know it. Let us imagine for a moment what happens in almost everyone's head when we wake up, i.e. after a period during which the conscious thought process was suspended. The minute we wake up, we become conscious of our body, the weight of it on the mattress, its odour underneath the covers, the heat it generates. We realize where we are, in bed, in our room, in the house, in town, etc. This process is not necessarily conscious but it is always there, at each and every moment of a being's conscious life. Without this constant locating and analyzing process, we would not know where we are, what we look like, what we are doing, if we are sitting, standing, walking or running, etc. Life as a whole is an endless analysis and interpretation of perceived feelings; life is only a dream. When a wise man closes his eyes and allows silence and peace to penetrate to the core of his being, he no longer thinks, he no longer analyzes anything, he is only the essence of life, a formless and endless consciousness. HE IS REALITY.

When someone's feet are above the ground, does that mean that he is flying?

MASTER

A person who possesses a knowledge superior to illusory learning.

A being desiring to leave an account of his subjective spiritual experience to those who could take advantage of it to achieve their own goal. The adept will choose a master only if he feels the need for one. The master is not an essential factor on the road to liberation. The adept is the only master of his own experience, success or failure. The master can help, but will not replace the observer. An arrogant or coercive master is not a real one. One can recognize a real master by his simplicity, honesty, wisdom, goodness, and above all, by his respect toward others. The master knows that there are countless paths leading to the goal and that his own will not fit others. Only the truth always remains unchanged. We all must be humble as if we possessed wisdom, and remain so even after wisdom is acquired.

What is the difference between the adept and the master?

MASTERY OF EMOTIONS

The ability to control one's emotions.

It seems practically impossible for ordinary people to control their continuously emerging emotions. They believe that they are those emotions, the good ones as well as the bad ones. Sometimes they successfully control them, but more often their attempts end in failure. If they are asked, they will answer that it is very difficult to change. The wise man recognizes emotions for what they are: assemblies of illusory aggregates which surface into the consciousness in order to make the body do what they want. When he feels such an emotion, he treats it as just another thought; he focuses on emptiness and gives the emotion free passage through the sky of his consciousness. When the emotion is ignored, it vanishes into the void without affecting the wise one. At one point or another in the course of his meditations, he sees them all pass by as orphans looking for parents and, not finding what they want, go on searching somewhere else. The wise man accepts nothing else but reality.

How can an action generate a reaction that will affect the initiator?

MATERIAL RELATIVITY

The characteristic of matter and thought that always depend on something else.

The material world is the creation of the collective mind. This is why we can interpret the world differently even if we all see the same thing. All that exists within the sphere of matter rests on the universal consciousness from which all emerges. In the beginning there was nothingness, then came thought. Thought produced elements, then dust, which in the course of its evolution has become suns and planets, and all that is on them, including human beings who are just animals barely more sophisticated than those walking on all four. All that exists at this very moment in the universe rests on what was the universe yesterday, and the day before. The mind is present at every level of creation; in fact the whole creation is its manifestation. After performing the fission of the atom core, great physicists never stop discovering new particles that they fragment to find even smaller particles. They finally end up doubting the very existence of matter itself. Could the source of matter be immaterial? Even they assure us that everything depends on everything and that nothing can exist alone in this universe. The observer remains an unknown factor in the experiment. They even say that at a certain point in the experiment, they seem to see what they want to see. They are surprised at the possibility of altering the behaviour of matter and matter itself by thought. The wise one knows that matter is only the mirage of the eternal emptiness of reality. He knows that all matter is only thoughts-images interpreted by the mental process. The wise man acknowledges that he is the creator of his world, as is everyone in the universe. He closes his eyes and as soon as the mental process falls under control, quiescence bathes the observer who witnesses the disappearance of the material world and the appearance of reality. He then experiments the stability of the immutable reality.

Why is it that matter seems so real if it is only thought?

ME

Mixture of aggregates that each individual believes to be himself.

What the sleeper believes to be his entity, his thinking and independent self. **I think therefore I am asleep.** The observer using spiritual analysis discovers that what he thought he was is in fact a grouping of various tendencies. He is an assembly of biological or genetic aggregates inherited from his ancestors, and of intellectual aggregates coming from all he has learned and experienced since birth. All those aggregates coexist in him and the brain interprets their interactions as its own. This is where the illusion of ME comes from. The illusion of me is totally mechanical and illusory. Spiritual analysis or deep reflection makes it possible to discover what is forming what we call ME. In fact, when someone takes a decision, it means that his strongest tendencies have won the dualistic battle against the weaker ones. The observer recognizes that he is only a spectator in the eternal theatre play. But paradoxically, he is also the writer of this play since he is one with the whole.

What becomes of the observed when he realizes that he is also the observer?

MEDITATION

Concentration of the attention on an object, a mental picture, a sound or on emptiness.

A discipline practiced in order to become conscious of the thought process, then to realize that it is uncontrollable and finally to ignore it. Meditation allows to reach a superior level of consciousness and in the end to transcend matter, pierce trough illusion and reach liberation. Meditation on emptiness is by far the most direct and quickest approach to achieve the goal. This type of meditation does not require any efforts or analysis. The observer concentrates on emptiness while he stays focused on a point spot in his head, an object ahead of him or on his breathing without letting the target invade him or becoming the target. In this state the adept establishes mental silence and in the internal peace, observes. Knowledge surfaces from the silence. The observer must avoid all efforts and, like a baby filled with wonder, look upon creation as it really is.

Is sadness in a dream less real than in life?

MEDITATION ON DEATH

A deep concentration on the cessation of biological life.

The death of the fleshy envelope can only be of importance to one who is still a sleep and has not yet realized that the body is not what he believes it to be; that in fact his essence is indestructible and immortal. The wise one sees the end of the physical life as a change, a transformation, the end of a cycle and the beginning of another. He knows that for a moment he wore a human mantle and the next it has vanished. He has discovered in past meditations that what he really is this spark of inalterable consciousness (the observer) who has nothing to do with the human body other than acknowledge its existence. From the depth of his meditation, only the observer remains and he knows that he exists as consciousness in the void since before the creation and will still exist after its disappearance. Body, death, birth, time and any other worldly notions can only be illusory and cannot hold any reality. These notions of the material world are all consequences of the analysis. They exist only if the mind recognizes them. When the mind ignores them, they vanish and one can only find the transcendental and eternal emptiness of reality. All that is matter will disappear; only void will prevail.

What becomes of the intellect after the death of physical body?

MEDITATION ON EMPTINESS

Concentration of the attention on mental emptiness.

Meditation on emptiness is the meditation of meditations. All meditations and disciplines lead eventually to this meditation on NOTHINGNESS. After discovering through his various studies, reflections and meditations that what he is looking for has no humanly recognizable characteristics, the adept meditates on nothingness. Reality, truth, First Principle, whatever the name we give to the divine source of the universe, all these illusory terms serve only the purpose of defining, for our limited understanding, the NOTHINGNESS eternally true and present. The wise man finally meditates on NOTHING. The meditation that cannot induce anyone in error. Where the observer looks directly into the source of truth, omnipotence, omniscience, autonomy and originality, "VOID". In the wisdom kingdom which transcends all meditations, the observer vanishes, the observer and the observed become one. Only the realization of this goal can lead the way to the great light of reality. This teaching is the most important of all. This meditation is the unique key allowing to reach the goal in the shortest time. It represents the door that opens directly on the truth.

Why would anyone meditate on anything but nothingness?

MEDITATION ON MATTER

Deep concentration on what matter is made of.

For people asleep or unconscious of the real nature of the world in which they live, matter is the only thing that exists. For them anything that can be touched is real. The wise one tries to answer some of his questions through meditation. What is matter made of? What are its components? He intuitively knows that matter can be divided into elements, and these elements can also be split into still smaller particles which can be separated into smaller ones, etc. When the wise one, from the bottom of his meditation, focuses his attention on the smallest components of matter, he becomes aware that they are but the fruit of thoughts, creations of the mind. Anything that is matter or takes its source in matter has no existence outside the mind that is the only cause of its presence in the world. Matter cannot exist without the universal mind, the First Principle. The material world is only the realization of the mind's thoughts. The illuminated wise man still sees and realizes the presence of creation, but he also simultaneously realizes the indissociable presence of the uncreated world. He is awakened to the unity of all, his eyes see through the veil of ignorance and allow him to contemplate the truth in all its glory. He has transcended matter.

Does illusion have its source in matter or matter in illusion?

MEDITATION ON THE MIND

Deep concentration on what the mind is made of.

Mind is an almost unknown entity in our world limited by an immeasurable mass of matter, an unimaginable confusion of colours, a cacophony of noises, an orgy of forms, and last but not least, an ocean of sensations in which humankind is immersed. It is said that mind is intellect and vice versa, that mind has a personality, qualities, etc. For the wise man, mind is the spark of consciousness persisting after muting the thoughts and external noises of his inner brass band. The individual mind is the observer with whom he identifies, but devoid of all material characteristics. The mind is a perfectly pure being observing the progress of the illusory world. The wise man meditates to discover its substance, form or colour. Does it have any recognizable faculties? Is it merely a phantom without any materiality? If it is not material, how can it take on so many different aspects? Who is its initiator? If mind were matter or depended on matter, it would be unstable and would continuously change as does all matter. The wise one discovers that it is impossible to identify, describe, understand or define the mind's composition, except to recognize that it is empty. But he cannot deny its existence since it is there in him. He deduces that mind is neither material nor immaterial. Mind is matter and void, void and matter, it is the state from which everything is derived, where all happens in one fugitive moment.

Why is the human being prisoner of space and time?

MEDITATION ON TIME

A deep concentration on the past, present and future.

If it is accepted that the past no longer exists, that the future does not yet exist and that the present, which is in fact only a momentary realization of the future, cannot be stopped or set in time and that it immediately vanishes into the past, one must acknowledge that the present is inseparable from the past and future. The human being who is a prisoner of space and matter has first invented time, then he divided it into three distinctive parts, past, present and future because he could not imagine the instantaneity of creation. He sees the world as through a window, one part of it at a time. He feels compelled to measure movement. The human being feels the necessity to identify and to explain in order to feel more secure. The wise man in deep meditation focuses on the notion of time and more specifically on the past, present and future to realize that they are one and the same thing. He understands that time cannot be real since the movement of matter that it witnesses is illusory. Time is only an invention of the mind as everything else when composes the material world. The wise man faces reality where all is instantaneity, where nothing happened yesterday or will happen tomorrow, but where all is occurring now. He enjoys the universal moment by excellence.

Why is the present a memory of the future that has become the past?

MEDITATION POINT

The state in which it is possible to meditate.

If the adept is conscious of the object on which his eyes are set, he is not meditating. If the adept is conscious of the point on which his attention is focused, he is not meditating. If he is invaded by thoughts, he is not meditating either. The adept meditates when all that remains of him is a spark of consciousness that does not think nor analyze, that only observes, that is there, that is all. Then and only then is the adept meditating, very close to reality and the truth. That moment can last for a fraction of a second, one or several seconds or minutes, rarely hours, but that is when the adept is meditating. Meditation is the art of silence and observation. When the cacophony of external noises fades away and the crazy dance of thoughts suspends its mad race, then the silence of meditation takes place and the mind rests in its natural state. In this state the individual mind communicates with the universal mind. In this moment of intense communication, the First Principle and the second principle form a unique and indivisible whole. Surrounded by this practically unbearable brilliance, the transcended adept realizes that he is what he was searching for with such passion. Meditation is this cosmic vessel taking the voyager toward a horizon always higher, always farther.

Why is it that some people who look at themselves in the mirror of life do not recognize themselves?

MEMORY

The faculty to store and remember past facts.

Mind as such possesses no memory since time does not exist in it. The notion of past, present and future can only exist in a dualistic environment where time is interpreted as a long series of events. The present is eternally modified and human beings perceive it as a central point between the past and future. One must not reject the past or future as unrealizable in the present. The wise one in a state of quiescence does not acknowledge any past or future actions, only an eternal present. In deep meditation where time is transcended, he can revive the farthest memories. He uses this discipline for self-analysis and to better understand the thought process. The wise man's memory is clear and transparent because it originates from the universe's instantaneity. Nothing for real has passed and nothing is really to come, everything is present for the one who in silence transcends time and touches the eternal present. The wise one uses his memory to remember that he must persevere on the path leading to the truth.

Must one remember to evolve in order to evolve?

METAMORPHOSIS

The passage from one state form to another completely different.

Many people falsely think that meditation is a dangerous discipline. That it is self-hypnosis, a system of depersonalization, a maker of people without soul. But most people who think that the effects of meditation are negatives have never experienced it. They are afraid of the unknown. Others see meditation as a relaxation method, a tool against stress and even diseases in general. Meditation on nothingness alone, without any other side practices, is in fact a method used to discipline the human being's thought process, which can only bring positive effects to the adept. The wise one knows by experience that meditation allows to reach inner quiescence, then transcend illusion in order to see reality in its natural essence. He is conscious that the human being is in fact a caterpillar hidden within its chrysalis awaiting the ultimate metamorphosis into a superior being. He believes this because he experiences it every day in the course of his meditations. Meditation is the human beings' metamorphosis tool.

Does the butterfly remember its life as a caterpillar?

MIND

The First Principle, the cause of all that is created.

The mind is the cause of creation. Without it, our illusory world would not exist. The mind is the First Principle, unique and indivisible, immutable and eternal. It is empty, "the uncreated substance or entity", non-existing but present. One could speculate about the mind almost indefinitely. The wise one does not waste time on speculations, and from the depth of his meditation he first realizes that the mind is invisible, since the only thing he sees is black emptiness. Then he acknowledges that the mind is not substantial, it is impossible to touch it, feel it or perceive it as matter. It is impossible to apply to it a concept related to the material world, one can only acknowledge its presence. One cannot define or describe it, analyze or dissect it. The wise man intuitively knows that what is described as individual mind and universal mind is in fact a different description of one and the same thing. He finally realizes that the mind is unborn, not made, that it is unalterable and cannot be destroyed. The mind is reality, the essence of all that exists. Even the greatest wise men of all times, who have realized the mind (who have intuitively known the mind) have declared that it does not exist in the worldly sense of the word. The mind is the source of what does and does not exist, of what is created and uncreated. The wise one knows that all who meditate with perseverance will realize, see or perceive reality at the end of their quest.

Who is the observer?

MISERY

A chain of painful and sorrowful events.

Anyone who is not conscious of living in illusion can only experience a life full of small joys and great sorrows. His happiness will seem very brief and insignificant compared to his sorrows. It is impossible to find peace while one is immersed in emotions. Since nothing is stable in this world, what exists today will not be tomorrow. One who clings to anything material is destined to lose what he thought he possessed and suffer because of this separation. The human misery rests solely on the loss of what was believed to be possession. On the contrary, someone who recognizes the world for what it is, an unstable illusion, does not hold on, nor desire to possess anything that he could lose almost immediately. He transcends misery and discovers serenity. He also realizes that acquiring worldly goods has no purpose since nothing endures. One with his eyes open on inner emptiness contemplates reality. He uses the illusory world to gather eternal wisdom rather than illusory and impermanent knowledge. This is the wisdom that transcends matter and allows one to see reality through illusion.

Why do some people take pleasure in their misery?

MISINTERPRETATION

The erroneous explanation and definition of something.

In a dualistic world where everything can be interpreted in a thousand ways, it is very important for the adept to be able to make the difference between an experience with an illusory content and another with a real content. A misinterpretation will lead to failure. Some adepts believe they reach the ultimate goal when thoughts cease their dance. Others believe they have illuminations when in fact they are subjected to hallucinations. The cessation of the thought process is only the first step on the long journey to the truth and has nothing to do with the ultimate quiescence of the infinite mind (which is the final goal). A hallucination is nothing but the brain's interpretation of physical or intellectual sensations. Every time the adept witnesses a phenomenon in meditation he must make sure that the event is not an illusory perception rather than a revelation or a glimpse of reality. The adept will acknowledge that even a real illumination does not last in our world. The moment he realizes that he had such an experience, contamination has occurred, the essence of truth begins to deteriorate. The analysis process that was suspended during deep meditation regains illusory consciousness and starts to analyze the revelation and interprets it according to the world's dualistic parameters. The adept feels the spark of truth fade away until it leaves only a vague memory of something absolute. The certainty is gone with the content of the experience diluted in illusion. The wise man knows that real truth is invariable. Thus before reaching the ultimate goal, he can only experience brief moments of inalterable truth during an illumination just before realizing its content.

Why is reality impossible to analyze?

MOMENT OF REST

A period during which activities and efforts accomplished to achieve a goal are suspended.

When the adept has succeeded in controlling the flow of thoughts constantly arising in his head, when he can remain outside the train of thoughts as an inalterable observer and contemplate the void, then he can take a moment of rest. He has reached an important step in his quest for truth. After all the work of discipline and control, after becoming aware that the solution lies in observation and non-intervention, the wise one becomes a spectator watching a film. He observes without trying to control and he is not influenced by all these illusory images. At this point he is free from the tyranny of the thought process, that used to invade him. He finally can stop and taste the satisfaction of success. He takes a deep breath in preparation for a quest that is even more inhuman, the quest that will liberate him from matter. Contemplation will be his vehicle to reach the other shore. During this new adventure, the wise man will slowly become aware of the reality, the reason behind creation and human beings. At the end of his course he will face the great ALL, the ultimate truth that will take him even further toward other achievements so extraordinary that no human being can imagine them.

Once the wise man is liberated, what becomes of his body?

MOVEMENT

Modification in a sense of displacement or transformation.

When the adept reaches the state of indifference towards the mental process, i.e. when he can remain insensible to the appearance and disappearance of images/thoughts, he enters a period of observation and intuitive analysis. In deep meditation he observes the nature of immobility or, in other words, the mind in its natural state. He studies the mind's immobility process, what happens when it moves. Does the state of tranquillity (quiescence) persist? Can he observe any movement when the mind rests in its motionless natural state? He observes the difference between what is moving (thoughts) and what is immobile (void). Are they really different? How does the movement become immobile? What is the difference between movement and immobility? The wise one, after countless observations and analysis, discovers that movement and immobility are part of the same phenomenon. He realizes that the observer and what is observed are identical, that one is the other and vice versa and that in fact they are absolutely inseparable. This state can only be intuitively comprehended, it is impossible to humanly explain it or recognize it because it is beyond the dualistic understanding of the material world. The wise man savours this intuitive knowledge, this window on truth, this illumination in the dark night of matter.

Must the wise man entirely reject the material world in order to grasp the truth?

MYSELF

Term used by an individual to identify him to himself and others.

The individual unconscious of his real state only sees his SELF, which he continually compares with that of others. For him, his self is an accumulation of qualities and faults, knowledge and ignorance, etc. But the major aspect which differentiates him from a wise man is that he identifies to this assembly of attributes (physical and intellectual aggregates) and he is convinced that he is all this and manages it all, that he controls his life. The wise one knows by experience that he does not manage anything and that he is in fact only an observer of life in progress. His research, in the beginning, is to localize his real self, then to analyze its composition. After numerous experiences he succeeds in isolating the constituents only to realize that they are only illusory devices and decorations. Finally, when he overcomes the illusion hiding the truth, he discovers that he is only a dim light of consciousness lost in mental emptiness, which in ignorance identified itself to illusory fantasies of the material world. But this dim light (consciousness) is still acknowledged as self. The self is still conscious of being conscious. The wise man will also have to renounce this last illusory pretence in order to reach the final illumination that will open the door to reality.

Does reality generate confusion within its own creation?

N

NATURAL

The essence of a being or a thing.

In its natural state, the First Principle (nothingness) is a homogeneous and total absence of motion. The perfect immobility represents the uncreated characteristic. Imagine the perfectly calm surface of the sea on a windless day at slack time between tides. This immense mirror represents the eternal mind's natural state. When the moon pulls the tide into action again, when the winds rise up and the surface becomes troubled by external factors, waves take shape and the naturalness of the sea is no longer visible, it is hidden under the waves. The waves' motion is the thought process in action hypnotizing the observer by its movements, power, beauty and promise. The waves are the illusory world in which we all live. This is why the adept must control his thought process in order to reach the natural surface of the mind (quiescence) and then scrutinize its depths. The seawater is clearer when debris from the continents and rivers (thoughts) are absent. Meditation on nothingness gives the opportunity to calm the waves and contemplate the smooth and homogeneous surface of the First Principle. Then the wise one is really in balance between reality and illusion. He calmly awaits illumination.

What does a seagull think when perched on the mast of a ship lost in the fog?

NATURAL STATE

An unaltered, non-modified beingness.

The state of the mind known to human beings is confused because it identifies with the thought process and the assembly of physical and intellectual aggregates forming the human being. Dominant aggregates use the confused mind to unify and control matter in order to achieve their personal material goals. One of the main characteristics of the mind is its capacity to identify with practically anything, simply because it is totally, perfectly neutral. It is the ultimate observer. It becomes what it observes. This is why human beings can say, "it is really me" or "I think therefore I am". Anyone can think as long as he wants, if there is no one inside to say, this is me thinking, nothing exists. Mind in its natural state does not think, meditate or control, it only observes. This is why when the wise man, by concentrating his attention on void, succeeds in establishing the inner silence and isolating the observer inside (the mind), this point of consciousness that is the origin of all. He starts getting glimpses of truth, of reality as it is without illusion. The mind in its natural state is the eternal and immutable emptiness, the source of all.

What are the constituents of complexity?

NATURE OF MEDITATION

The different elements that compose meditation.

Meditation is first absolute inner silence and total inner emptiness. Second, meditation is absence of thoughts, reflection and analysis. Any form of will, tensing, frustration, effort or desire destroys meditation. Meditation rests on perfect neutrality, the state in which only subsists a spark of consciousness called the observer. This spark, this minute presence that rests on nothing, that is in fact nothing since it cannot be compared to anything else, simply rests there, suspended in the infinite void and observes the eternal reality. When the wise man meditates, all his bodily sensors are turned off. He no longer takes part in the operation of his body and he is no longer conscious that he inhibits one. His thought process is on hold. His attention is entirely focused on inner emptiness and silence. He remains only this spark of consciousness with no more name, shape, presence or location, he IS! Then the wise man realizes that he has not reached his anticipated goal yet. When the time comes, this last feeling of beingness will vanish and the observer will return to his just place inside reality where his consciousness will become infinite.

What is the nature of reality?

NEED

The feeling that it is essential to obtain something.

Apart from his natural requirements, the human being creates for himself hundreds of different needs and appetites that he considers vital to his survival. Some daze themselves in a whirlwind of noise (music, leisure or social activities etc.). Others prefer to bury themselves under wealth, residences, cars, boats, and luxury in general. All these activities or possessions are in fact only illusions, they form a fog so thick that the human being no longer sees reality; he only contemplates unreality and transition. One who lives only for material things is like an animal blinded by a light in the night: he is blinded by his desire to do and acquire and that desire keeps him from seeing anything else. On the contrary the wise man's goal is to abolish false needs and requirements.

Through meditation he learns to control his thoughts and actions, then he realizes after taming matter that all creations are only dreams and illusions. In reality there is nothing to acquire, but the desire for sensation and possession, which is itself unreal, projects the object of its dream on the infinite empty screen. Finally the wise one reaches his natural state and enjoys the absence of illusion.

How thick is the veil of illusion?

NEGATIVE EMOTION

An affective reaction due to a false interpretation of an experience with an evil tendency.

When the word emotion comes up in a conversation, people usually refer to negative emotions. The ignorant does not see positive emotions as objects of attachment to the illusory world. Generally, people see themselves as an assembly of positive and negative emotions. They divide the world in two groups, the good ones who hold more positive emotions than negative ones, and the bad ones who, on the contrary, hold more negative emotions than positive ones. They do not realize that both types of emotions have the same goal: they both attach human beings to the material world and prevent them from seeing beyond the veil of illusion and finding happiness. The wise one realizes that those who use their negative emotions to spread evil around them, work in fact against themselves, since all negative actions will produce negative reactions which will inevitably return to their initiator. Before he can find peace and happiness, the initiator must be subjected to the return impact of all his past actions, or he has to transcend them.

How can one transcend a negative charge?

NEUTRALITY

The characteristic of someone who does not judge or take position.

The state of a being not playing the dualistic game. The universe is an hypnotic assembly of seductions via sight, sound, smell and various other stimuli that mankind qualifies as good or bad according to the latest moral criteria. The adept threading the path of truth is conscious that he must not become enslaved to worldly seductions. He knows that they are solely short-lived, and will all disappear one day leaving in their wake a more or less acute feeling of distress. The wise one lives in the inner silence of neutrality, where nothing can affect him one way or another. He experiences the unity of what is created and non-created.

Why practice neutrality in a dualistic world?

NOISE

A non-harmonic vibration picked up by the hearing mechanism, often distracting and annoying.

Most people do not tolerate silence, they must hear something (music, songs, street noises, etc.). They want to create the illusion of a presence because they fear solitude, and silence is synonymous of isolation. The more a person wishes to hear loud sonorities, the more important his need for others is. Human beings find security in surrounding noises. The obtuse in silence gets quickly bored, and then falls asleep. The wise one in silence becomes more alive and analyzes the farthest corners of his intellect and being. The external noise is often the enemy of the adept when he attempts to establish silence inside of him, but he quickly learns to ignore these distractions and concentrate on the inner silence. The inside noise, if we can call it so, or the constant movement of thoughts-pictures ceaselessly emerging and disappearing from the mental web, is an enemy far more difficult to conquer that those few cacophonies of life. The adept must never lose courage and give up or become blind to the ultimate goal of his search. Those who practice meditation will develop, with time, a perfect concentration without any distraction. But before reaching this perfect focus of consciousness, the adept must enjoy every moment of silence, which lasts longer, with each session of meditation. He must savour every moment of silence between distractions.

Does a noise without an audience exist?

NON-ATTACHMENT

The action of not enslaving oneself to worldly things.

The wise man makes great efforts not to be ensnared by illusory possessions of the material world (the comfort of a home, the love of close ones) as well as by the dictatorship of social relations and work schedules which usually succeed in blinding the searcher, condemning him to waste his time away in futile expenses of energy to achieve useless endeavours. The awakened one will not go back to sleep. The adept will unceasingly work on his non-attachment by meditating on the impermanence of all that exists and on the inevitable end of everything that has a beginning, the unavoidable end of all, which generates only sorrow. Any acquisition ends in dispersion, any construction in destruction, any meeting in separation, any birth in death, nothing subsists. The wise one realizes that he has to walk the domain of life and taste all good and bad experiences to understand that worldly things no longer satisfy him, and finally reach disillusionment. Life does not offer him what he desires; it no more answers his needs. This realization alone causes the opening of the door onto the truth that will give him an indestructible satisfaction for the years he has yet to live and the moments preceding his death. The wise man has discovered something no worldly possession could ever offer.

How can vanity and vexation lead to the awakening?

NON-DOMINATING AGGREGATE

Group of secondary thoughts which do not dominate the brain.

All thoughts passing through your head, more or less influencing the aggregate in power without dominating it. They are a person's tendencies that do not succeed in expressing themselves. For example, a person may dream all his life about becoming an airplane pilot, but never fulfills his dream. This aggregate does not have sufficient power to win the battle for brain dominance. In fact, to achieve his dream, this person would only have to decide to take a pilot course now and follow the course to the end. However he cannot because this aggregate is not at the command station. The wise one learned in his numerous experiences how to proceed to fulfill a dream, to allow a secondary aggregate to become a dominant one. While a secondary aggregate may not have the power to take the ultimate decision to do something in particular, it is often strong enough to order secondary actions or tasks to be executed. In order for this aggregate or tendency to grow, one only has to work on it. Reading on the subject, practical actions leading to its achievement, spending time with people who already have fulfilled this dream will help to reinforce an aggregate until one day it is powerful enough to dominate all other aggregates and order the brain to do what it wants. On that day a dream will be fulfilled. The wise man never stops studying, analyzing and meditating to reinforce the aggregate which wishes to reach the absolute truth. If this tendency (aggregate) is not cultivated, it will be forgotten.

Why is it impossible to do anything else than what one is currently doing?

NON-INTERVENTION

Inaction, non-interference, indifference toward a person, an event or a thing.

One of the spiritual discipline's objectives is to reach a state of total indifference and non-intervention toward physical and mental sensations. This is how the wise one becomes insensitive to the material world, totally neutral in the face of illusions and how he is able to face the state of the absolute truth. This is the path of the braves and the courageous who are not afraid to defy illusory mountains in order to walk the plain of reality. However, the non-interference stage is not the ultimate goal. In fact, it is only another step on the road leading to the searcher's liberation. In his last analysis, the wise man will realize that illusion (the created) and reality (the uncreated) are in fact inseparable from each other and that they form the universal mind, the First Principle. From the depth of his contemplation, the wise man opens his eyes and realizes that illusion and reality are both extremities of a duality that will be revealed to him as a unity upon liberation.

What is the link between human being and reality?

NOW

The moment currently occurring.

Now is certainly the most important moment in the life of any living being. The present instant is the only time during which it is possible, for the ignorant as well as the awakened, to act upon the outer world and upon himself. This is a great revelation that could change someone's life. Only remember the following statement, "nothing will get done if nothing is done". Most human beings regret not having done some actions in the past that could allow them to reap what they desire now. But still today they are not doing what they should and tomorrow they will regret it. If an action is not executed when it should, chances are that it will never be executed. The adept awakened and aware of the importance of the present moment will always do what he has to when it has to be done. Someone who does nothing today cannot expect to harvest something tomorrow. The wise man lives in the "now" at every moment of his existence. For him, only the present moment exists and has any value, because he knows that he cannot change what was done yesterday, and cannot do now what must be done tomorrow. Thus he concentrates on doing now what must me done today in order to take advantage of the results tomorrow.

How can one overcome the time barrier?

O

OBSERVATION

The action of looking with interest with a view to learn.

The adept does not stop at meditation; he carries with him, in every-day life, the results of his long silences. He lives now with a new capacity to observe illusion. In fact, meditation is a tool which allows the user to transform his way of seeing and understanding his being and the universe. Slowly the adept observes his own transformation and realizes that as he withdraws from matter, matter loses in importance. The impact of matter on someone who practises meditation gradually decreases. Meditation allows him to take on a natural behaviour unaffected by illusory analysis. The adept becomes tolerant towards himself and others, he totally respects the laws of action-reaction and lives and let live. The wise one looks at the world around him as if he were an observer inside his head. He observes the world through the eyes of the body he inhabits, he observes without any kind of analysis, and that enables him to see the truth. The illusory world passes in front of his eyes as a movie in which he would play the part of a stranger, while knowing that he is also its initiator and the actor. He notes that by detaching himself from worldly things, he progressively frees himself from his fears and anguishes. He, at last, sees the great cause of this world's sorrow, the attachment to things totally without value.

How can one measure the success of his meditation?

OBSERVER

The consciousness that remains when all thoughts are calmed down.

The essence of consciousness remaining in the emptiness of meditation. The observer is the one who remains in place and focuses on the void. He is consciousness without identity because he cannot compare it with anything else; it is unique. Furthermore, since the observer does not think, he does not have the capacity to compare and analyze. But the consciousness has two well-defined characteristics, namely existence and observation. The observer is here, he exists for himself, he is conscious of his existence but cannot express it. He observes the vast expanse of emptiness of which he is an integral part. The observer does not make any efforts nor does he let anything emerging from emptiness distract him. He looks on without asking any questions. The wise one knows that the expression of emptiness is illusory and impermanent, therefore he does not react to images emerging from emptiness and disappearing into it. The observer is like a buoy on a raging sea, he does not let himself be influenced by what is happening around him, he waits for the storm to subside and the calm to return. Finally, one day, the observer realizes that he is observing himself, and the division vanishes in the light of unity.

How does the observer express himself?

OBSESSION

The state of someone who cannot control the fact that he constantly perceives images or words.

The people who live in this material world are obsessed by various emotions and passions such as desire, envy, fear, hate, etc. These are the passions and emotions leading the world we know. Any impartial reasoning is unknown since all analysis is based on false data. In the modern computerized world, we use the expression "garbage in, garbage out". That goes for human beings as well: their analysis centre is in good order but the data (sensations) entered is false. The adept uses meditation to stand back a little from his own emotions. After some time he realizes that passions and emotions disappear when they are ignored just like the thoughts which emerge during his meditation. During the day when something occurs and induces an emotion out from his unconsciousness, he acknowledges it for what it is and concentrates of what he thinks is important at the moment. That is when the emotion starts slowly to vanish and finally completely disappears. The wise man knows that everything in the world appears and disappears, including him.

What does someone who has stopped his analysis process perceive?

OBSTACLE

Anything impeding the accomplishment of an objective.

The adept ceaselessly meets obstacles on his path towards his personal goal. But everything that seems to be a hindrance to his spiritual growth can be used as a tool to progress towards his ultimate objective. Those obstacles remain a nuisance to his progress only if he tries to control or, eliminate them, or if they influence him. In order for these obstacles to become improvement tools, the adept will consider them for what they are (thoughts) and will not reject them, become attached to them or let them influence him; he will remain indifferent while he observes them. He simply acknowledges their presence and what they are. This practice will allow him to recognize the observer (void) and the observed (thoughts) and their common and indissociable nature. He learns to recognize the real essence of the observer and the observed. The wise one in deep meditation knows that he cannot be influenced by either positive or negative thoughts since the observer (himself) is perfectly indifferent. The meditative observation of the material world may lead directly to the realization of the universal unity.

What should be the wise man's behaviour when he faces a sudden apparition on his path?

OPPORTUNITY

Favourable occasion to do something.

Generally speaking, human beings should realize the importance of the opportunity represented by the possession of a body. This body is a machine that allows, through the interpretation mechanism (brain), the superior aggregate to act upon the created world and try to achieve its own dreams. For the adept, this is a very precious period during which every moment is used to progress toward the emancipation of his entire being. The wise one in possession of a body and aware of being a prisoner of the life and death cycle will not rest before the final illumination moment, when he will have the ability to contemplate both aspects of reality without discrimination. He is aware of the importance of the body in his quest for truth. He treats it adequately, without yielding to its primitive fancies, but gives it what it needs to ensure that it stays active for as long as possible. He knows that when he will leave the tired body, he will no more be able to act on the material world and will live in the death world where assimilation and contemplation reign as masters. The wise man considers that birth and the use of a body are the greatest opportunities for someone who is looking for the ultimate truth. The body is the tool necessary for the research, study and meditation leading to the liberation from the life and death cycle to which all human beings are linked before they experience eternal reality.

What role does chance play in the emergence of an opportunity?

ORDINARY LOVE

THE Physical and intellectual affinity between two human beings.

A purely physical attraction (sex). The satisfaction of sexual appetites. An intellectual attraction (platonic love). The satisfaction of intellectual appetites. An attraction of opposites, where one brings to the other talents, personality traits, material possessions, etc. the other craves for. These three types of attraction are only temporary and illusory. They can only lead to deception and pain. The observer will realize that material love can only be detrimental to his awakening. Physical love takes root in the desire to possess and illumination can be achieved only when desire is totally transcended.

What is the difference between love and hate?

ORIGIN

An imaginary point where reality and illusion start.

The First Principle has no beginning or end. Originally, there was ignorance and ignorance produced the thought process, which generated knowledge that in turn beget corporeality and its sensations, then desires and finally action. The process of birth, maturation, ageing and dying is the vehicle of this illusory system. When the wise one finally returns to the first sensation, he realises that the First Principle would not be perfect if it could not express its originality without altering its indivisible unity. Careful though, we are facing a paradox when we state that the First Principle is active in the expression of its originality. That means that it is not totally static as we would be tempted to believe about a perfect entity. It is possible to grasp this paradox in deep meditation and realize that divine expression is not an activity as we understand it in the material world. At this point, one must not attempt to express the inexpressible; everyone must go see for himself.

Why is stability a prerequisite to perfection?

P

PARADOX

An idea contrary to the established logic.

The long road leading from ignorance to wisdom is strewn with paradoxes, which for some people are the blatant proof of the non-existence of a path leading to the ultimate truth where all is understood. For them, only solid and tangible things are real. For others, these paradoxes are challenges compelling them to conduct further research and meditation in order to successfully grasp the essence of these mysteries. These individuals will reflect deeply on the suggestion that all that exists emerges from emptiness, or on the essence of the unity in the whole and the whole in the unity, on the image of the First Principle and that of the second principle, etc. These paradoxes are completely incomprehensible as long as the searcher tries to analyze them from the illusory world point of view based on duality. And even those who intuitively in deep meditation grasp the essence of these great truths are incapable of explaining them with the limited means of the material world. The searcher will have to discover his explanations and his own truths. Meditation on emptiness is the key to opening those doors. The fastest method to achieve the targeted objective.

If everything emerges from emptiness, how can emptiness be empty?

PARASITE

An organism disturbing perception.

The parasite elements (thoughts) that inhabit human beings are directly generated by the analytical instrument called brain. Different aggregates interact and the brain tries to interpret and identify the sensations (or signals) it receives, thus creating mental images that we call thoughts. These images seemingly coming from nowhere suddenly appear in the adept's awareness and distract him from his quest of silence and peace. Anyone who practices meditation soon realizes that these parasites must be eliminated in order to find peace and continue on contemplating without distraction. This work may be long but it is feasible. The wise one lets his mind rest in its natural state of total calm and non-intervention. Totally relaxed, he watches thoughts pass by in his head without being the least distracted. He does not try to control them and neither falls under their influence. He uses his will to remain concentrated on the void without fail. He lets his mind act as a spectator and carries on his contemplation. After a while, thoughts vanish and silence take precedence. Finally the mind rests in its natural state and the wise man contemplates in peace.

What produced the thought that caused a thought?

PARENT

A person linked to others by the same ancestors.

People are most closely linked to their family first, then they are particularly conscious of the persons close to them, friends, partners, acquaintances, etc. An ordinary person will be emotionally affected by the happiness or sorrows experienced by his parents or close ones. But this person will practically be indifferent to the fate of strangers. The reason for this is that he is living in ignorance and believes to be isolated from the rest of the world. His vision is limited to his own being and his close ones, he does not have the capacity to see further because his perception is restricted by the veil of illusion. The wise man in meditation sees through the darkness of ignorance and realizes that all human beings are closely linked together and form in fact a single entity. He deduces from this that when one of these beings is affected, the whole community is subjected to the consequences. No one is interested in self-induced grief; nevertheless, the ignorant does get hurt when he hurts another person. The wise one lives in the respect of others and lets others live their own life, he does not attempt to do either good or bad, his respects for everything that exists mirrors his own. His reason for being is to progress on the path leading to the truth and to participate in keeping it open for those who look for it.

What is the basic difference between one being and another?

PASSING THOUGHTS

A method allowing the observer not to be distracted by thoughts.

Thoughts that take over the consciousness of people around you, including yours, are those with the most energy, the others only pass without attracting your attention too strongly, so you can ignore them. When the adept realizes this fact, he acknowledges that it would certainly be possible to ignore all thoughts even if they are more powerful. He begins to practice the technique called "passing thoughts". He closes his eyes, savours a moment of silence, then thoughts come forth, he observes them (without analyzing them) and he accepts them for what they are (illusions, thus without importance) and he lets them continue their journey until eventually they disappear. It is important that this exercise be practised delicately and effortlessly. Any effort will only generate more thought energy. The adept liberates the passing thought and returns slowly to his quiet observation. For example: The adept's attention is virgin, without thoughts. Then he notices thoughts passing as running stars in his inner sky. He looks at them without thinking, without analyzing, he only observes whatever thought it is and he says to this thought: "you are only illusion, go your way", (return to attention). This is followed by a period of observation, then another thought appears and he says the same thing to it and so on. The adept will persevere and prolong these periods of quiet observation for as long as possible without getting too tired. During these periods of silence, the mind returns to its natural state. These are moments of truth leading to quiescence.

Is thought the creator of the observer or is it the other way around?

PASSION

Phenomenon ensuing from uncontrolled sensations.

Passions lead the world, since all beings, unconscious of their nature, only rely on their sensations in their daily life. One, who does not know that his passions, the product of his sensations, are not real, surrenders to them since he does not know better. The wise one learns early that passions come from duality, from the "I love" and "I hate", or the "I accept" and "I refuse" factors. Passions dominate the ignorant but not the one who dissects them in order to learn what they are made of and how they behave. The wise man does not allow passions to interfere with his quest. He knows them for what they are, the fruit of sensations that come from illusory signals interpreted by a confused mental process generating absurd results: passions. Thus for the wise one, passion does not possess any reality, it is only a thin fog on the horizon of one who studies the infinite depth. In deep meditation he watches his passions melt under the sun of reality. In the void of meditation, nothing material can subsist, everything vanishes, only truth remains. Someone who is dominated by his passions cannot even realize the existence of the path leading to the light. For him, there is only illusion, matter. The wise man has compassion for him but ultimately rejoices knowing that even the passionate will one day cross the bridge which will take him beyond the river of dream.

Must one suffer with those who suffer or be happy with those who are happy?

PATH

Method used to reach enlightenment more rapidly.

A method or guidelines left behind by liberated beings for those who are just awakening to reality. The objective to reach is unique and the same for everyone, but the path differs from one searcher to the next. To follow the path, the adept will **study** the literature on the subject of truth, **reflect** deeply on this truth and **meditate** in silence. Careful though, the searcher will not let himself be trapped by book knowledge, which leads nowhere, he will experiment every bit of knowledge by himself through meditation. Only silence in meditation can transcend worldly knowledge and let divine wisdom teach the adept the science of recognizing true from false, reality from illusion. The wise one rejects knowledge in order to experiment wisdom, the ignorant holds on tight to his little transitory knowledge while he misses the eternal truth.

Why do all paths lead to the truth?

PATIENCE

Capacity to wait, persist on doing or endure a thing, a person or a situation.

The quality to keep on doing work without rest toward the realization of a project or a dream. Patience is a quality that must be cultivated by anyone who meditates and wishes to reach his goal. In silence, the observer patiently waits for the light, the coming of daylight. The adept does not get bored nor does he lose his patience. The work of meditation is long and difficult, but one who persists will achieve what he is looking for. No one can deny the truth to the one who searches sincerely for it. It is often in the most critical moments, when the will is weakening, that the greatest revelations come forth. One will never abandon, one will take the position, close his sensation windows and open the inside eye that possesses the capacity to see all, even the invisible. Observe relentlessly to see the light illuminate the world of shadows and confusion.

How long is an hour in meditation?

PEACE

Harmonious relations between various beings.

Peace in the world will be impossible to achieve until human beings come to understand that they are all ONE in the great cosmic machine. We all come from the same source, and we all share the same images of the world. We all are controlled by more or less evolved or absurd aggregates. Peace is impossible as long as there is one being in the world who does not realize this fundamental fact. We are all individually linked to the universe and the universe to each one of us. Peace will shine on the world when all illusions are transcended, when the created being will be able to confront the impartial light of inner quiescence. Peace takes place in the wise man's heart the moment he focuses his attention on the surface of the uncreated mirror. When he looks at his neighbour he sees himself. Confronted by human stupidity, he sadly smiles, and focuses his attention on nothingness with an even more powerful vigour and determination. Peace grows one being at a time.

What does one gain when, for the sake of vengeance, he kill his mother in order to eliminate his father's murderer?

PENDULUM

Oscillation between two points or between two states.

Non-liberated human beings balance between two states of consciousness, life which is the active state and death which is the inactive or passive one. During their active period, human beings can interact with the rest of creation. This is the period during which we gather concepts and mental materials. When we die, we lose the machine that allowed us to experiment and also to think, so we relax. In this corporal nudity similar to sleep, we process data acquired during our life, a little like dreams process previous experiences during sleep. When this process becomes exhausted because there is no more data to process, our being will take on another body to live a new active oscillation of his illusory existence cycle. The adept's goal is to terminate this perpetual and monotonous cycle and forever stop the oscillation movement. This cycle can be stopped only if everything is consumed and when desire is completely abolished. The crazy race toward understanding and evolution can only cease when the wise man realizes that life cannot offer him anything anymore. Only then can the wise man look directly at the blinding light of truth.

How many lives must a wise man live before he realizes the truth?

PERCEPTION

The function allowing to understand the result of an analysis.

The individual or divine mind (First Principle) does not possess any particular characteristics, thus it is impossible for it to analyze or understand; it can only be. It does not realize either that it is, since realization requires analysis which in turn entails comparison. However, it knows that it is. The First Principle cannot compare itself or be compared to anything since it is ONE, thus alone and unique. The individual or divine mind cannot see itself, it is not a thing or a concept of any kind, its essence is wisdom. The wise one acknowledges that perception is only possible in the dualistic world because from the depth of his meditation all discriminations vanish and leave room solely for the observer. A small flame of consciousness stripped of every worldly characteristics, bathing in eternal wisdom, and keeping only the consciousness that he is. The wise one draws from this wisdom allowing him to understand the reason for the great cosmic machine.

On what does human beings' perception rest?

PERFECTION

A state of perfect immobility or staticity. The quality of the whole, unique, infinite, eternal, omnipresent and omnipotent.

What is nothing and is everything. The First Principle or the creator of everything visible and invisible: God. The adept realizes that it is impossible to define perfection with words and that any attempt to do so is bound to fail. But the observer knows that perfection inhabits everyone and everything. He does not attempt to explain what is perfect, his goal is to experiment what is perfect, to become perfection. No one knows what is perfection and the wise ones who have completed the long voyage, who have reached what we call liberation, state that they are only at the beginning of an adventure even greater and more impossible to express than the one they have just lived. Perfection is the ultimate goal for the moment. Who knows what the future has in store.

How could perfection evolve?

PERMANENT

The quality of anything that lasts eternally.

Anything that is **not** material or managed by the mental process is permanent. Nothing exists permanently in this material world; everything appears, matures and finally disappears. Creation is in constant transformation, in a continuous state of change. Impermanence is the major cause of humanity's problems, because nothing is ever really acquired, nothing is ever sure, everything earned will be lost one day and losing causes pain. The wise one, knowing this, tries to discover what is permanent, things that endure, things that he will never lose, and when he finds one he knows that he has acquired a piece of the puzzle, a part of the truth. The observer quickly realizes that his meditation's emptiness or void does not move, never changes and cannot be altered, contrary to thoughts that are constantly appear, transform and disappear. After a while he has no choice but to admit that only emptiness or void is always perfectly static, thus permanent. How can emptiness be reality?

PERMANENT MEDITATION

Meditation in the course of ordinary daily events.

The meditating adept quickly understands that he has to extend as much as possible his meditating state. His desire to see and understand the world without dualistic analysis grows; he wants to see the world as it is and not according to erroneous interpretation. In order to do so, he tries to remain concentrated and to be present at each moment in the course of various activities he must perform during a normal day. The moment the adept is conscious of his beingness in the present, and not influenced by the thought process, HE IS MEDITATING. In the beginning, the adept must, as soon as he realizes that he is distracted by thoughts, re-focus his attention and become present again while accomplishing what he is doing. The adept needs a great deal of courage, and without losing patience he must re-focus every time he is distracted, until his consciousness becomes natural. Then the adept lives the present moment in its totality. His breathing can help him in difficult moments. He can mentally follow the rhythm of his breathing while he focuses his attention on being present: this will help stabilize his concentration and will make the task easier.

How can motivation be the goal?

PERSEVERANCE

The action of not losing one's courage and to continue without fail.

The adept perseveres in his quest and does not let anything weaken his will to reach his anticipated objectives. He ceaselessly studies, listens and meditates on what is created and what is not. He does not let his concentration falter; this is the price to pay to experience sudden-awareness moments. With patience he always controls his thought process and does not let thoughts pollute his contemplation. He watches them go by without defining them. When he feels mental fatigue, he perseveres in his effort until all his being is re-energized. He persists in meditation until he reaches the restful state of quiescence. From this state, he applies his energy to prolong the duration of peace and repeat it at will. Even when misfortune hits, he uses it as a development tool. He meditates on the impermanence of what is considered good or bad. He continuously fights his attachment to worldly things and remains in contemplation until he feels the indefinable sensation of compassion for all beings of the universe. At this point he is at the threshold of realization. Nothing can influence him anymore; he is invincible in his armour of peace and wisdom.

Why is perseverance a guarantee of success?

PERSONALITY

The intellectual characteristics by which an individual recognizes himself as a being.

The personality comprises all intellectual aggregates (or sensations) experienced by an individual in the course of his past and present lives. Each one of the aggregates and assemblies of aggregates possesses some degree of power and the dominant one is the one that catches the brain's attention, it is the one at the command station ordering the body around. An assembly of aggregates can represent what people call a trait of personality or a person's tendency. This trait of character will be more or less predominant according to the power of the overall aggregates composing it. Everything a person has learned and realized in the past concerning spirituality, for example, forms an assembly of aggregates.

Its importance will determine its predominance over other assemblies and thus the spiritual tendency of this being. The aggregates composing someone's personality are in constant transformation and, according to interactions occurring in the course of this being's life, one of these aggregates will become predominant or will lose its dominant place. The wise one knows that he experiences a predominant spiritual assembly of aggregates at certain times. His goal is to increase the power of this aggregate and, in order to do so, he takes advantage of the moments when it is in command to initiate the greatest possible number of interactions on the subject through study or meditation. These activities will increase the volume and strength of the aggregate that will eventually remain in power for longer periods of time. A day will come when the spiritual aggregate will be permanently at the command station. The wise man will have reached the presence, which means being conscious and in control of any occurrence at all times, even during his daily occupations. Then he will experience quiescence all day long, he will be in a state of constant meditation, on the road to realization.

Why must we dissect matter in order to understand nothingness?

PLACE

An appropriate location for meditation.

Someone with the desire to meditate will choose a place fitting his taste and tendencies. No one can dictate to anyone else something as intimate as a meditation site. For the physical place of meditation, the wise man recommends a calm place, safe from distractions. A quiet place, a little aside from the action. But the adept immediately notes that meditation happens in the mind and nowhere else and that once the attention is focused on reality, the physical surroundings lose most of their importance. Meditation occurs in the great inter-cerebral emptiness. He also notes that meditation not only consists of a few minutes of presence in the morning and at night, but in a continuous presence or consciousness at every moment of life. The adept tries to remain present in his head at each instant of the day and night. As soon as he realizes that he has been totally absorbed in his actions (whatever they were), he becomes conscious of his presence. He will not divide his consciousness in two parts, one for the work and the other for the presence (this would only lead to a fragmentation of his consciousness, which is not the goal of the exercise), but he becomes aware that he is present during the accomplishment of the action. This allows the adept to avoid becoming lost in the past or the future and identifying with an illusory action. Instead, he remains conscious that he is doing something in the material world and recognizes it for what it is. Thus the adept meditates. Illusion is unconsciousness.

Why is it the same to meditate on a pile of manure than on an embroidered cushion?

PLANNING

The working out of an objective and the actions needed in order to achieve it.

The human being builds his world from well-planned projects. The planning helps him realize his dreams and expectations of success, wealth, well-being and happiness. But all this planning forces him to live in the long-term. He thinks that he will finally be happy after this beautiful achievement, and he forgets that no one can be happy in the future. The only place and time where one can find and live happiness is here and now, since nothing else exists but the present time. Anyone who does not taste the sweetness of peace and serenity here and today is condemned to chase after it for the rest of his life without ever catching it. The wise man has understood that, and this is the reason why he lives each moment of each day as if it were the last one of his life. With his eyes closed to illusion and opened to reality, he takes the time to stop and assess his state of peace and serenity. In constant contact with the truth, he radiates calm and happiness, he realizes creation, he does not suffer it anymore.

What is the difference between searching for happiness and finding it?

POINT OF CONCENTRATION

A mental point on which attention is focused.

The goal of concentrating the attention on a mental point is to separate the thought process from the consciousness of the being, to detach the observer from the mass of intellectual aggregates he believes to be. Most people's attention is located in their eyes. Anyone who closes his eyes and observes what happens for a moment, becomes aware that his attention is not in his nose, nor in his ears, nor in his mouth, but in his eyes. With an effort it is possible to transfer one's attention to any part of the body, but no effort is necessary to bring it to the eyes, the attention goes back there automatically. This is very normal since the eyes represent the most important data sensor in the whole human machine. Thus, it is reasonable to want to be more present at this information centre. When the adept focuses his attention on a mental concentration point, the eyes and other sensor centres become secondary, the adept is present at his concentration point and nowhere else. The most current concentration point is located at the top the head, and higher if possible. From this point, it is possible to control the thought process and to progress toward the recognition of the human being's real nature. From this point of view, the wise man meditates on wisdom and contemplates the infinite emptiness of reality.

What is attention made of?

POINT OF VIEW

A particular way to see or understand.

A person in good health sees life very differently than a sick person. Everyone interprets the world in his own way, whether it is an experience, a television program, a film, a book, a piece of art, etc. Furthermore, one's interpretation constantly changes according to the mood or newly acquired knowledge. Everything is a question of point of view in this world of dualities and illusions. The unenlightened beings perceive these different interpretations and points of view as being perfectly normal. They are under the influence of things and interpretations of this world because they only see the multitude, the difference between things of the creation. The wise man with wide-opened eyes knows that the difference is imaginary and that all is immersed in the unity of reality. Thus the unenlightened one sees the world through a filter which makes him believe that all is real, while the wise one looks upon and interprets the world for what it really is, namely the projection and interpretation of the mind (an illusion). He resists being blinded by all those dreams of glory and wealth since his only thirst is for wealth of knowledge and pure view. His only dream is to reach the eternal truth. Meditation on nothingness allows him to glimpse beyond the hypnotic filter and see partial truth. Then with time the eternal blinding truth shines upon the observer.

Why is the observer part of the scenery?

POLLUTION

The result of dirtying, soiling a thing or the environment.

Anything that can be harmful to the true vision of reality. In the beginning there was void in all its transparency and purity. Then came ignorance that permitted the advent of the material world. Then, for ages, the mind, under its human form, experienced what is created, the illusion; and as a sponge absorbed all those erroneous concepts. Today, the human mind is so totally polluted that it has increasing difficulties understanding the real purpose of the universe in which it lives. In order to liberate the mind from pollution, the adept will first acknowledge that the material world is nothing but concepts and illusions. Then he will realize that the illusory world is only an image projected on the void's canvas by the individual mind. Liberation will be possible only once the thought process is mastered, once the mental movement comes to a full stop.

What happens in the mind when one stops the comparison process?

POSITIVE EMOTION

An affective reaction due to a false interpretation of an experience that has a beneficial tendency.

Most people will say, I understand that emotions are the source of the world's sorrow, but there are not only bad emotions, there are good ones also. The vision of the ignorant is limited to the illusory world, thus his point of view is dualistic: for him there is good and bad. The wise one accepts without difficulty that positive emotions are far less destructive than their negative counterparts. But he also realizes that emotions, whether positive or negative, are erroneous interpretations of the world and enslave to materiality anyone who gives them importance. He clearly sees that his fellow creatures use gold (good) chains as well as iron (evil) chains to tie themselves to the world of illusion and sorrow. In deep meditation he sees positive and negative emotions vanish into nothingness as smoke coming out of a chimney on a winter night. But he also realizes that those using positive emotions to spread good around them accumulate a positive charge that will eventually bring them some happiness.

What becomes of someone who has transcended his emotions?

POSSESSION

Disposing of something at will.

The material things in which most people search for the solution of all their problems. Individuals who do not recognize that the only valuable possessions are not from this world unrelentingly accumulate illusory goods. Yet they see around them people who have built fortunes in the hope to find peace but are only unhappier under beautiful dresses and fake smiles. The misery of the rich and idolized is real, but often they do not feel their unhappiness for a long time because they are so blinded by the sensations and emotions they feel. The wise one stores up real possessions, those that are intangible in this world. The glimpse of wisdom he gathers at the turn of his meditation gives him the peace the ignorant beings are unsuccessfully looking for. He owns nothing, has nothing, but in reality can dispose of it all. If everything were given to you tomorrow, what would you do with it? You would probably leave it where it is. This is the situation of the wise man. Only those possessing a little want to keep it for themselves. One who has all, wants to share it joyously with everyone. He is rich because he is no longer a slave of matter. It offers itself to him under all kinds of aspects. The wise man smiles and returns to his contemplation.

How can material possessions harm a searcher of the truth?

POSTURE

Particular body position.

The beginner must first find a good body position to meditate. A position in which he will feel comfortable while it follows certain rules. These few rules are: 1) the back must remain in a straight line with the head with the chin parallel to the ground; 2) the chest is lightly projected to the front; 3) arms are relaxed and the hands rest on the thighs with the palms facing up, or the hands can be joined together loosely without crossing the fingers. The person practising can sit cross-legged on the ground (tailor like), but this position is often very uncomfortable for North-American people. It is preferable to sit on a straight-backed chair, where it is possible to keep the back straight and the feet flat on the floor. It is important that the head remains straight, in balance, not resting on the back of the chair. It is also possible to meditate while lying down, before going to sleep, but this posture is not recommended for meditating in general, especially early on because the beginner can fall asleep too easily. The wise one meditates in a comfortable position, without being too relaxed, his body in a stable equilibrium. He can keep this posture for very long periods of time without tiring too much. Furthermore, he keeps on meditating during all his daily physical tasks and even during his sleep. But care most be taken: meditation is not a physical gymnastic but rather a mental one.

Will meditation take one as far as self-destruction?

POVERTY

The state of a being who lacks the resources to achieve his objectives.

Contrary to what most people think, real poverty is more spiritual than material. Because very poor indeed is the one who does not realize that worldly wealth cannot bring him happiness and that he cannot take it with him when he dies. Very poor is the one who is a prisoner of his passions and who does not hesitate to harm his fellow men to achieve his goals. Unhappy is the one who believes that physical or intellectual love can bring happiness to his life. Anyone who does not possess spiritual wisdom, after an interval of joy, falls into a state of sadness and unhappiness. Since everything in the material world has a beginning and an end, nothing escapes this universal law. The wise one is free as the wind because he is not attached to anything and does not desire anything worldly. Because he does not desire anything, everything is offered to him, everything is within his reach. His only goal is to reach the truth through meditation. After studying and analyzing creation by means of his limited consciousness (intellect), he goes on an in-depth study of the thought process (the world) by means of the transcendent universal mind. He analyzes the microcosmic mind under its human mask and finally realizes that all humans are part of the truth, of the great cosmic machine; they would only have to open their eyes to understand the greatest mystery of the universe. But the wise one knows that everything passes in this world and that creation as a large wave rising above the sea will inevitably return to it. Each human being opens his eyes to the truth when his time has come, when he has finished burning all of his actions' reactions. Meditation is a shortcut allowing to reach the goal faster.

What happens to the one sitting on his golden throne when he realizes the futility of wealth in the great scheme?

POWER

The ability to do things.

Some ignorant beings who dimly start to see beyond the illusion often make the mistake of using meditation tools in an attempt to acquire powers over matter. They falsely believe that powers will bring them the happiness they are looking for. They are mistaken because if they are successful in acquiring some powers they will not have the wisdom to understand that these powers also are part of the illusion. They will use them, will attach themselves to them and in order to continue on the evolution path will have, as with any other material thing, to transcend them and shed them. The wise one is not searching for powers. His goal is truth and reality and he knows that a search for powers would only delay him on the road leading beyond illusion. If he acquires powers, through his efforts to reach illumination, he will not give them any attention and will focus even more on his quest. At the end of the journey he knows that he will possess all imaginable powers and more, by human standard, but he also knows that he will have the wisdom to understand their futility.

What is the power of a wise one in the quiescence state?

PRACTICAL KNOWLEDGE

Knowledge acquired by experience.

For everyone, whether in the material or spiritual world, practical knowledge implies that it is acquired through direct contact between the one who wishes to learn and the thing to be known. Practical knowledge is the opposite of theoretical knowledge obtained by proxy, by means of a person or object related to the matter under study. The student never communicates directly with the mass of what he wishes to learn. For the wise one, practical knowledge means that wisdom is obtained through direct contact with the essence of all that exists. This experience is only possible for one who, in the quiescence of deep meditation, frees his individual essence (individual mind) to become immersed in the essence of all that there is (universal mind). The wise man intuitively knows that his mind in its natural state, true, pure and unaltered is an infinite stream of consciousness uncreated and indestructible that emerges from and immerses itself in the ocean of the universal mind (First Principle). During this intense moment, he experiences a sudden inner awareness and a conviction that the knowledge acquired is one and unique, eternal. For him, it is impossible to learn the truth without direct contact with the void.

Why is universal wisdom an inherent part of the searcher?

PRACTICE

Doing something physically in order to gain experience.

Reaching: The material world is full of people using eloquent words in an attempt to convince their neighbours of the knowledge they believe they own and the so-called wisdom they preach. Be careful: there is quite a difference between words and truth. Most of these people have simply invented or acquired their knowledge in books; they practically never acquired it through practice. It is easy to profess without practising what one preaches. These people are usually profiteers. The wise one does not try to convince, he is satisfied with the practice of his art of meditation, and when the time comes he shares his experience with others if he deems it necessary. His only advice is not to believe anything at first sight, and to verify everything through the practice of meditation. The adept will not be fooled into believing that his book knowledge is sufficient. Any intellectual knowledge is contaminated by the mental analysis process; thus useless to the sincere searchers. The only valuable knowledge is the one emerging from the depth of meditations as a lightning setting the contemplator's mind on fire. No one can deny the ultimate wisdom and, in order to be really ultimate, it must never come into contact with duality. Only practice can lead to intuitive knowledge.

Why does intuitive knowledge bear the seal of reality?

PRACTISING PERSON

An individual observing a spiritual discipline.

Any individual with the intelligence and the knowledge to understand the physical, intellectual or spiritual benefits derived from meditation can practice this discipline. Meditation does not interfere with the religious beliefs of a practising person because it is not another religion but a mental discipline allowing to acquire a clearer vision of the world in which we live or of someone's religious beliefs, as the case may be. The practising person focuses his attention on nothingness with the intention to control his mental process and reach an inner peace called quiescence; a state of inner silence where thoughts have ceased to appear and disappear from nothingness. In quiescence, he focuses his attention on his personal questions or problems without analyzing them, in the hope of obtaining answers that are not the product of dualistic analysis. Finally, in deep contemplation he wishes to gain the understanding of the cosmic mechanism and grasp the essence of all things. The wise man sees any form of meditation as the first step toward truth and ultimate illumination.

What is the difference between a human being and an animal?

PRAYER

A formula used to ask favours from a superior being.

The ignorant immerses himself into adoration and prayer to one or several superior beings in the hope of gaining material or immaterial things. He even goes as far as to bargain for his favours: if you give me this, I will do that for you, one mass for good marks on an exam, etc., as if the superior being could ever need what he has to offer. The human being creates his own superior beings and develops laws that manage them. The illusion is totally hallucinating, so well indeed that he firmly believes that someone is listening. He does not realize that the only listening ear resides within himself. The beginner in meditation will not get caught in the prayer's trap and will realize that as soon as he is <u>asking</u>; he no longer meditates, he is in fact praying. No request favours awakening; it rather promotes dependence. The wise man knows that results depend on prior actions and that no superior being is influencing these results one way or another. He knows that he can only rely on himself to reach his ultimate goal, and that prayer cannot replace the experience of life's events. As soon as he closes his eyes and that silence emerges, any doubt is erased, and there remains only the indomitable will to experience reality.

Where does the power of prayer come from?

PREACHER

A person who promotes some facts and words.

The world is full of preachers of all kinds and various beliefs. Whether they are true or false is of no consequence, they all fill a particular niche in the great game of life which would be empty without them. Any form of preaching is good as long as it is based on honest experiences and beliefs. There is an audience for each existing preacher since the diversity of our world in unlimited. A preacher's voice will produce an echo, there will always be people to gather around someone who pretends to possess answers to questions about existence. It is important for the adept to understand that he should not become someone who preaches what he does not practice or believe in. This is an illusory path leading to only more illusion and sorrow. No knowledge is really assimilated nor will it give the expected results before being experienced. The adept can share without restraint his meditative experiences with those who wish to reach the same goal as his. He never declares anything absolute but advises those listening to experience by themselves before accepting anything as a true fact. Only the void of meditation is the bearer of absolute truth.

Why is the fruit of duality always changing?

PREREQUISITE

A series of facts that must exist before another thing can take place.

The path to liberation is open to all, but only a few have the necessary qualities and will to set out on it. Most people do not even see this evolution highway, because they are totally blinded and dominated by the illusion. Meditation is known to a great part of the population and only a minority acknowledges its value and its capacity to solve material problems. Not all people are ready to take a short-cut to reach the truth. Those who consider the possibility to embark upon the road to reality show certain characteristics. When someone feels that he is ready to take the direct road leading to the eternal light, he must, before everything else, be convinced that the material world can only generate confusion and disillusion, and that it does not lead to peace and serenity. He must also be absolutely sure that there is a way to achieve peace and happiness. From this point on, one only needs to practice the art of meditation; this great purifier will do the rest. Thus disillusion in the material world and faith in a better world represent the spring-board toward the truth.

How can one explain that human beings are equal and unequal at the same time?

PRESENCE

The awareness of being there when an event occurs.

Our world is filled with great absentees. Everyone does thousands of things without being present. When at work, they are in fact on vacation; while eating, they climb mountains or flirt with the girl next door; when they seem to be listening to you, they are preparing their own speech; when they look happy, they think about their problems; when they relax, they are concerned about the payment of their rent. In fact they are never there, because where ever they are, they want to be elsewhere; whatever they do, they would prefer to do something else. Meditation is a catalyst allowing the adept to be present at all times. During his meditations he is present there, right in the centre of his mind, in the middle of the cosmic void. Meditation teaches him that it is impossible to do something well if you are not there to do it. In his life the wise man is conscious of walking when he walks, of talking when he talks, of laughing when he laughs, of eating when he eats, etc. He lives each moment to the fullest, he is not preoccupied by what will happen in five or ten minutes, or tomorrow, or next year: he simply lives what he is currently doing without letting his analysis process destroy the essence of the present moment. By being present at all times, the wise one meditates constantly.

Where does meditation on void lead?

PRESENT

A moment located between past and future, that contains the result of past actions and the potential of the future.

The present moment is the unique thing that a human being possesses in his short life, the only moment when he can act. The wise one is conscious that he is harvesting what he has sown in the past, and that he is responsible for everything that happens to him. All thoughts and actions initiated in the past, including those of the present moment, are the creators of an individual's future. The present moment is the most important period for a being, because he cannot change the past but his present actions can alter the future and make it better or worse. The observer knows very well that his present meditation is the seed that will grow into the ultimate observation. He sows in this day and already foresees the harvest to come.

Does an action have a tendency to repeat itself?

PRETENSION

The claim of excessive knowledge, abusive statement that a goal has being reached.

Pretension is the disease that contaminates anyone who shows too much faith and who lacks intellectual capacities. This person thinks that the moon is made of cheese and believes he has reached the goal when in fact he has only had a glimpse of the truth, sometimes not even that. The demagogue does not meditate enough and thinks too much. He rationalizes the little truth he pretends to hold and believes that he possesses innate wisdom. This mix creates the great demagogues who pretend to be the only bearers of the so-called real truth. These people's dogmatism demonstrates clearly that they have not achieved anything besides disillusion. The wise man does not believe he is the only carrier of truth, he realizes that in the dualistic world each living being has its own irrefutable truth. He is someone who progresses on a continuous search within and not outside himself. The inner silence leads to the truth, the outside noise is only illusion. The wise one knows that the path to the ultimate truth is endless and that all that exists in the illusion is treading this path toward the only real confrontation. It is no good to pretend, one must be able to confront reality.

Why is pretension a form of progressive projection?

PRIDE

Erroneous assessment of one's own value compared to someone else's.

The corporeal, intellectual and even spiritual composition of the human being makes him the centre of the universe. Everything revolves around his person; he is, in his view, the only spectator of life's progress. All that surrounds him can only be secondary because he is, according to his senses, the central point of creation. Inflated with his pride, he faces this illusory self-importance, believing to be the central pivot holding the ultimate truth. When the mystery starts to get clearer, the illusion dissolves a little and one can have a fugitive view of the true nature of the universe. That is when human pride receives an injection of humility. The adept sees himself as a minute particle lost in the infinite cosmic ocean. His pride vanishes to leave in its wake the collapse of his self. Confronted with the immensity of this divine thought of which he is only a spark, the adept realizes that all beings of the universe are one in the sidereal cauldron of creation, and that when something affects him, it affects the whole created world. Then light becomes brighter and he realizes in deep mediation that he is infinitely small and yet infinitely great. He is the creator and the created. Within the emptiness of reality, there is no more comparison; measures or quantification, there is only unity in which the searcher bathes, where he is everything and nothing all at once.

Why would it be impossible to hurt one's brother when pride is absent?

PROBLEM

A difficult and often painful situation that requires a solution.

Some human beings under the control of their emotions often act wickedly toward their fellowmen. They do not have sufficient wisdom to grasp the seriousness of their actions. Anyone who does not respect the universal law (an immutable law) stipulating that one should consider others as if they were oneself, creates problems for himself on two planes of the illusory world. First, he runs the risk of being punished by the social law of the moment. Second, he accumulates negative charges that will inevitably return to their origin (action/reaction). If every individual could regard his neighbour as himself, we would be living in some kind of paradise. But this seems to go against creation's duality where positive and negative charges must balance one another. The wise man realizes that any negative action represents a self-imposed problem. He knows that he is responsible for all his actions and thoughts and that he will be subjected to each positive or negative charge. But the wise one can hardly act negatively because he sees the whole creation as part of himself. When he closes his eyes, he observes the absence of space-time and realizes that he is in the universe as the universe is in him, that what is down here is up there and that what is up there is down here.

How can the universe be in oneself?

PROGENY

The product or offsprings of a union.

The ignorant blinded by illusion sees only separated things, independent from one another. For him, an action appears to be alone and separated from other actions, a human being right after birth is no more linked to his mother, a thing can only be isolated from another. Thus he lives in a world of total confusion where unity does not exist. This is the reason why his environment becomes more and more complicated until it collapses under its own complexity. The wise one looks for unity and singularity. Without fait he meditates on duality in order to unify these two opposite poles into one and the same principle. He goes from complexity to duality, then finally discovers the unity of all that exists, the First Principle. He meditates on the sea and its product the wave, to realize that any phenomenon happening in this material world sprouts from a previous phenomenon. Everything is progeny, everything comes from an ancestor, everything is the fruit of something. Nothing in this world is independent from the rest of the universe. The wise man in the course of his meditations sees parading in front of his eyes a long chain of interdependent beings and events forming in fact a single unit of which he is part. Then, when he abolishes space and time, he realizes the instantaneity of this chain of life. The illumination reveals to him the instant of creation, this incommensurable space-time where everything is occurring.

In what way are the waves and the sea different?

PROGRAM

Description of actions planned in advance.

Anyone who wakes up and opens his eyes to a brand new point of view on the created world will prepare his program of actions in order to reach the spiritual goal he states for himself at more or less long term. The beginner sincerely searching for the truth intuitively knows that he can reach it. He acknowledges that a path must exist and that others before him have certainly treaded it. He takes the time to discover the first glimpse of knowledge that will allow him to progress. Anyone who believes in the truth will find it; this is a universal law. When someone is ready, his mental projections and physical actions lead him directly to the object of his search, whether it is documentation, a guide, etc. Then armed with his brand new knowledge, he programs his course, plans his journey. This program will change on the way, it will be modified, transformed in relation with the new knowledge and wisdom acquired. The wise one has discovered during his long voyage some characteristics guaranteeing success. He first learned about himself, his qualities and faults, he developed unwavering faith in the goal to be reached and an infallible mental concentration; he has remained humble even when confronted with the greatest worldly successes and insensible to the assaults of matter, he has always tried to be sincere in his objectives and in doing the necessary actions to achieve them, he has never lost courage and has always worked and still works on his liberation for the greatest good of humankind.

Who is the stranger inhabiting every living being?

PROGRESS

A slow transformation of a being caused by the development of knowledge and wisdom.

During his normal life, every living being makes an effort, consciously or not, to acquire new knowledge that will enable him to better survive in his environment. The entire biological evolution of the human being rests on the precept that one has to learn to survive. Thus man has developed a specialized body and a superior intellect to dominate every other living beings on the planet. But while his biological and intellectual faculties evolved rapidly, his spiritual development seems to have progressed at a slower pace. It is certainly easier to survive today than it was a thousand years ago. But despite this ease, the human being is as unhappy today as his ancestors were. He is still subjected to the same ancestral emotions such as fear, egoism, anxiety, obsession and aggressiveness: nothing has really changed for him regarding his inner well-being. Spiritual evolution is not the business of mass movements, but the history of individual actions. Even if it seems that people in general have practically not evolved spiritually since the dawn of time, it takes only a moment of attention and a little observation to note that many individuals have taken the road leading to inner happiness. The wise man's spiritual progress in inversely proportional to the strength of his illusory passions.

What causes illusory passions?

PROGRESSION

A continuous sequence of events bringing one from one level to another.

The slow progression allowing a being to leave a state of ignorance to reach the realization of truth is long and often difficult, but the result is an unchanging and permanent sanity, the understanding of ALL. 1. After many long lives, the being suddenly realizes that what surrounds him is not enough anymore, that something must exist other than this world of pain and misery. Worldly possessions satisfy him no more. 2. He begins his search for another truth, different from the one he believed in until then. His quest may be long and difficult before he can find the path leading to enlightenment. But eventually he will find it, everyone does. 3. He begins his journey of discipline, willpower and perseverance. Finally, he silences the thought process, and begins his inner analysis. 4. He realizes that the thought process is illusory and can only lead to disillusion and unhappiness. He becomes conscious that everything that exists is the fruit of thought that is the result of interpretation. 5. He learns that in order to reach its goal the mind must be purged of concepts accumulated during aeons, cleaned of the pollution that prevents one from seeing reality as it is. He can perform this spiritual analysis after reaching the state of quiescence of the mind. 6. Finally, he abolishes all differences; his mind is clear and transparent in its natural state. The mind in its natural state is one with the First Principle. The wise man realizes the unity of all that exists, the unity of creation and void, the instantaneity of the universe, and what it all is and contains. He contemplates reality with naked eyes.

How can all of mankind be on the path to liberation?

PROJECTION

The action of throwing an object forward or a thought toward the future.

Any thought or action is a projection into the future, since this thought or action will interact with its environment, and will produce results in the future. A thought is a mixture of elements (aggregates) in constant transformation because it is in contact with other thoughts. The wise one knows that **he is** the result of his past thoughts and **will be** tomorrow the result of his present thoughts. There is always an purpose behind a thought and this purpose will become illusory reality, according to the level of power used to initiate it. Look out: one's dreams and desires will come true. This is why one must be careful with dreams, desires and overall thoughts. The material world is the creation of thought by our individual and collective thoughts. Thought creates illusion that we interpret as reality. But illusion can only be reality to another illusion. The adept projects what he desires since he knows that his projection will become reality and he will harvest the fruit of his effort. The wise man projects his own goals and acknowledges only the reality that is illusion to the sleeping world.

How can one be what he thinks?

PROVENANCE

The source from where something originates.

For some people, a superior being who, for some unknown reason, has decided to set this machine in motion created the material world. They do not see the possibility to be even partially responsible for this tragicomic theatre play. Thus they feel isolated from others, they live separated from reality. They are like this gentleman who after losing his wallet does not look for it simply because he does not know that he has lost it. The majority of human beings, not knowing that they are beings of eternal light, have no reason to try to regain this superior state of wisdom. The wise man knows that he is mind and that mind creates thoughts which in turn produce other thoughts which finally produce matter, the material world and even the body in which he lives. Through meditation he has detached himself from matter to discover his provenance, his natural essence and an all-new evolving adventure that will lead him beyond the imaginary to the country of reality.

Why should each individual assume full responsibility regarding creation?

PUNISHMENT

The action of sentencing an individual to a penalty because he broke the justice code of a dualistic society.

Only the illusory reason for initiating an action can able to judge that action good or bad according to a dualistic moral code. A policeman who, in the course of his duty, kills a criminal is not considered guilty of any offence even if he has made the same gesture as a notorious assassin who will hang for his action; his motive was different. Worldly justice will steal the freedom of the one who steals. The judiciary system is polarized by a group of people who decide what is punishable and what is not. The adept realizes that a society punishing its members punishes itself. Even if individuals while working for justice are not subjected to worldly justice, they are subjected to the law of action/reaction and they are individually responsible for their actions. The wise one's position is well above such moral and justice code, and all his actions and thoughts are focused on the well-being and evolution of all beings in the universe. From the depth of his meditation he knows that he is working for the harmonization and liberation of mankind. As an individual sheds his aberrations, the universe becomes less and less confused.

What is the solution to crime?

PURE

The quality of something devoid of any foreign substance.

Everything that exists in the material world, without exception, contains foreign substances; nothing is really pure. Nothing is unique, thus everything is composed of at least two substances or things, which are also made of other elements or components. The adept is searching for the unity, the non-composed, the purity, and in order to do so he meditates. In meditation, he will not imagine, think about, analyze or reflect upon anything. He will keep a pure and natural state of mind, perfectly neutral but still intent on everything. When a wise one reaches the state of conscious non-thinking, the state of tranquillity such as that of a sleeping baby, the eternal light pierces through darkness and enables him to experience instantaneity, the state where one becomes conscious that ALL is happening in one instant without ever ending. Then he realizes his participation in the creation and his link to the uncreated, finally his true place in the great cosmic machine. Only those who first transcend their identification with matter can hope to become aware of the ultimate truth.

Why are hands washed in dirty water not cleaner than they were before?

PURPOSE

The goal or reason for a being or a thing to exist.

Humankind believes it is destined for great things, that it will build eternal civilizations, spectacular cities, invent miraculous techniques, control its environment, force happiness upon itself if need be. But all it has succeeded to achieve is to exploit nature, destroy the natural balance of the world, build concrete mountains where no one wants to live anymore, invent technical gadgets that enslave him ever more to machines. As for its civilizations, they are all equally absurd. Finally under all its masks of illusory happiness, it is as sad as a crow looking at its first born, who fell from the nest, dead at the foot of the tree. The wise one knows the purpose of creation and wishes that all beings of the universe search for their own inner paradise instead of trying to find the impossible while taking the chance to destroy their life support. He also acknowledges that everything is there for the taking for those with enough courage to open their eyes and see reality as it is. But more soberly, he is conscious that only those who can, will embark upon the path leading to the truth and that all others will have to continue to bear the consequences of their past and present lives until the day when, exhausted of running in circles, they will finally see a light at the end of the tunnel. Then the path will be there for them and, as all the others did, they will learn to close their windows on the world to contemplate in silence the eternal reality and acknowledge absolute happiness.

Will the robot learn to meditate one day?

Q

QUIESCENCE

Realization of intellectual silence or absence of thoughts that one can achieve by concentrating his attention long enough.

Quiescence is the first step toward liberation. After trying in vain to control his thoughts, the new observer realizes that it is impossible to control thought formation or to wipe them all out. Then comes the knowledge not to try to stop or control thoughts but rather to ignore them while keeping a constant attention on the meditation point. Little by little thoughts will lose their intensity and after a certain time they will only appear occasionally as birds passing through a cloudless sky. Finally the great silence takes all the space and the observer knows quiescence, a moment of rest on the road to liberation. The adept must not confuse quiescence with the permanent realization or final liberation. Only perseverance will enable him to reach the eternal light.

Where do the thoughts that constantly form in the mind come from?

R

REACTION

The impact of an action. The result of a good or bad action or thought on its originator and the environment.

It is essential to understand that everything in the material world exists only through interaction. Nothing in this world can move or change without altering the whole universe. The creation is a unique and indivisible whole, and within that whole there is total interdependence. Everything rests on something else, everything depends on some other things; nothing can exist independently in this world of illusion. The adept understands that his actions will impact and react with the whole universe, thus he initiates only positive actions and thoughts. Reactions cannot influence one who has no desire for things of this world. In the absence of desire for sensations, the observer realizes the impermanence of things said to be solid and the reality of what most people believe to be unreal and intangible. A blind person sees nothing even in daylight.

What can a person doing nothing expect from life?

REALITY

The characteristic of what really exists, without relation to dream or fiction.

Reaching: Reality is not what one sees, touches, tastes, etc., because those are only interpretations of the brain in an effort to identify sensations it receives from various body perception centres. Reality is not the human intellect, nor this assembly of thoughts he usually accepts as his identity. Reality is the inner observer who is aware of the continuous flow of thoughts. The wise one knows that meditation is the only method that can helps one to become aware of the thought process and realize what he ultimately IS (the observer) and not the assembly of thoughts continuously emerging in his mind. Void is the antidote against the thought process. If the adept remains long enough in a state of perfect concentration on emptiness, he will experience perfect contemplation. Void, as a pair of scissors, cuts the never-ending line of mental images and allows the adept to bathe in the inner peace. Reality is the absence of creation; reality is the immutable and eternal void, the essence of illusion.

How can illusion be rooted in reality?

REALITY OF THE ILLUSION

The tangibility of the unreal.

It is very difficult to qualify as unreal what can be so hurtful or cause so much pleasure or such overwhelming pain or happiness. One merely has to touch a rock to realise that it is real. There is nothing more real for an illusion than another illusion. This is why when a being looks upon the world with his illusory mechanisms and analyzes it with his illusory brain, he can only see reality inside the illusion; everything he touches and feels is true and real. He has no other viewpoint. But as soon as the adept stills his external impulse sensors, suspends the random movement of his thoughts and contemplates the silence of void reigning inside of him, his vision of the world is transformed. He realizes that what he believed real and stable is not in fact very tangible and is subjected to constant transformations. He sees that what he used to believe as important and essential is in fact insignificant and even childish. When he comes out of his meditation, he sees the world differently, he feels fewer desires to possess, dominate, and enjoy his illusory senses. When desires are reduced, happiness and peace increase. He realizes the importance of searching for the truth and its unimaginable potential even though he has only glimpsed it. From this moment on he uses the illusory world as a tool to progress and liberate himself from the chains of appearance tying him down in this valley of tears. Liberated from his chains, he will rise toward the light of reality.

Why is reality so elusive?

REALITY-ILLUSION

The unity of what really exists and its dreamlike product, the creation.

Some people have a tendency to believe that the wise man in his search for reality and his abandonment of illusion is attempting in fact to deny the existence of the material world. Others will go as far as to believe that he is simply looking for his annihilation, and that his meditations on void will ultimately lead him to the dissolution of his being. They are quite mistaken. The wise man realizes very well that the material world possesses a form of reality limited to illusion. This means that illusion is real as long as one is submerged in it. It vanishes as soon as it is possible to see beyond the fog of emotions. It is approximately the same for the reality sought by the wise man, in which he will find the eternal and immutable void, but also the essence of illusion that is part of it. The wise man states that the illusion originates in void and that void is perfectly pure, free of any pollutant, that it is unique and unchangeable. This paradox can only be realized in deep meditation: it is a notion absolutely impossible to express with the limited language of humanity. The wise one acknowledges that creation is the living expression of void.

When will creation disappear altogether?

REALIZATION

The achievement of an idea or project. The goal reached after a long process.

The realization or liberation is the objective of all adepts in search of reality. After becoming master of his thought process, the adept in deep meditation will experience various minor realizations before reaching the ultimate realization and finally the liberation. As the observer's ignorance disappears, creative thoughts cease their activities, creation itself vanishes, then the dualistic power which gives it substance loses its energy supply and existence. Without its dualistic energy supply linking it to the material world, the individual mind realizes its real divine nature. The wise man has attained realization, and that is the result of a limited mind realizing its infinite potential.

What does the observer gain from a prolonged meditation on a specific topic?

REALIZATION OF REALITY

The fact of understanding what really exists.

Reality does not exist in this world of illusions and fleeting spectres. Anyone who thinks he possesses a little bit of reality soon observes the illusory dream dissolving. Disillusioned, he witnesses his own dissolution into absolute forgetfulness. The wise man can only realize true reality while deeply immersed into meditation, where he bathes in uninterrupted peace and silence. In this state, the mind returns to its initial state, immune against polluting thoughts. All body windows are closed to the external world and do not let any impulsion or message enter for interpretation. The mind rests in its natural state of perfect tranquillity. This is the state in which the wise one realizes that there is no searcher nor object of research, that the ignorant is not different from the wise one, that all concepts do not really exist, and finally that there is no duality but only one single cosmic mind, the First Principle which expresses itself through life.

Why does the wise man consider the most ignorant being as liberated?

REBIRTH

Coming back to life in a different body as a child.

Rebirth is an undeniable law of nature for one who believes in the law of action/reaction. This law states that everything rests on an infinite network of actions immediately followed by reactions directly influencing the environment and the cause. This law can be verified at any time in the entire universe. Thus all beings and their faculties are the result of an assembly of physiological and intellectual causes and effects (aggregates) going back millions of years. And the human being of tomorrow will be the result of all our actions of yesterday and today. A human being slowly creates himself in order to be the entity he wishes to be at each moment. After being the cause of millions of actions and the impact point of millions of reactions, the being leaves his tired body, used during the active period of his cycle, to start a passive phase in death (without the acting machine). Then, when he has finished processing all the data from his previous life, the being starts another active phase in another body to perpetuate the life and death cycle. The wise one's goal is to transcend this cycle of life and death by reaching a higher state of comprehension through meditation on nothingness.

How many times must one die to become an infant of light?

RECALL

Something coming back to one's mind.

People who are not searching and are still imprisoned in their world of sensations use the word recall to designate their past memories. However, this word for the adept means that he must constantly remind himself and never forget four essential factors for him to progress on the path which leads to the truth. First, he will always remember to control his body's every action and never let it interfere with his social environment. The body is the tool used by the dominant aggregates to express themselves in the created world. Second, he will never forget that he is searching or let his senses run free, he will remain in control at all times. Senses are the captors forwarding the information they collect in the external world to the brain, which interprets them by means of comparisons. Third, he will at all times keep his thinking process on a short leash, and never let it ramble endlessly. The thought process is the mechanism that reacts to any sensation by projecting mental pictures. Fourth, he will never forget and will always be aware of the first three. In order to do so, the adept will continuously reinforce his spiritual aggregates by reading, researching, analyzing or meditating on matters related to his objective. The aggregates still subjected to the material world will be set back and the spiritual aggregates will dominate the body.

Must an awakened mind never sleep in order to reach its goal?

RECOGNITION OF EMPTINESS

Awareness of the absence of thoughts; the mental silence.

It is sometimes difficult for numerous people, who sincerely wish to practice meditation, to experience the absence of thoughts, or mental silence. Several of them are afraid of the idea of not thinking. They think: What will I become? Or still, they imagine they will be deprived of their will. Others simply think that it is impossible to stop the thoughts and contemplate mental emptiness and silence. Here is a simple and instantaneous method to assist beginners in experimenting mental emptiness: In a quiet setting, with his back in a straight position, the relaxed beginner executes a complete respiration, he slowly breathes in until his belly comes out a little, then without waiting he slowly breathes out until his belly comes in a little. At the end of the expiration he counts to three while he lets himself become aware of the mental emptiness and silence. He will contemplate the silence for a few seconds before the thoughts return. This short experience can be repeated at will, then when the beginner is convinced that the absence of thoughts is possible and even pleasurable, he only has to prolong this period of silence using his respiration or not.

What is the nature of mental emptiness?

REFLECTION

Concentration of the attention on a thought form in order to understand it.

After the indifference state where the wise man is no longer distracted by thought movements, comes a state of quiescence favourable to reflection. At this stage, the wise one has practically reached a total inner peace, even if he still recognizes the mental activities of thoughts. But his mind having reached its natural state is perfectly indifferent to illusory activities. The wise one then undertakes a period of reflection. He is ready to acknowledge the unity of complexity, to tear down the wall separating motion and rest, he is ready to taste the elixir of instantaneity, this unique moment during which the whole creation appears, lasts and disappears, this instant where all is consumed. Careful: reflection does not mean the analysis of a particular thought, but strictly the concentration of the attention on the latter in order to grasp its essence and to intuitively understand its message. The wise man synthesizes and creates a mental image of a thought, for example the notion of motion and rest (the question at the end of each teaching can be used to this end). When the thought form is clear, the adept enters into deep contemplation and concentrates entirely on this mental image without trying to analyze it or not analyze it, in a perfect state of neutrality. The observer focuses on the mental image until an illumination occurs. The time of great reflections and great illuminations is near by.

What happens when the observer becomes the reflection?

REFORM

The action of changing, transforming, for the purpose of improving a being, a situation or a thing.

Since the human being believes that he possesses the truth and the right way of doing things, he constantly tries to change and improve (in his view) those who do not know better and with whom he shares the world. Nothing is ever absolutely well done, nothing is ever really well said, if it is not done or said by him. This is the behaviour of someone who does not respect others as he wishes to be respected by others. This is the behaviour of someone who does not realize that other people really exist. A person of this type is so selfish that he does not realize that other people also believe that they do and say things the right way. The adept who opens his eyes to the world and notices that other people exist does not waste time trying to reform them. His goal and reason for living are to work on his own transformation, for the greater good of others. He uses the silence of meditation to reach an ever-deeper comprehension of creation's mechanism.

In what way does a wise man differ from an ignorant?

REFUGE

A safe place where one can be secure.

In the course of his quest, the adept finds refuges (certainties) which are a great help to him in difficult moments (when the power or attraction of matter gets stronger). His refuge can be, for example, the certainty that something better than the material world exists and that it is possible to reach it through meditation; that others before him have treaded a similar path and reached the eternal light; that he participates in the creation of the illusory world, and that it is possible to experience reality through meditation; that the entire world needs help and the best way to help is to lighten the confusion charge weighing on the human race by becoming himself less confused through the understanding of the cosmic machine; that only the erroneous interpretation of creation produces human beings' sorrow; that the silence of quiescence, produced by the absence of thoughts, is the screen from which will emerge revelations, and finally illumination; that the meditation he practices is the shortest and most direct route from confusion to sanity, from illusion to reality, from sleep to wakefulness. These refuges allow him to persist without fail in his meditation, without ever letting illusory images influence him, and they help him wait patiently for the results of his efforts. The adept will follow his intuition and do what he has to when he has to in order to achieve his goal.

What is the only refuge where the wise one can be invulnerable to illusion?

REGRET

The sensation of not having done what should have been done.

Regret is only another illusory sensation of this world. People experience this sensation when they believe that they cannot obtain something they could have obtained in the past if they had acted differently. Only fools feel regrets, because they are useless since they generally concern past experiences, and in this material world it is impossible to modify the past, only the present and the future accept changes. Furthermore, the wise one realizes that anyone who regrets not being able to do something in the present is someone who refuses to assume his beingness. This is why he concentrates on the present action. He also knows that someone who regrets something, in fact does not forgive himself for having or not having done an action. This creates a worry harming the searcher's concentration. The wise man regrets nothing, he lays down action after action, moment after moment like bricks in a building that will, in its right time, surpass the limits of the material world. He observes his mistakes and corrects his motion, his thought or situation, then continues on his way knowing that he has accomplished a positive action. He tries not to feel sorry for himself or for what would have been his position if he had acted differently. He acknowledges and acts upon what is within his reach and ignores what he cannot modify. The wise man is looking for absolute truth and knowledge, taking advantage of every moment of his corporeal life. He does not let illusion influence him, never forgets that he is part of the human unity and does not let youth, maturity or old age distract him from his quest. He researches, studies, reflects and meditates in order to obtain, at the end of his quest, the right to look reality in the eye.

Why is a mirror reflection in the darkness less real than in the light of the day?

REJECT

Attempt to throw away from oneself what is undesirable.

As soon as the adept closes his eyes in an attempt to focus his attention on a point inside his head in order to reach silence, he feels like he is invaded by thoughts of all kinds, coming from nowhere, appearing and disappearing without end. The adept feels like he is bounced around by this continuous flux on which he seems to have no control. Then he starts what is called a period of rejection, meaning that for a while he will try to eliminate, by will power alone, the stream of thoughts. When he feels or sees a thought he rejects it, chases it far away. The thought disappears, but the rejecting action itself generates another thought and this cycle could go on eternally. Tired after a while, the adept realizes that this method of rejection does not work at all as desired. Then, he abandons rejection for indifference, he focuses his attention on a mental point and tries to ignore the thoughts assailing him and soon he realizes that he has some good results. The more intense his concentration, the less thoughts distract him. He watches them passing far away, as birds in a cloudless sky. At this point, he relaxes, increases his concentration without applying force, and accepts thoughts as they go by. If one of them distracts him, he does not push it away, he only returns to his focus and the thought vanishes into nothingness. He becomes the impassive observer of passing thoughts. After a while, he reaches quiescence, a state of peace where everything is perfectly calm, from where even bird-thoughts are absent. He has reached the natural state of the mind at rest.

If the adept does not control his thoughts, who does?

RELATIONSHIPS

Sustained frequenting of various persons.

People in general base their relationships on their own needs. Some are looking for company, others want friends or someone to admire and sometimes to hate, or they wish to meet someone who fulfills their emotional needs. Yet others are looking only for sex or escape from boredom, etc. All these relationships are part of the illusory actions that human beings strive to continuously repeat until complete exhaustion of the energy that each and everyone assigned to them. The wise one also looks for relationships with people who practise, as he does, the search for truth. He takes advantage of their comfort and moral support. Then he realizes that his search for relationships is futile, whatever his initial reason for seeking them out. In meditation he discovers that the only things that count are focusing the attention on the void and searching for the real truth, and that all beings of the universe, while looking for futile or spiritual relationships, are in fact searching for the same truth. Everyone is on the path to reality. The only difference (in this illusory world) is their level of consciousness about the adventure they are living.

Can the level of comprehension dictate the impact of an action?

RELIGION

Spiritual research during which a human being tries to conquer a better world.

All forms of religion are obvious signs that a human being is not satisfied with his condition and wants to change it. The practice of religion is different for everyone since we all have an understanding of our own needs and aspirations. Everyone finds the spiritual search that he can accept and understand. In this case we can come back to the old saying "one can only understand what he can understand when he becomes aware of it". Meditation is meant to be a tool for searching the truth. The implication of meditation on emptiness is very clear: a person focuses his attention on his inner emptiness; that is all. This meditation on the first hand allows anyone who focuses his attention on his inner void for a sufficient period of time to "control" his thought process and reach inner silence. On the other hand, it enables him to experiment sudden awareness of the reality of his surroundings. Meditation makes it possible to differentiate what is created and what is not, then to unify these two poles into one and the same unit that is the source of everything in existence.

Who determines the difference between one's god and someone else's god?

RENOUNCEMENT

The action of abandoning one's desires to possess.

In the so-called "normal" world, possessions often represent the social status of a person. The more things someone possesses, the more successful he is according to material world standards. But in fact, any possession can only bring deception since it cannot be permanent, i.e. one will lose eventually. The adept who embarks upon the path leading to reality must experience this sensation in order to understand it and transcend it. He will study, analyze and meditate on possession and renouncement. In the course of one of his experiences he will acquire something of value to him and will analyze his feelings and the process of attachment to what one desires. Then he will abandon this thing, he might give it away for example, in order, to consciously discover the tearing caused by the rupture between the owner and the owned object. He will also notice the feeling of freedom of someone who withdraws from a particular attachment. Then he can generalize this experience of renouncement and extend it to everything the material world has to offer. What is the feeling of someone who has abandoned everything, who is unattached to anything? The wise man's goal is total renouncement of worldly things, the elimination of all material desires. His meditation allowed him to glimpse a state of liberation impossible to describe, a state of inhuman peace and happiness. He realizes that the price to pay to permanently bathe in this state is the absence of ties to the illusion world. The wise one is willing to die to one world to be born again in another.

What drives human beings to accumulate possessions?

REPETITION

Something happening again and again. Tendency to occur once more.

After long periods of observation the observer discovers that actions and thoughts have a tendency to repeat themselves or to produce offsprings more of less similar to their parent. If you run, you have a tendency to keep on running, if you sit, you have a tendency to remain sitting. Everything has a tendency to repeat itself, thus the wise one, aware of this fact, takes advantage of this universal characteristic by initiating thoughts and actions which, by repeating themselves, will produce the intended results, even if the thoughts and actions are slightly altered. However, nothing can happen exactly as projected, because of the effect of chance incorporating its lot of unknown factors (aggregates) into the original equation. The wise man creates tendencies that will lead him to his objective in the material world. By initiating a meditation, he knows that he creates the probability to meditate again and again until he reaches what he is looking for.

Why does life seem to continuously repeat itself?

RESEARCH

The action of trying to discover, find and acquire knowledge or goods.

It does not suffice to search, one must know where to look. Most human beings are conducting some kind of spiritual research on a various scale. In all cases, this research on a various scale is good and useful because it separates us from animals. During his research, the searcher will only find what he can understand. No one can understand what is beyond one's grasp. Everything is well and good in the best of worlds. The wise one is not unlike ordinary people; he too understands only what he is ready to understand. Those who search for answers in their inner selves are already well on their way to the truth. When the adept finally ceases to search outside in order to find himself, he embarks on the illuminated path leading to the truth. Then, from the moment he realizes that answers, in addition to coming from within, automatically emerge from the silence following the interruption of the thought process, he is on the royal path, on the great alley of the awakened and realized ones. He has reached the point of no return; the moment of the great confrontation is close.

What does find one who succeeded in bypassing preconceived ideas?

RESULT

The consequence of a series of actions.

In the material world, all actions produce a reaction and all of humankind is submitted to this law. It is the same for the wise man working on liberation from the dualistic illusion. The efforts he undertakes in this world are also subjected to the action-reaction law. What result does the wise one real once he has reached his goal, at the end of the present stage of his voyage? He gains the perceptiveness required to accurately view the universe. He reaches the comprehension of the world in its primordial state unaltered by the thought process. Thus he perceives reality in its essence, which is absolute unity. He realizes that any thought process never altered the limitless, eternal and immutable void; he sees perfection. Furthermore, he understands where matter is coming from and is capable of observing creation from the viewpoint of the uncreated. He is there without ego and yet still conscious, in balance between reality and illusion, in an instant of perfect instantaneity. The entire universe, without beginning or end, is open to him as a great book made of only one page. He has come through the illusion wall to actually understand that nothing is separated from the unity, that the WHOLE is ONE and ONE is the WHOLE. The wise man's mind is now free from the illusion, the cause of all the word's problems. He is pleased to realize that the illusions of today will be the reality of tomorrow. Nothing or anybody can escape this fact.

Why fight to dominate an illusion when one simply has to stop thinking about it?

RETREAT

The action to retire in a place of calm favourable to introspection.

The wise man can choose to live a life away from the world in some monastery and enjoy the solitude propitious to inner research. He also can choose to live an active social life dedicated to relieve his brothers and sisters from their sorrow or to share his spiritual experiences with his fellow men. But whatever kind of life he embraces, he enjoys constant retreat since the eternal truth is always present within him. He realizes his solitude and closes his eyes to enter his refuge where, distant from the world he can enjoy this incredible peace. The wise man's retreat is permanent since it comes from within. He looks at the world as a great school that he can use at will to progress on the path. He walks alone, as does every other human being; on the road he decided to follow in order to reach his goal. He looks upon his inner horizon that seems to border an infinite space. This horizon is so far away that it seems practically inaccessible, yet the wise one will have to touch it in order to see himself in the mirror of void.

How many roads lead to the truth?

RICHES

The accumulation of terrestrial wealth.

Wealth is the ultimate objective of one who is hypnotized by the material world appearances. All his desires revolve around his needs or what he interprets as his needs and his desire to fulfill them. Because all in the illusory world is unstable and changing, one blinded to reality suffers from an incurable insecurity. In his attempt to appease his hunger for stability and security, the ignorant fills each instant of his short life working to gather goods that in fact are only loaned to him for a short period. The human being in general numbs himself with illusory purchases in the hope of finding happiness, but these purchases are only gratification tying him even more to his problems. Everything is illusory, nothing is real in this world, riches vanish before the ultimate reality. What is the use of a nice home when you are dead? What is the use of a fortune that you will lose or that your family will fight over immediately after your last breath? What is the use of friends who will forget you eventually after you are gone? What is the use of working trying to earn something that you cannot keep after this life? The wise one invests in the world what is necessary for his survival and then works on his own realization. He spends most of his time searching the mysteries of life and death, of the created and the uncreated. Finally he focuses his attention on an inner point which he finds permanent, stable, perfectly motionless, REAL. He discovers that what is stable and permanent really exists. Reality is eternally present and immutable. Happiness can only be reached in reality.

How can one gain by losing everything?

RITUAL

An assembly of gestures, postures and verbal practices.

Adepts belonging to most religions or philosophical movements develop their own ceremonies and rituals that allow them to create an atmosphere or a feeling of belonging. Rituals have always been awakening tools for people who otherwise would not have been able to become aware or to belong to a movement promoting the existence of spiritual experience. The adept shall not hesitate to use rituals to help set himself in the right frame of mind or to boost his awakening potential. But he must not forget that the goal is not the ritual, and that any ceremony is only a tool to accomplish something else. As for the wise man, he is not much concerned by rituals or any other type of practices. His ritual is the simplest; he finds a comfortable position, closes his eyes, concentrates his attention on a mental point and observes the creative void, nothing else. He knows that all rituals, as valuable as they may be, are part of the great illusion. Thus, they too have to be transcended.

How can a ritual be a form of attachment to the illusory world?

S

SATISFACTION

The pleasure to have accomplished something desired.

Everyone living in the illusion is searching for satisfaction in the possession of wealth, powers or honours. Moreover, ordinary people never stop mutually congratulating and gratifying themselves for their accomplishments, wealth, talents or good deeds. All that noise, light and glitter hiding the real meaning of life will be forgotten at the end of the feast. The sleeping human does not understand that the greater glory is, the more difficult it will be to accept not being remembered, the greater wealth is, the more difficult it will be to lose it, the greater the talents are, the more difficult it will be to watch them vanish. Happiness always escapes those who look for it in the material world, and yet they will attempt in vain to catch this unrealizable dream until one day they realize its futility. The wise one has understood and does not accept to be blinded by things that do not last. He prefers to search for truth in his inner maze. With the power of his will, he dominates the internal noise and establishes silence that becomes the foundation of his exploration of a world beyond human analysis. He focuses on the uncreated emptiness and, liberated from worldly temptations, contemplates his real and permanent satisfaction. What the searcher acquires here will last forever; even death is powerless before the eternal light.

When will the actor of the great play cease to play his role?

SCIENCE

A body of knowledge that touches a particular subject.

As soon as the word science is pronounced, everyone sees approximately the same mental imagery, machines, vehicles rolling, flying or navigating, others which analyze, weigh, or print; then buildings, houses, roads, etc. These are the images of our civilization, which for us represent the science of human beings. But with all that science, is the human being any happier? Has he changed? Has he improved? Does he know himself better today than yesterday? No, not really, the human being has a thin layer of civilization that has a tendency to wear out at the slightest stress. Then he shows the same weaknesses and primitive instincts as our ancestors. The world has changed a lot, but not the human being. Our science of the material world is illusory, it cannot be reliable or stable, it is its nature to constantly change, it can only lead to deception. What is true today will be false tomorrow. The wise man studies the science of man, the science that changes what is happening inside the human being. He studies a science that in some cases reaches back thousands of years and still has not been changed; it has not been altered by time. The wise man of today meditates as the wise one meditated three thousands years ago. Meditation is the science that allows the human being to look inside of him and change, alter his essence by experimenting and understanding the mechanics of the universe and his own being. No other science allows that. Wise men of yesterday and today find the same thing: reality.

Why is meditation an exact science?

SEARCHER

Individual who works at discovering something.

In society, people are searching for wealth, security, rest, love, etc. Everyone is attempting to discover something that could make their life less painful. Everyone without exception, whether he is considered good or evil, honest or dishonest, tries to better his condition. The problem is that they ignore universal laws, and their actions that should bring them a little temporary happiness often immerse them into permanent sorrow. The searcher who has acquired a little wisdom understands that happiness experienced in this world, whether large or small, will not last, and will eventually vanish. Thus he searches for happiness through actions that will close the gap between him and reality. By respecting the universal law of action-reaction, his achievements only bring him benefits and progress in his quest for truth. In deep meditation the wise man realizes that the search, the object of research and the searcher are a single unit.

What is the difference between the search of an ignorant and that of a wise man?

SECURITY

Well-being brought by the absence of danger.

A human being constantly feels in danger of losing his security. Since he acknowledges only the material world, he cannot look anywhere else to find what he believes he must have in order to fulfill his needs. All human beings are walking on a road leading to an unknown goal. This road is strewn with pitfalls, difficulties and suffering, a little like an obstacle course without a finish line. It seems without end because most walkers are under the influence of illusion and do not realize what is happening. They navigate as ships without a compass in a fog of ignorance, fear and submission. Since they fulfill their needs with illusory things, their desire to possess is immense, they are so afraid of losing what they own that they yield as slaves at the foot of their master, matter. The wise man looks for his security within the silence and the absence of space, matter and time. He discovers that the detachment from worldly goods eliminates the notions of danger and possession. The wise one who does not own anything cannot lose anything. His security is the light of truth he contemplates during his meditations.

Why don't worldly things bring security?

SELF-CONFIDENCE

Believing in our own capacity to do something.

The ignorant beings are so blinded by illusion that it is impossible for them to truly believe that they can reach a superior state of mind. They always link such an evolution with gains of power that will allow them to rule the world and acquire colossal wealth. Their attention is concentrated on the material and all is perceived and analyzed according to illusions. The adept who slowly opens his eyes to reality begins to believe in himself and to cultivate this belief in his evolution that will allow him to reach unknown summits of wisdom and bliss. Without this belief, there is no hope of evolution beyond matter. It is impossible to achieve anything unless we believe in it. The wise man's progress lifts the veils of illusion one by one, allowing him to see reality more clearly. Inside him burns the fire of faith in the goal and in his capacity to reach it. In deep meditation he concentrates on the light that transforms him little by little into a superior consciousness capable of embracing the whole universe. In the silence of his retreat he smiles at people who believe in themselves.

What an unbeliever searcher can find?

SELF-OBSERVATION

The action of someone who observes himself.

The adept works tirelessly at concentrating his attention on his inner mirror, empty of any thought or reflection. The adept must remain present at all times and particularly in the course of his meditation. Without presence, there is no meditation. Thus the adept will be conscious that he observes the void. Attention, danger: most beginners make the error of self-observation. The adept in meditation observes his inner emptiness, he does not think, he does not analyze, he is present within the infinity of void. Then, all of a sudden, "I am meditating and I am conscious that I observe the void, I am conscious of being conscious that I observe the void", etc. This is a frequent mistake. If someone is conscious of being conscious, there is thought, there is analysis, thus there is NO meditation, the silence is polluted. In order to meditate the adept must be present and observe the silence; that is all. In silence the truth emerges from the void and illuminates the observer.

Why does illusion vanish as soon as the attention rests on reality?

SELFISHNESS

The action of giving too much importance to the self to the detriment of the whole.

When the adept finally establishes and maintains a state of quiescence, there is danger that he develops an egotistic weakness that will prompt him to believe that he has reached the end of his quest and that he has arrived at his final goal. The adept must always be suspicious if he starts making egotistic statements such as: "I will never come back to earth. I do not wish to live in a body anymore. I want to quit material life forever. I have reached the great illumination. I am realized". If an adept entertains this type of thoughts or statements, it is obvious that he is still very far from the great truth. The goal cannot be reached as long as the smallest trace of individualism remains in the searcher, as long as he has not transcended all egocentric tendencies. The adept must then meditate on the unity of the created and uncreated. The illuminated wise man is a totally altruistic being who has transcended the complexity and assimilated the unity of the creation. The entire universe becomes the body and mind of the one with open eyes and this universal being must also pursue the same quest as the individual being. No one will be totally liberated until the entire universe completes its liberation. All is the same, nothing is different, nothing is lost, all is transformed, only points of view change positions.

Who is the inventor of the difference?

SENSATIONS

Cerebral interpretation of external and internal stimulations sensed by the body's various sensors.

Sensations make what a human being is and how he reacts. Among the simplest sensations managing every human being's life, there is sight, hearing, smell, taste, touch, etc., in addition to notions of time, weight, space, etc. As the adept progresses in his search for quiescence, he sees each type of sensation and notion vanishing to reappear when he comes out of meditation. Sight, touch, taste and smell are the first to disappear, then the hearing goes too. The adept experiences a state of great calm and serenity, but he is still conscious of his body and environment (space). Pure attention, not distracted by thoughts, focused on emptiness eliminates different notions including the notion of time. One hour in meditation seems to last a few seconds. The consciousness (attention) of the beginner is imprisoned inside his cranium, then as thoughts calm down, the space in which the attention is present grows, but keeps an horizon, thus a limit, until finally when the great silence takes over the adept experiences an infinite space which transcends into an indescribable void, where the notion of space does not exist. This is one of the most extraordinary experiences that a person can live. When the adept closes every sensation door and silences all his notions, he at last finds himself alone in the sidereal emptiness. He has reached the threshold of wisdom; he now only has to open the door on the eternal truth.

Why does consciousness without landmarks have a tendency to dissolve?

SEPARATION

The action of isolating one thing from another.

In deep concentration, the adept attempting to eliminate or control the ever-emerging thoughts must first recognize them as such in order to make the decision to eliminate them. Since recognizing the existence of thoughts can only perform this elimination process, it automatically creates other thoughts. Thus contemplation is continuously marred by this procession of emerging and disappearing thoughts inside the adept's consciousness. The adept must therefore abandon his faculty to recognize things as well as the recognizer and let his mind rest in a perfect state of passivity. The time has come for the great separation: the adept must isolate his mind from all other physical processes. His state of spiritual relaxation and his will are so developed by now that he can, without any effort, be totally indifferent to whatever happens beyond his point of consciousness. Only the observer remains unique and unalterable. Nothing can distract contemplation anymore.

Why does every effort produce a counter-effort?

SERVITUDE

The state of submission of an individual entirely subjected to another person, a situation or a thing.

Emotions chain humankind without it being aware of it. Without knowing it, people are slaves to their desire to possess. They want everything, happiness, wealth, pleasure, possessions, a woman, a man, etc. They are never satisfied with what they have and they keep looking for newer and different things in their quest for illusory happiness. Human beings are enslaved because they desire and because they want to keep on desiring. Yet, as long as a person desires, he runs the risk that his desire will not become reality. When someone wants to keep something or someone, he loses it; when he desires to acquire something, he cannot; when he thinks that he has reached happiness, he soon realizes that it is not the case, etc. Thus all beings who desire live in a world that takes the shape of a roller-coaster: at the top, a little happiness, at the bottom, a lot of sadness, at the top a little joy, at the bottom a great deal of sorrow, etc. The wise man puts an end to this crazy race by eliminating one by one his desires to acquire, to possess, to keep, etc. Through meditation he learns to stop desiring things, rather to live the present moment with its contents, no more, no less. He realizes that each human being is the maker, one link at the time, of the chain that ties him to sorrow. He learns to let the light of reality invade his being. He contemplates the illumination that teaches that real wealth does not enslave but rather liberates.

What does one who renounces win?

SETTING POINT

A point on which the eyes are set during concentration or meditation.

The adept may prefer to meditate with his eyes open or closed. In the first case, he sets his eyes on an object placed in front of him at close distance (approximately 1.5m). It is preferable that this object be simple otherwise it could distract his concentration. Then he focuses his attention on a mental point. It is very important that the attention does not remain in the eyes because the adept could identify with the object and this attempt would be a failure. The goal of concentration is not to become an object but to achieve the silence necessary for meditation. In the second case, the adept closes his eyes and focuses his attention on a mental point other than the eyes which then become neutral, they only sense black. In this case, it is also essential for the attention to leave the eyes. If not, they could certainly offer a very nice sound-and-light show to the adept, but this is not the purpose of this exercise and again it would be a failure. The eyes have nothing to do with the process of focusing the attention on a mental point.

How can the attention become what it wants?

SHORT CUT

A shorter way to go from one point to another.

There is the slowest way, the ignorant way, which, although it leads to liberation, entirely bathes into the illusion. Completely submerged into the unreality, the beings progress at a very slow pace. There are quicker ways, such as different forms of meditation on sound, words, images, etc. But eventually these forms of meditation will have to abandon illusory tools which slow progress, and concentrate on reality, the void, in order to reach their stated goal. Meditation on void is the quickest method first to reach knowledge about oneself, then the realization of reality. This mental discipline leads directly to the goal without using illusory mechanics or detours. Emptiness (void) is the source of creation and anyone who meditates on emptiness communicates directly with the source of creation. Void is the only immutable, infinite and eternal thing that human beings can experience in this impermanent world. Meditation on void is simple and contains no rites or ceremonies. The adept concentrates on the inner void, without effort, without thinking, without analyzing, and he contemplates reality from which will emerge the truth.

How can the relationship of void and reality be explained?

SILENCE

Absence of noise. When there is no sound.

In order to learn what is silence, one must first realize that it is quite difficult to find in the material world. The adept experiments on his own and tries to find silence. It is almost impossible to succeed. Even if he goes in the remotest corners of the world, he will always hear the sound of the sea, a stream, a bird singing, etc. Shut alone in a sealed room, he will always hear the sound of his breathing, his heartbeat, etc. Is it possible that silence is absent from this world? The adept finally finds silence deep inside of him when, after calming his thoughts, quiescence allows him to experiment real silence. The observer in deep meditation closes the external sensation doors by means of his powerful concentration and, isolated from the illusory world, he contemplates void in perfect silence. A small spark of consciousness in the middle of eternal emptiness and silence, he waits, detached from illusion, the emergence of light. This is the silence sought by those who wish to experience reality because this is where the blinding light of truth originates. When thoughts are calmed down, silence takes place, and the world vanishes. When the mental process starts anew, silence disappears and the illusory world immediately reappears.

Why must there be noise in the material universe?

SIMPLE THINGS

Something uncomplicated, without embellishment.

People of the world prefer what has a lot of material value, anything that can demonstrate their status in society. They will even scorn quality and prefer a wealthy appearance. In fact they use worldly goods to impress their circle of friends, indicate their superiority in an illusory world where everything is superior or inferior. The wise man recognizes worldly things for what they are and has few concerns regarding the appearance of things or their impact on people around him. For example, he recognizes that a house is a shelter against bad weather and a protection against aggressions, nothing else. He sees no reason to own a castle too big for his needs. He knows that an automobile is a means of transportation from point A to point B and nothing else. He sees no reason to own a luxury car to show off. He recognizes money for what it is, a tool to obtain what he needs to ensure the survival of his body and allow him to study, analyze and meditate in order to discover the real nature of the universe.

Why is consciousness part of reality rather than illusion?

SIMPLICITY

The character of what is not complicated, of what is composed of few elements.

The material world tends toward complexity. What is simple one day becomes with time more and more complicated, more and more difficult to understand. In the beginning there was the mind, and from the mind emerged duality which generates multiplicity. Thus the adept and the wise man, both wishing to experience the essence of unity (mind), must simplify everything until they reach this unity which is invisible yet omnipresent. The adept who simplifies and decomposes various elements of creation to find the first element is on the right course, the one which leads to the truth. The wise man abandons complexity to contemplate the void in his meditation. Without really meditating, without thinking and analyzing, in a state of natural rest, he observes the essence of all, emptiness. The void is unique, unalterable, impossible to break down, permanent and impossible to explain with words. He has discovered the only thing with which he can make contact and which includes all those characteristics that do not correspond to any product of the created universe. The wise man bathes in the great simplicity, mother of all things.

How can a material being observe the uncreated?

SINGULARITY

The nature of what is unique, without counterpart.

The similar interpretation and representation of the universe by the various members of the world community is due to the source singularity (First Principle). Only in an illusory world is it possible to experience differences, distinctions, dissimilarities and contrasts. All in the same manner perceives the illusory world because they all use the same reading instruments whether it is the eyes, ears, tongue, hands and other mechanisms that pick up various sensations. Then when the wise one erases the difference by letting his mind rest in its natural state (silence, absence of thoughts), he meets only one state: Is it a being? Is it a thing? No one knows and no one can interpret it since there is nothing to be interpreted. But the wise man realizes that all beings of the universe spring from this inexplicable reality. Thus the dream ensuing from it can only be identical for everyone since ALL are in fact ONE and the SAME when they take off their cape of illusion and dream.

Why does a human being continuously reinvent the world?

SLANDER

The action of expressing lies in relation to a person.

Slander is a social occupation practised as a game in the illusory world. The ignorant ceaselessly criticizes, attacks and depreciates his neighbours. The slanderer does not know that he projects his own image onto another person. Furthermore, his mental and audio projections produce an impact that will return to its starting point with its negative consequence. A proverb says that only a thief will call another a thief. One thing is certain, slanderers are people slandered against. They will realize one day that others' flaws as well as theirs are the result of their past thoughts and actions and that their future flaws will be the product of their present thoughts and actions. The wise one acknowledges his personal flaws and does not attempt to project them onto others. Instead, he tries to understand their nature and composition in order to transcend them. He deeply meditates on the various factors that slow him down in his quest for truth. The wise man realizes that as everything else emerging from duality, all negative factors vanish as soon as the mind rests in its natural state. Silence cures everything; silence purifies everything.

When someone slanders against his brother, is he attempting to destroy his own reflection?

SLAVE

A person controlled by his passions.

Passionate people with only contempt for the rest of the world, because they are totally dominated by their emotions, can display behaviours that must not be mistaken for discipline or detachment. In the eyes of a beginner, these persons may seem indifferent and liberated from social laws that manage the illusory world. In fact, they are absolutely not liberated from anything, quite the contrary; they are slaves to their excessive emotions. The wise man, liberated or not from worldly conventions, will take care not to offend or hurt any of his fellow men. He understands that social laws do not concern him because his own law covers all human conventions and more. The wise one considers every human being as part of him and his attachment to material goods is non-existent. The ethics of this being have no roots in the interpretation of sensations, his truth emerges from the infinite void of reality. He has no desire for possessions or sensations, his goal is to confront the uncomfortable, the reality that is void and still generates illusion.

Why forgive one who hurts his fellow?

SLEEP

The suspension of consciousness and cessation of physical activity.

The electro-biological machine requires rest after a certain period and sets the brain function off. The thought process and the physical activity are practically totally suspended to allow rest to take place. The observation and analysis of sleep reveal that when the device (brain) used to pick up and interpret aggregate sensations stops working, illusory consciousness disappears at the same time. This indicates that the consciousness of being, of existing, depends only on the brain capacity to compare and interpret sensations. The awareness of existing vanishes when the brain stops to analyze, whether it is during sleep or meditation. Upon awakening the brain starts working again and the awareness of existing emerges. The dreams that happen during the night are aggregate interactions trying to find a new equilibrium after a certain period of body awareness where they were able to act upon the physical world through the brain and body. The wise one can maintain his spark of consciousness (quiescence) when the machine sleeps, in order to meditate through the hours of rest. Death is another form of sleep where the whole body disappears and the assembly of aggregates that formed the entity that believed it existed (me) finds itself without a sensor and interpreter. Therefore during the cycles of death there is no consciousness of existence, as we know it. But upon rebirth the brain of the new body starts again the cycle of analysis and interpretation and creates the illusion of existence and a new me.

Why is the reflection of a dreamer in a mirror no less real than the dreamer himself?

SLEEPER

Someone in a state of unconsciousness.

A person who acknowledges only the material world and lives totally immersed in the illusion. The whole universe is immersed in the First Principle. The sleeper, as well as the awakened and the liberated, are part of the eternal cosmic dream. The wise one knows that all sleepers will be awakened and liberated one day and that there is never any difference between the liberated and the sleeper. Everything is happening at the same moment in the unity of the universe and the sleeper is at the same time asleep, awakened and liberated. Let us not forget the instantaneous nature of the creation, only illusory measures lead us to believe in time.

In the middle of a meditation, what time is it on the universe's clock?

SMALL-TEACHING

The communication of erroneous information from a person to another.

The preachers of a small-teaching impose partial views and beliefs about the world or the evolution. They pretend to share wisdom, happiness and various powers with their followers without having to prove their teachings. These teachings are often used as entry doors by people looking for power and wealth at the expense of sincere searchers. The precepts of a small-teaching rest on the ignorance of reality and on the reinforcement of illusion. These teachings usually call upon the adepts' dreams of happiness, greatness and power in order to exploit them. The basic principles of such teachings often originate from hallucinations or illusory dreams of greatness of the founder. Any teaching that requires faith without asking questions, which forbid any doubts, is false, and can only lead to deception. Another type of small-teaching is one which pretends to be the only one of value and which rejects all other teachings. The adept in the stage of awakening looks for a great-teaching. One that advises to personally doubt, analyze and research the teaching. A teaching advocating that real truth will be found only when the final goal is reached.

Why does a small-teaching have to demand infallible faith?

SOLITUDE

The state of being alone.

Solitude is a staple sought-after by wise ones and other individuals with expanding consciousness. A being awakening to something else than the material cacophony looks first for peace, a little silence and solitude, a little time to think. First there is the physical solitude, when a being is no longer in the presence of other beings. This is the behaviour of the adept looking inward for the answer of answers. Then he closes his eyes, focuses his attention and reaches the inner solitude where the being is alone without a single thought in an ocean of peace and quiescence. It is in this inner peace, so soft and so perfect, that the wise one realizes that the multitude is indivisible and that the so irritating noise of the sleeping mass of beings is in fact only the humming of confusion. One has only to disregard erroneous words and focus only on the tone of homogeneity. The wise man hears only the great cosmic wind that links all beings into a permanent and immutable unity.

How can the wise man's solitude help humankind?

SORROW

An event considered as a negative experience by an individual.

All sorrows, from the most insignificant to the most important ones, are mainly caused by the loss of something that a person does not want to lose, or by the impossibility to obtain what a person wishes to acquire. Thus, sorrow is based on the desire to possess and to keep. For some, losing something can seem unbearable and life without it impossible, while the same loss may not be very important for others. Everything depends on the point of view. Therefore, in everyone's life, there are things, which if lost, would cause a great deal of sorrow. While, on the other hand, the loss of some other things would have no impact, such as things that one is not attached to. The wise one in meditation learns to recognize what would be a cause of sorrow for him and one by one transcends those desires of possessing. The more the wise one progresses in his quest for truth, the less he is influenced by loss or gain of illusory goods or anything else. When the desire to possess illusory things vanishes, sorrow loses its ascendancy. The wise man's happiness rests in his search for truth, in every glimpse of truth he achieves and in his quest for the ultimate illumination.

Why is emptiness the lifebuoy of humankind?

SOURCE

The origin of a thing or idea. Where we find what results from it.

The source of truth and reality the adept is looking for can only be found in his own mind. Meditation must be done at the mind level since it is the source of reality and the cause of illusion. Philosophy must rest on the mind, which is nothingness, which contains everything and from which everything comes from. Liberation can only be found in the mind, the source of fettering illusions. The adept's attention must never leave the inner void of truth. When the wise one has found the source, he ceases his preliminary research and abandons his secondary practices to concentrate all his attention on his mind, the pure reflection of the First Principle, the ultimate source of what is created and uncreated. With perseverance he awaits the fusion of his mind with the divine one, the source of dream and reality. When the wise man turns his sight within, the effects and illusions vanish. He realizes that his mind as the First Principle does not possess any specific characteristics. The boundless and eternal void transcend all that exists, even the observer. Finally, when the observer does not find the observer anymore, differences have no more power and divine wisdom emerges. The observer is now the creator, created and uncreated.

How does a wise man see the material world after experiencing the reality of void?

SPARK

Small point of intense light.

The spark, also called the observer, is this faint light of consciousness that persists after having dominated all random thoughts cropping up from emptiness. The spark is the consciousness that observes the limitless void in the state of quiescence, it is the real "I", the prolongation of the First Principle. Meditation is the discipline through which the spark can emerge, and cease to identify itself with thoughts. Without the discipline learned through the practice of meditation, the spark is subjugated by "thought-plays" and identifies itself with their eternal back-and-forth motion. In this state it loses its real vision of the universe and is subjected to the limited and erroneous view of analysis. It does not possess the long view of the world anymore but the relative view of action-reaction. This state prevails all over the material world, where everything is interpreted, where knowledge is never absolute. When the adept practices meditation on emptiness, he succeeds in stopping the mental process and by erasing the illusion, he can emerge from ignorance and see the universe in its real aspect again. At this stage, the wise one is no more fooled by the illusory world "monkey-plays", and leaves behind his load of sorrows.

In the hereafter, does the wind make any noise when it bends the tree tops?

SPIRITUAL ANALYSIS

Concentration of the attention or consciousness upon a question, problem, etc. without relying on thinking process.

The goal of this concentration is to ask a question and wait for an answer which will be purely intuitive thus exact and real. The searcher must concentrate his attention on a particular question, problem, etc. without dissecting nor analyzing it. In silence, he contemplates the question without distraction or efforts, and he relaxes, waits for the answer. Concentration allows to experience the focused object. When the searcher focuses his attention long enough on nothingness, he experiments the essence of reality and truth.

What makes the sleeper's judgement erroneous?

STABLE DATA

A permanent truth with unchanging characteristics.

The world bathes in confusion because the demands on human beings are too great for their understanding capacity. Illusory data is so numerous that human beings are incapable of understanding the purpose of things and events anymore. A human being is totally overcome, thus confused and disoriented. He believes or refutes anything and everything without taking the time to assess the essence of it. The human brain can only process a limited number of impulses.

A human being's confusion is proportional to the quantity of data he needs to process. Lost in this confusion, the human being forgets that he is mind and stable. The wise man in meditation focuses on only one thing (void) and therefore touches his real eternal nature again. Reality rests on void, the only stable data that one can experience in this world, everything else is unstable, changing and illusory. The wise one ignores what is unstable and focuses on his inner emptiness, which will eventually open the door to reality and universal truth. By focusing on one thing the wise man reaches the highest level of sanity.

How can an ignorant escape confusion?

STAGE

Intermediate step between departure and arrival.

The liberation path comprises two main stages divided into different steps. The first stage is called quiescence. At this stage the adept sees his life being transformed, he begins to understand the material world mechanisms and glimpse the blinding reality. At this stage the adept catches his breath before embarking on the ultimate goal, realization. It is at this level that he casts off the aberrations of this world and the cape of matter influences. He witnesses the disappearance of false emotions, his mental and physical health improves a lot. Quiescence is also the stepping board used by the adept to project himself toward the second stage which is realization. At this level the wise one completely detaches himself from matter and confronts reality as it is from all eternity. Realization is also called a step because it is not the end. It is false to believe that the wise man has to lose himself into eternal nothingness once he is confronted with realization. He is rather totally liberated from illusion, and prepares himself to confront an even greater adventure than the one he has just lived. Liberation is only the end of a stage and the beginning of another.

What is the difference between departure and arrival?

STEP

A particular and successive period of something in progress.

The progression the potential adept must experience to go from ignorance to wisdom is a long and often difficult one. It is possible to divide it in different steps punctuating the path leading to the conquest followed by the searcher. Step 1. Ignorance: the level of most human beings. The potential adept is still satisfied with the illusory reality, his small happiness and misfortunes. Step 2. Awakening: the adept experiences disillusion, he is looking for a way out, for a better world. If he is ready, he discovers the path that will lead him to the discovery of truth and reality. Step 3. Involvement: the adept embarks on the path; he understands the challenge. He realizes also that he will have to become entirely involved if he wants to live the greatest adventure in the universe and reach the goal. He sets to work with discipline; he practices with perseverance. Nothing can distract him from his goal. Step 4. Wisdom: the adept abolishes the difference and faces the absolute emptiness. He realizes himself in the blinding light of eternal truth. He understands everything. Step 5. Superhuman: at this point the wise one possesses knowledge well above normal worldly knowledge. He understands the mechanism of matter; his place on this theatre stage, what he can do is practically unlimited. What he does depends on his new goal. He is one with the created and the uncreated.

Where can the potential adept find the path that leads to liberation?

STOP

The action of immobilizing something.

During the process leading to the control of thought movement, the adept becomes gradually more successful in remaining indifferent to the thoughts trying to distract him. But regularly he succumbs and one thought or another invades him. After a while, he realizes that he has wandered and he focuses his attention back on emptiness and carries on with his meditation, to find however that he is subjected again to the same experience a moment later. At this stage in his progression, the adept must make a very important decision; otherwise he might stagnate at this level, as someone imprisoned in a vicious circle of "silence" and "thought" incessantly succeeding one another without ever really emerging into the emptiness of quiescence that is the next step to reach. The moment of ultimate "arrest" has come. The adept regains his self-control and firmly decides to arrest the movement of thoughts, to become totally immune to their actions. And from this moment on, he will pour the required amount of energy into his concentration so as not to be invaded by wandering thoughts anymore. This decision is final and without appeal, the break is clean and final. The adept's attention, strong as tempered steel, surpasses this stage to finally bathe in quiescence. He experiences an extraordinary sensation well-being and communicates with all the elements of the universe. He is in the ray of light, which illuminates reality.

Why does a thought disappear when it is ignored?

STUDY

The action of learning and analyzing new knowledge in order to better understand.

Those who study and acquire new knowledge are on the road of a better understanding of his world. The more knowledge a person has, the more his capacity to survive and succeed increases. Study does not only mean book knowledge but also natural knowledge of the world in which human beings evolve. The searcher realizes that the deeper he goes into grasping the nature of reality, the easier it will be for him to reach wisdom. The adept and the wise man are both continuously searching for new knowledge. They constantly study the message of all great wise ones of yesterday and today. They deepen their spiritual knowledge through study, analysis and deep meditations until they feel its essence. The wise man in deep meditation studies the emptiness of the creative mind. When in the course of a particularly successful meditation the wise man's microcosmic mind comes into contact with the macrocosmic mind, he experiences a moment of sudden consciousness. An intuitive understanding of what is reality, the ultimate wisdom.

Does a human being acquire new knowledge or simply remember knowledge he has forgotten from the past?

SUPERIOR BEING

A being who dominates matter.

The ignorant demonstrates his smallness through his pride and envy of others, his desire to accumulate wealth to the detriment of his fellow men, his lack of respect for laws and for his own commitments, etc. He is totally dominated by matter which makes him act as a puppet suspended to the ends of strings. His suffering his proportional to his attachment to illusion. On the contrary, the superior being is simple in his words and actions; he is neither proud, nor envious, nor hypocritical. He abides by the laws and keeps his own word. He wants only the good of others, whether they are good or evil. The objective of each and every one of his thoughts and actions is to awaken the world to reality and eliminate emotional suffering. The wise man looks upon suffering as a scourge to which humanity is submitted until it understands its mechanics and learns to dominate it by looking at truth squarely. He is detached from matter, which has no more ascendancy on him. Meditation is the antidote to attachment to worldly things.

How can an ignorant meditate?

SUPERIOR CONSCIOUSNESS

The faculty to acknowledge facts other than what is generally accepted.

In general, knowledge comes through the education acquired from family, school and society. Then a being also possesses a stock of knowledge, the product of previous lives' experiences. Between these two sets of knowledge emerges the being's personality. For some this knowledge produces the emergence of a superior consciousness that doubts the accuracy of the material world's limited logic because it sometimes glimpses the absolute logic. For example, someone realizes that each and everyone is right in his personal context, that in fact no one is really right or wrong, or that the death of a familiar person is not different from the death of a stranger, that only emotions make one interpret them differently. He also realizes that a perfect being could not have created our world, which we see as imperfect. Either the world is perfect or the creator is imperfect. Then he sees that perfection can only be perfectly passive since the smallest of motion would produce modifications and changes, thus imperfection. Perfection cannot change since it is perfect, then it is perfectly static and passive. These are some of the first realizations an adept experiences at the beginning of the adventure that will lead him to wisdom. In the course of his quest, he will discover meditation as a disciplinary tool for his thought process, then silence in the inner quiescence that he will use as a springboard to reach his objective, the absolute truth. This superior consciousness will not cease to grow until it becomes the absolute consciousness, knowing ALL.

How can a mother looking upon a battlefield covered with corpses cry for anybody else but her son?

SUPERIORITY

The quality of anyone who thinks that he is above those around him.

Everything in this world is organized into a hierarchy, and each individual fills a well-defined place within the social machine. The position of a being within a society is determined by various factors, among which his education, race, religion, intelligence, resourcefulness, etc. However, each individual deep within himself believes that he is the one to be right, that he would do better than anyone else in a situation or another. Each human being feels that he is the centre of the universe. This certainty allows the illusory machine to operate. Without it a wave of despair would wash over the world and few people would survive, if any. Furthermore, it is true that the human is the centre of the created universe; his only error is to think that he is separated from the whole. At each instant he reinvents the illusion of multiplicity, of difference and diversity. The wise man first intuitively knows, then he experiences that the universe's multiplicity is a false interpretation of reality. In fact, the material world is only a mental projection of its constituting members. The wise man in meditation sees the fog of illusion evaporates, unveiling reality in all its singularity. Then he realizes that nothing is superior to anything or anyone, that no hierarchy truly exists and that superiority is an illusory notion integrated into the great universal dream. Anyone who focuses his attention on the void understands the futility of aiming for superiority. It is better to search for reality.

How can inferior understanding leads to domination?

T

TECHNOLOGY

The use of scientific knowledge to improve human beings' condition.

From all times, human beings have used their superior intelligence to better their position in their environment. From fire to weapons and machines to the atomic bomb, humans stop at nothing in order to secure what they believe to be well-being and happiness. Yet after all these efforts, the expected results are not there. Ho! they are more comfortable, but certainly not happier than before. They have invented thousands of machines to free themselves from the slavery of daily labour, yet they spend more hours working today than ever before. Sometimes, one being awakens and all of sudden realizes the impossibility to find happiness through the possession of material things. Then he turns to the study of his physical, mental and intellectual being to realize that happiness is right there for anyone to take if he only opens his eyes to the truth. He takes refuge in the silence inside of him from where he soars up to the highest spiritual horizons. He acknowledges the created world, including technology, for what it is, only a snare ready to trap the ignorant beings as honey traps the hungry fly. Meditation opens for him the door to self-improvement and to an unalterable happiness.

Why can't material world bring real happiness?

TEMPORAL RELATIVITY

Fluctuation of time duration according to some factors of influence.

Time is nothing but the measure of movement. Stop all movement and time no longer exists. Humans are a little maniac regarding time and have invented thousands of ways to measure it inaccurately. Perception of time, which is relative to the displacement of bodies in space in relation with other bodies, is also subjected to the emotional state of the observer. A few days before vacation time may seem like weeks, even months, while a few days before a visit to the dentist always seem to pass too quickly. Ten minutes spent in a hot bath and ten minutes in the hands of a torturer have a very different temporal reference for the subject. But the watch will indicate that the same amount of time has passed in each case. But what is really important? What the watch measures or the perception of time duration the subject experiences? Do we measure time for the benefit of machines or human beings? If those measures are executed for human beings, they are totally inexact and erroneous since they are based on the movement of celestial bodies and not on the movement of human emotions which manage the perception of time. A wise man experimenting quiescence, has absolutely no notion of time, simply because in the emptiness of quiescence nothing exists, no matter or emotions, thus nothing can move, nothing can be measured and nothing is relative, all is real.

Why can emotions make the perception of time fluctuate?

TENDENCY

Predisposition to act in a certain way according to what one likes or dislikes.

The overall intellectual aggregates determine what a person likes or dislikes, what he wishes to do or not do, etc. Being an integral part of the aggregates, the individual tendencies or tastes likes the aggregates fluctuate significantly in addition to appearing and disappearing according to the moment, or depending on the dominant aggregate. Since aggregates are in constant transformation due to their interaction, the tendencies that depend on them are continually modified. One moment we want to do this, then it gets boring, we want to do that; this game of tendencies depends on the aggregate commanding the brain. The observer does not take any kind of decision here; he is simply a spectator. The brain interprets the aggregates' sensations and orders the body to action. The wise one knows that any tendency is illusory and appears and disappears without any more reality than a thought in the sky of his quiescence. He does not let his momentary tastes interfere with his search for truth. He works with determination to the realization of his ultimate goal, reality, and in so doing makes this spiritual aggregate assembly more powerful and predominant. The adept becomes sane when all fluctuating tastes are relegated to inferior positions and the spiritual tendency dominates the brain permanently.

Why can't the surface of the pond of serenity ripple without destroying the observer's reflection?

TENSION

Continuous force applied with the possibility of failure.

The beginner in the art of meditating without meditating, i.e. while concentrating his attention exclusively on the inner void, often applies excessive tension and risks becoming tired and losing the desired control. But on the other hand he must not fall into laxity and under the influence of the thought process. Too much laxity or tension can only be harmful, thus one must find equilibrium. In the beginning the adept will tire by trying to make thoughts disappear as soon as they appear in his head. But when fatigued he will relax and use another method where he will let thoughts do as they will, while trying not to be influenced by them. By alternating tension and relaxation methods he will remain fresh and will not take the chance of losing control over his concentration. The wise man closes his eyes and totally ignores thoughts. Lacking attention, they stop their frantic dance.

What gains the wise man out of the absence of effort?

THEORETICAL KNOWLEDGE

Knowledge intellectually acquired through persons or objects.

All knowledge acquired in books, on television, with the help of professors or any other medium which interpose themselves between the student and the matter to be learned. This knowledge, even for survival in the material world, is mediocre and only gains value after the student has practical experience of the subject matter. For the wise one, intellectual knowledge based only on sensations is spiritually irrelevant. For him, any knowledge that can change, be altered, transformed, even a little, has no spiritual value. This is the very essence of his search, to find reality. However, theoretical knowledge is of some importance to the searcher, since it can serve as a guide during his quest. But it cannot replace practical knowledge, the wisdom the adept discovers through his meditations. After many years of inner silence, the wise man reaches a very important TRUTH, a truth that never changed and that will never change. Only EMPTINESS (void) is the same for all. When the adept succeeds in establishing silence within, the void surfaces, and it is the same for all adepts and wise men of all times. It is unalterable, immutable, indestructible, infinite and eternal. It is reality.

How does the material world appear to the wise man's eyes?

THOUGHT

Mental image produced by the meeting of different aggregates or stimuli.

No thought can be composed of only one sensation. Everything in the universe is multiple and thoughts do not escape this law. They are composed of different aggregates, which when meeting other aggregates, produce a new sensation interpreted by the brain. The brain usually produces a more or less furtive image of its interpretation. The thought formation is a purely electronic process in which volition plays no part. The awakened observer realizes that he is witnessing the passing of his life.

What can one observe after the thought process has been stopped?

THOUGHT PROCESS

Normal mechanical work of the mind in reaction to outside or inside random stimuli.

The thought process is the mechanism that produces the interpretation of the material world. This mechanism, based on various sensations, creates the images that we believe to be real and permanent. The illusion in which we live is the fruit of a dualistic and discriminatory interpretation issued from the thinking machine. The wise one acknowledges that illusion is the only barrier, the only screen that separates him from reality. He uses his capacity to act to concentrate his entire attention on the absence of thoughts, on the void. He focuses on nothingness and the illusory canvas tears apart to show the truth. Meditation on the void is the fastest method to wake the sleeper.

What is the mental mechanism interpreting?

THOUGHT-MATTER

The solidification of mental projections.

Our thoughts are only images without value, only passing through without touching anyone. A thought cannot hurt anybody. What is the purpose of thinking about it, I will never make succeed. Why keep on dreaming, dreams do not become reality. Our thoughts have no impact on ourselves. These are a few expressions that one can often hear around the people who ignore the power of thought. Thought is so powerful that all that one sees, all that exists is thought, nothing else. Everything is thought-matter. The wise one knows with certainty that any thought triggers an infinite series of reactions that influence the initiator and the entire world. Thought precedes any action as thought precedes any matter. Just try to do the simplest of action without first wanting it, desiring it and ordering it. Without thought nothing exists, we are the matter of thought, we are thought-matter. Thus everything we think or mentally project programs our tomorrow, our thoughts of today shape our future. The wise man deep in meditation intuitively perceives that thoughts have a tendency to gather and form groups he calls aggregates. When a group of aggregates is sufficiently important, he witnesses the appearance of matter.

How can silence annihilate thought?

THREE VIEWS

Three levels of perception of the universe.

Level 1: The ignorant sees the material world as the only thing, which has any bearing on him. He is matter and feeds on matter. His only goal is the accumulation of goods because he believes that possession is the source of happiness. He takes this so seriously that he makes himself miserable until the day of the great disillusion that opens the door to the research of happiness outside worldly things. Level 2: The adept sees the world for what it is, an illusion of every instant, continuously recreated by humankind. In meditation he discovers emptiness and realizes that this void is in fact reality and that nothing else really exists outside this uncreated state. When he comes out of his meditation, he returns to the illusion. He is astride between the created and the uncreated and he does not realize yet the essence of the great cosmic machine. Level 3: The wise man realizes the unreality of matter and the reality of void and goes further in his understanding of the universal play. He realizes that truth resides in both facets of the world he can experience, namely in matter (the created) and void (the uncreated). When he unites these two states, he succeeds in grasping the essence of the whole. For him the union of emptiness and illusion forms the unique and infinite reality. One is the expression of the other. He experiences then the moment of creation without beginning or end, the instant during which everything occurred, is occurring and will forever occur.

How can unity be composed of void and creation?

TIME

False notion of duration caused by the constant transformation of the material world.

Time is a measure of movement. There is no fixed standard of time. Time in essence is limitless, without beginning or end. Therefore past, present and future do not really exist. Time does not possess any reality. The thought process invents the notion of time in order to measure movement. Time is only relative and does not possess any existence of its own. An instant lasts forever and eternity last but one instant.

What is the difference between a minute spent relaxing in your bathtub and a minute spent waiting for the dentist to pull out one of your teeth?

TOLERANCE

The absence of interference toward persons, situations or things.

Half the world in general does not agree with what the other half of the world does or believes. People want to change their fellow men so they would act and think as they do. Half of humankind wants to dominate the other half. No one believes that anyone else is doing anything right; everybody criticizes his fellow men. The wise one searches for tolerance since he understands that nothing is really bad and nothing is really good, everyone has his own vision of what should be appropriate or inappropriate for the moment. He focuses his attention on nature in order to realize that there is nothing in it that can be defined as good or bad. Everything is happening, as it should, all is in a perfect state of balance. All is action and reaction. The wise one looks upon and accepts what is and what is happening and continues with his meditation on the void. He does not refute nor support anything. He accepts the material world for what it is, the reflection of the individual mind on the surface of the infinite sea of the universal mind.

What is the level of life of one who does not live in the present?

TONALITY

A scale of comprehension of the illusory world.

It is possible to consider that there is a great evolution gap between the ignorant, the prisoner of sensations and matter, and the illuminated one, liberated from all physical links, insensitive to the assaults of the dream world. Nevertheless, several great wise men state that once the goal is reached, nothing is changed; only the interpretation of the world is modified in order to render a real image of the mystery of the universe. Thus, there is no evolution as such, but rather a slow transformation of our perception of the world. A slow elevation of the level of comprehension, a shade of difference with each sudden moment of awareness. This elevation of tonality is produced as follows: the adept 1. has a glimpse of truth (partial illumination) during meditation or at any other time, 2. as soon as he realizes what is happening, this truth is contaminated by the analysis process which immediately dissects it, verifies it, weighs it, compares it, etc. and, 3. finally files it. This truth has lost a great deal of its purity, it was subjected to a rape performed by duality, in the course of which it lost its unity, and was made into a lesser thing. But something will always remain of it, and that something is integrated into the adept's personality (aggregates) who will be changed forever. He is now a little higher in the comprehension range. The tonality of his vision of the world is a little superior. This slow progression will inevitably lead to the great illumination where the adept, now wise man, will understand the world and its mysteries.

Why does analysis destroy truth?

TOOL

A device used to perform a task.

Tools are one of the marks of a human being's intelligence. He pretends that because he uses tools to bend the environment to his needs, he is the most intelligent living being. Draped in this illusory interpretation of intelligence, he believes to be the king of the earth and the dictator of the others species inhabiting this planet with him. However, when a wise man assesses the results of the race toward modernization, he quickly becomes aware that if at first sight survival odds may seem better than in the past, when he looks closer, he realizes that the future survival of the race is not at all certain. Man has forgotten that he was part of nature and unrelentingly destroys it. Let us hope that he will awaken in time to remedy a situation where he will simply be deprived of an ecosystem into which to flourish. One has only to study the working of an anthill or a beehive to understand the stupidity of a human being full of himself. The wise man's tools are of a different order. He uses study, analysis and meditation to understand the mystery of creation and reach the ultimate truth. He does what he feels he should be doing at the time and where he feels he should do it. Then he uses the results of those actions as tools to further progress on the path to liberation.

How can one recognize a pro-survival action?

TRAINING

Apprenticeship intended to acquire knowledge.

At birth, a human being registers in school and after his death he takes advantage of the vacation as he progresses on the evolution road that will lead him to the realization of truth. Life extends a just training and results are always accurate.

Each being experiences exactly what he needs to understand a little more, a little better the futility of the material world and the mechanics of the great cosmic machine until the day he will understand everything. The alternate cycle of life and death allows the observer to experience, then to assimilate these experiences in the silence of in-between-lives. When the information to be assimilated runs out, it is time to come back to life and start again producing new data which will be used to advance one more step. The wise man at the moment of understanding everything realizes that his new task is to guide those who open their eyes to a glimpse of reality. He understands that he has just received his degree and that from now on he is part of the universe's adult world. He looks upon humankind and a benevolent smile illuminates his being.

Why must we unlearn in order to learn?

TRANQUILLITY

State of calmness and serenity.

The adept finds tranquillity when his body is at rest, relaxed but in a state wakefulness. His brain is off and does not embark upon any analysis or interpretation; it does not attempt to understand what it perceives. His intellect does not produce any thought forms or imagery; the intellectual aggregates are resting and waiting to take over the brain again. The mind or observer contemplates reality in a state of quiescence; he focuses on the infinite and eternal void. We call reality, nothingness or void what the adept contemplates but these are only illusory words attempting to <u>interpret</u> what the observer is experiencing. Only experience can give an accurate idea of this reality. For the adept all is at rest and bathes in an infinite peace from which emerges the instantaneity of all that is created and not created. During the ultimate moment when the adept does not imagine anything, think about anything, meditate on anything, reflect on anything, the mind returns to its natural state and offers the observer a panoramic view on reality as it is and not as imagined. The adept discovers the reality which is the cause of all that exists.

How could emptiness, as a medicine, cure someone who suffers from ignorance?

TRANSCENDENCE

The character of what is surpassed.

In order to reach the final illumination, the searcher must realize the essence of all that exists, whether in the illusory or real state. He must transcend all that is dualistic as well as his sensation of independence from the rest of the world. He will realize that his identification is only another way to cling to the material world. Thus he will reject all forms of identification, possession and interpretation. Only when stripped of all that is illusory, all that has only short-term duration, naked in the limitless nothingness, will he be able to confront the eternal light. At that moment he will open his eyes on reality and understand what is happening behind the illusory veil. He will experiment the universal instantaneity, the state of immateriality in no-space-time. The wise one knows that he must transcend illusion, and to do so he explores the emptiness of his inner self. Experience is the key to success. He knows that his degree of realization reduces the level of ignorance in the world. The liberation of the world can only happen after all the universal ignorance is transcended.

Why is the ignorant trying to hide behind a transparent wall?

TRANSCENDENTAL KNOWLEDGE

Superior knowledge related to a level of consciousness beyond the material world.

Transcendental knowledge is divided into two levels of wisdom. On the first hand the adept realizes, after a long period of study, analysis and meditation that the physical body is a complex system of aggregates only generating sorrow and unhappiness, and that it contains a "conscious" individual entity in constant transformation. His greatest discovery is certainly the fact that everything believed in disappears at each instant to immediately reappear changed, transformed. He is only a being in permanent modification. On the other hand, the wise one, after in-depth study, analysis, meditation and sudden moments of awareness experienced during his quest for truth, realizes that the material world, the entire universe, is by nature empty. He also realizes that in fact the world is not created, does not possess any foundation and does not rest on anything. At the end of his journey, the wise man knows that everything is void, and that what people believe to be matter is in fact emptiness. There exists only a state of consciousness bathing in the infinite void.

How can the tolerance of the wise one lighten the ignorant being's confusion?

TRANSFORMATION

Passage from one state to another with improvement.

The status of everything existing in the material world. The creation is totally unstable and impermanent. Matter and idea movement and friction cause the transformation, wearing and mutation of everything in the created universe. The wise one is aware that everything around him is in perpetual mutation and that not one thing keeps a permanent state. Everything changes, everything moves, everything is transformed, including the observer. Only the emptiness (void) on which the wise one concentrates his attention in mental silence is permanent and unchangeable.

Why does anything not perfectly static change?

TRANSITORY

The characteristic of what is brief and without real value.

Despite numerous undeniable proofs of the impermanence of everything that exists in the created universe, human beings persist in believing in the reality of illusion. They acquire today what they will lose tomorrow with great sorrow. Even when faced with the ever-changing world, the ignorant convinces himself that everything is stable and stopped in time. The wise man does not attach himself to his body because he knows that he will lose one day. He does not accumulate a fortune because he knows that he can lose it at any moment and that he cannot take it with him upon his death. He does not attach himself to his friends because they cannot be of any help to him as soon as he closes his eyes. The wise one does not seek material success because he knows that it is only transitory. He does not look for glory because he sees it as the illusion of the transitory illusions. The purpose of all his actions is to increase his state of awareness, because he knows that in order to find happiness he must wake to reality. The wise man knows that the created world is in transition between the finite and the infinite and that only the essence of consciousness (the observer) will endure time.

Why must one renounce every illusory thing in order to gain happiness?

TRILOGY OF HAPPINESS

Three different states that ensue from the same theme.

Human beings endlessly spend their energy in an attempt to measure their different level of happiness. They see sorrow as the worst thing and they consider it is very different from happiness. Is it possible to measure at what point a person begins to be unhappy? The wise man recognizes that sorrow and happiness are extremes of the same emotion related to the physical and intellectual well-being of human beings. He also notices that this state continuously fluctuates and passes from plus (happiness) to minus (sorrow) from one moment to the next. He knows that illusory happiness, like sorrow, is temporary, the happiness of today takes the shape of tomorrow's sorrow. Then the wise one realizes a superior state of happiness he calls «felicity». This is a state, which he glimpses or momentarily feels when he meditates deeply. This state of happiness is real, permanent, it does not wither away, wear off or tarnish. Within his inner silence, the wise one tastes the elixir of eternal felicity. His ultimate goal is to one-day bathe completely into the ocean of infinite light and truth.

Why can't human beings control their own happiness?

TRUTH

Something conformed to the immutable reality. Something that cannot be denied.

The truth is what the adept is searching for, and he will find it only inside of him, behind the images and concepts accepted as reality by the individual. The truth is not part of the space and time kingdom. The truth is that the universe is the product of thought and someone meditating on this fact discovers that reality is mind. The First Principle is the potential from which all individual minds emerge as well as all the illusory worlds in which they live. Everything in the universe has roots in the great eternal and immutable void. The universe is the First Principle's offspring, its expression. It is impossible to separate the idea from the thought and the thought from the object since they all emanate from the divine mind. The individual mind energizes the body and the divine mind energizes the whole creation. Everything rests on thought and when thought stops, everything disappears and leaves only the real potential, empty but capable of anything.

What is the difference between something true and something false?

U

UNCONSCIOUSNESS

Impossibility to acknowledge reality because of analysis founded on unreal facts.

The characteristic of the sleeper who only acknowledges the material world and lives totally immersed in the illusion. Unconsciousness as well as consciousness are an integral part of the First Principle and both have their respective place in the great material machine. The whole universe is on the road to liberation and in perfect void, and because space and time do not exist, we are simultaneously conscious and unconscious, this is a paradox that is possible to grasp only in the deepest meditation, where duality does not rule. Illusion alone stops us from achieving perfection and reaching the divine source. The silence within rises the veil hiding this truth.

What is the first cause of unconsciousness?

UNCREATED

The characteristic of what has no material existence or has not been invented. Something that has not been pulled out of nothingness. Nothingness.

Mind is uncreated because the wise man who confronts it realizes that it is nothing, it rests on nothing and is not objective nor subjective. The mind is perfectly empty but is the reservoir for everything since one in quiescence sees things of this world emerge from the mind and immerse in it. Expression is the essence of mind and the creation's goal is evolution. The uncreated is eternal, immutable; nothing can alter it. It possesses no form or quality of the creation. The mind is without objectivity or subjectivity and cause, without origin, unborn and yet self-existing. Mind transcends creation. The wise man meditates on nothing because his ultimate goal is the light of nothingness in which creation bathes. In order to reach nothingness, one must meditate on his inner nothingness.

Why must one meditate on something that does not exist in order to find the only thing that really exists?

UNION

The grouping of various elements in a whole.

All human beings, despite their individual beliefs and their tendency to divide and separate things from each other, are looking for an ultimate model with whom they could identify. Since the beginning of time, they have been searching for the protection of a superior being who could defend them, protect them against the enemy or simply against themselves. A human being searches for this comfort outside of him when, since the beginning, all he has to do to silence the cacophony of his thoughts to discover that the essence of creation (God) lives within. The wise one acknowledges that the human mind is inseparable from the universal mind and that both form a unity. The prime objective of contemplation or meditation is to allow the union in instantaneity of the human and divine aspects of the mind. This goal is only achievable after the human mind is liberated from the confusion caused by the thought process. When mind is no longer influenced by illusion, it learns to know itself for what it really is, emptiness. The highest level of wisdom is achieved when the wise man can recognize each individual thing while knowing that all things form an immutable union.

Why does each human being believe he is alone and unique?

UNITY

The characteristic of what is one and indivisible.

The First Principle as a unity cannot possess a thought process mechanism; it is the ultimate and unique thought. If it could, it would then be a manifold being, and part of the world of dualities. It would not occupy the first place, it would be second or at the least diversified. Thus, we must conclude that what is complex can possess a thought treatment mechanism and that unity is thought itself. The thought process, like intelligence which is only an electro-biologic analytical and understanding mechanism processing illusory knowledge, has its source in unity and not the other way around. Let us not forget that what has the capacity to think is not thought itself but a being with the faculty to process thoughts. Thought is the unity that embraces all that is existing and non-existing. The ultimate thought generates the world forming images.

Why does a human being carry the essence of the universe in himself?

UNIVERSAL BALANCE

The confrontation of positive and negative forces that establishes stability.

First there was unity (First Principle), which gave birth to a bipolar thought (- and +) and this thought generated complexity composed of an immeasurable quantity of positive and negatives units. Creation's integrity rests on the universal balance. As soon as an event occurs, the universe immediately proceeds to rebalance forces in order to return to stability. A rock thrown in the air will eventually fall to the ground and stabilize there. As a sun exploding far into space will ultimately return to stability, everything tends toward stability in the created world, its continuity depends on it. The scientific community demonstrated to us that nothing is ever lost or ever created in our world, which infers that the universe is closed and depends on a "limited" quantity of energy or positive and negatives units. If a certain amount of positive energy is transformed into negative energy, automatically an equal amount of negative energy will be transformed into positive energy in order to ensure the stability of the whole. The wise man in meditation acknowledges that the created universe cannot be totally positive or negative. This would destroy the balance of creation, which could no longer find its stability. He also knows that when all beings of the creation will have transcended their passions and will face reality, the created world will vanish as mist in the morning sun. The material world does not really exist, we think it at each instant.

Would it be impossible for the universe to exist if we were not there?

UNIVERSAL BODY

The assembly of everything that exists in the universe.

Is it possible to visualize the whole universe and all that it contains in one mental-image? Is it possible to become aware of every movement, every thought, every element or assembly, every living being and lifeless thing? Is it possible to grasp the essence of the great scenario in which every being and thing has a well-defined place? Is it possible to learn the reason behind this cluster of confusion consumed by emptiness in which, as if they were blind, human beings always perform the same motions, always repeat the same errors? Are they imperceptibly progressing toward an inhuman goal that is the abandonment of all similarities in order to enjoy unity? These are but a few of the questions that the wise man is attempting to answer. He meditates to refine his intuition, to render it capable of perceiving the imperceptible. He is trying to realize the unity of all that is part of the creation, from the most insignificant particle of dust, the most microscopic plant, the lowest creature up to the illuminated wise one who has become a glorified entity of the eternal truth. The wise man uses every moment of his life in studies, analysis and meditations that will take him to the supreme goal.

Can an element foreign to the enigma hold its key?

UNIVERSAL MIND

The assembly of all mind perception activities in the universe.

Is it possible to perceive what a daisy feels when someone pulls one of its petals, or what a stone feels when it is burst open by a hammer, or what a mother losing her child at birth feels? Is it possible to penetrate the reason for created matter, to understand its composition, its arrangements, its diversities and its similarities? Is it possible to explain why the world is the same for all, while it is being defined and understood in as many ways as there are living beings? Is it possible to share the pain of an amputated leg, the happiness of a mother delivering a baby or the surprise of a child opening his eyes for the first time? Is it possible to understand the reason for perception organs? The wise man, through meditation, is attempting to unify the expression of the mind in the universe from the most insignificant creation, from the most instinctive function or reaction to external sensations in things and beings. First he studies sensations of lifeless matter, then that of plants, animals, human beings up to the sensations of the illuminated being with his totally awakened mind bathing in the eternal light of truth.

What is the link between the microcosmic mind and the macrocosmic mind?

UNIVERSAL VOICE

The assembly of all sounds that exist in the universe.

Is it possible to hear the noise of colliding stars, the sound of a child smiling in the womb, the sound of a severed head falling to the ground, the sound of a bird passing in the sky? Is it possible to hear silence in the crush of an angered crowd? Is it possible to prick up one's ears to the sound of the ignorant and not hear his cry of pain, or to listen to the wind without hearing the wail of grass crushed under our feet? Is it possible to hear the noise of the ants working, or the noise of the celestial bodies' friction in the void, or the sound of the furious stars in fire? The wise man, through meditation, tries to unify the expressions of sound from the most elementary sound made by nature, trees, human beings, things, stars and planets as well as the deafening sound of thoughts up to the sound of truth which reverberates in the void of absolute infinity. In meditation he is flawlessly attentive to silence because silence contains all sounds in the universe as white is composed of all colours of the spectrum.

What is the sound of a sabre beheading a thought?

UNIVERSALITY

Assembly of beings and things forming a whole.

Since all beings of the universe form only one and the same universality, it seems impossible for one of them to forsake the assembly and enjoy a treatment different from the mass. The illuminated, the one who achieves what he called his objective, his ultimate goal, realizes that there is no end to the experience, but only stages of evolution and of transformation leading a human being (who does not keep his present shape for very long) beyond his wildest dreams. The First Principle from where emerges all that exists is eternal and limitless, thus the evolutionary adventure is without finality, it always existed and will always exist. The illuminated, as the ignorant, is part of the same evolutionary machine; the only difference between the two is their respective degree of awakening to reality. As long as there will remain one ignorant in the farthest corner of creation, the wheel of life and death will go on turning in order to refine consciousness and express the Great Dreamer's imagery. The wise one knows that sorrow's existence rests only on a false interpretation of the world. He also realizes that he is present in everything and that everything is present within him. Nothing exists outside the observer.

Why are people different from one another?

UNIVERSE

The cosmic manifestation of the First Principle.

The adept must not consider the material world as a prison from which he must escape because this world is nothing else than the manifestation of the First Principle in constant evolution. Instead he must regard it as a supreme chance to participate in this transformation. When he is confronted by emptiness, the wise man realizes that matter and void are indiscernible and in fact are two facets of the same whole.

What is the cause of the universe's materiality?

UNLIMITED INTELLIGENCE

The faculty to know and understand acquired through meditation when the thought process is absent.

The human capacity of unlimited intelligence allows it to grasp the greatest mysteries of the creation and non-creation. But only beings starting to awake and the awakened ones can take advantage of it because the thought process hides its presence behind a cacophony of miscellaneous thoughts. Only a person in quiescence can perceive and use this faculty. The unlimited intelligence does not use erroneous analysis to achieve comprehension but rather an immersion in the eternal pool of wisdom. The observer knows that his intelligence is unlimited as soon as he closes the door of sensations and observes reality as it is. He realizes that as long as he was separated from the whole by the veil of illusions, it was impossible for him to assimilate divine revelations. At the beginning, the unlimited intelligence allows him to perceive bits of absolute truth when he is in deep meditation; then comes the realization of the absolute wisdom of reality.

Why is humankind more intelligent than the animal kingdom?

UNPREDICTABLE

The characteristic of what is uncertain, unstable. The nature of what is under the influence of chance.

The whole created universe is based on uncertainty, nothing is ever sure, nothing is ever certain. Everything changes, everything is transformed from one moment to the next, nothing is ever the same. The wise one acknowledges this illusion's characteristic, and is not fooled into believing that what seems on the way to happen will happen, in fact it can be quite different. This is only another life's facet ensuring the wise one that he took the right decision when he started to look for homogeneity inside rather than outside. No one can predict the exact future because chance is constantly at work transforming beautiful dreams into deception or sadness into happiness. In his heart of hearts, in the silence, the observer realizes that only stability can bring him further ahead in his quest for the truth. The one without desire for worldly possessions is invulnerable. The wise man lives the unique and eternal present moment, nothing else.

What is chance?

V

VEHICLE

Anything that can transport someone or something from one place to another.

Research, study and reflection are all vehicles able to carry the searcher part of the way. But the greatest vehicle is meditation, which as a raft, allows the pilgrim to cross the river of illusions and land on the shore of reality. The oldest and most effective method of meditation is the one in which there is nothing, only the silence of emptiness and an observer. This is the vehicle of the great liberated, the shortest road to fulfill the supreme goal. The observer holds on to nothing, he is there in the void, a tiny presence ready to be lost in the great nothingness. Meditation is the vehicle of the greatest adventure offered to mankind. The adept is a modern time adventurer exploring his inner worlds in order to overcome them and reach the infinite spaces of the non-created. The wise man realizes that, once he is on the other shore, the vehicle is not useful anymore and he must leave it behind. There, another adventure awaits him.

Why is meditation on emptiness the fastest vehicle to reach liberation?

VICE

What is wrong and goes against the moral of a dualistic society.

Vice and virtue are part of the great duality of this world. Vice must exist if we want the universe to remain what it is. Vice is the negative pole and virtue the positive one. Upon losing its negativeness, an atom would crumble to nothingness. The same thing would happen to the universe if it would lose its negative pole. Without vice how could we evaluate what is virtue? The wise one realizes that vice impedes the progress of the one who searches for the truth. But he also realizes that in the silence of his inner void, vice and virtue do not really exist and that they are only the mirror image on one another.

How can someone's vice be someone else's virtue?

VIGILANCE

Attentive and continuous consciousness.

When the adept has reached a pure level of concentration that is no longer tarnished by distractions caused by the emergence and immersion of thoughts, he must then work on his vigilance. The state of alertness of one in contemplation must be unalterable. The adept must be capable of being present without depending on anything; he is there in the inner space and rests on nothing. The observer does not think, meditate, nor try to control, he is simply there and observes the void as a waking child, fascinated by the light playing on his bedroom walls. In this state, the adept can experience sensations of presence, hear voices; see more or less real forms. When he loses the notion of his body and intellect, he can feel that he is floating or flying in the air. But the observer must absolutely neither identify, like or dislike or even hold on to these sensations. He must be vigilant and never react to the various sensations, even if they are ecstatic and fill him with happiness. The wise one awaiting illumination is totally relaxed and indifferent to anything other than the void he is contemplating.

What becomes of the wise man who totally ignores matter?

VIRTUE

Everything right according to the moral principle of a dualistic society.

All dualistic societies believe that their virtues are infallible, and they deny that of others. It is false to believe that virtue alone can lead to the elevation of a being. Virtue and vice are an integral part of the world's duality, one positive and the other negative. The wise one knows fully well that the universe could not exist without its two opposite poles. Thus good and bad are desirable if one wants the universe to continue on its way. The adept studies, analyzes and meditates on the effects of good and bad and discovers that they both attach mankind to the material world and that the only and real answer is found in the transcendence of the two, in a perfect neutrality. The wise man practises virtue because it assists him in his search. The unification of positive and negative is the pilgrim's ultimate goal.

Why is it that virtue alone cannot lead to liberation?

VOID

That which contains nothing material or perceptible.

Void, not the spatial or temporal emptiness but the great spiritual void is the state that the wise one acknowledges as immutable, perfectly immobile, simply perfect. For him void is the only real thing of which contemplation reveals the great truth. However, this void is nothing, has no qualities or characteristics that would allow us to understand or grasp its essence. Void is absence of everything; it is eternal silence. Nevertheless, this void generates what we call the world, and despite the illusion or non-reality concept of this world, it still possesses a relative reality for all those who inhabit it. Justly, the wise man explains that the material world is in fact eternal emptiness and what we are living is only an illusion that we project upon the void's screen. He also states that the created world is the result of the meeting of two opposed polarities, the positive and the negative, and that their unification is in fact the eternal ALL, and forms a perfect unity. Void and creation are a single thing. Those who succeed in reaching the inner silence and contemplating the void become aware of the eternal truth. In order to understand the truth in these words, one must personally experience it. Meditation opens the door unto horizons that few humans have visited.

Why is the ignorant who refuses the notion of absolute void still a part of it?

VOLUBILITY

Great quantity of words spoken rapidly.

A great intellectual capacity combined with a poor understanding of the nature of the universe prompts some people to practice volubility. Captivated by sensations that make them indifferent to silence, they submerge themselves and others in an endless river of words. The wise one, on the contrary, recognizes the unreality of the intellectual feats and concentrates on silence, the bearer of illumination. He realizes that words, as any other created forms, are illusory and that the intuition that comes from the uncreated void takes root in reality. For him meditation is the source of intuitive knowledge, the wisdom that does not rest on analysis. In the silence of his meditations he becomes aware that he is an integral part of all beings which form the great evolving machine.

Why is silence capable of transcending words?

VOYAGE

The action of going from one place to another.

The human being comes from far back and will go even farther than all his wildest dreams may lead him to believe. From cosmic dust to inert matter, and from inert matter to animated matter and whatever more. The human being is but one step among many others of the divine evolution. Since the beginning of time, the search has always been the same: to understand ever more in order to go farther. Meditation on nothingness allows the eyes to open on the conclusion of an adventure and the beginning of a new search of the unknown as yet incomprehensible. At the end of his road, when the wise man reaches illumination, he knows that this is not the end of the course and that in fact the final objective does not exist since the ultimate goal is the expression of the eternal reality, without beginning or end. Even the realized one cannot understand what awaits him in the course of this great new voyage, because no one can grasp what is beyond one's understanding. On his way out of the illumination stage, the wise man looks back and ahead, then realizes that in fact nothing has changed, except that the tone of the divine hymn is a little higher.

What is the one word that can define beginning and end?

WANDERING

The action to move away from the targeted goal.

In order to reach the meditation state, the adept will first have to succeed in concentrating his attention on emptiness without being distracted. Distraction is due to the fact that his attention (consciousness) identifies itself with a passing thought, taking him away from the targeted goal; he is then wandering. In the course of meditation, pure attention observes emptiness (void) and sometimes a thought rises from the horizon and passes through the silence of the inner sky. An appearing thought calls the attention and if it packs enough energy and if the attention does not have the power (discipline) to remain concentrated, then the thought dominates and the attention identifies with it. At that moment the adept thinks this thought, he believes to be this thought, and the meditation is broken. Wandering is an important obstacle to conquer. When the adept realizes that he errs, he immediately returns his attention (gently) to the observation of emptiness. He will reinforce the wall of his attention in order to be able to support subsequent attacks and ignore passing thoughts however strong they might be. The wise man has practised this return to the observation hundreds, thousands of times before he can maintain his attention clean of any impurity and taste the fruit of quiescence.

What is the nature of attention?

WASTE

The action of squandering one's assets.

Generally, all that human beings accomplish in the course of their physical life is part of the long road that leads them to the appeasement of their material desires and the discovery of a superior dimension of understanding. In the spiritual sense of the term, no life is ever wasted. Everyone does what they have to do when they have to. Thus, waste does not exist, error does not exist, all is integrated into the great evolution journey of illusory beings toward truth. Nothing is lost, nothing is gained, all is transformed. The same principle applies to beings as well as things and energy. Those who think that they are wasting their life forget that they do what they think is right for them with their stock of knowledge and wisdom, as poor or rich as it may be. A person who does what is called good gathers a positive charge, thus reactions to his actions are positives, and that makes his life less miserable than the life of someone who carries a heavy load of negative endeavours. But in either case the purpose of these actions is to bring them always closer to the truth. Nothing is truly wrong or right, the real purpose for everything that happens on the road is evolution. The wise man does not reject nor accept anything positive or negative. Meditation has allowed him to transcend good and bad into a unity. He sees his life as a long chain of experiences leading him continuously closer to his ultimate goal, liberation.

What is the mechanism that allows a being to make a decision?

WISDOM

Knowledge acquired without physical sensations, analysis or interpretations. A knowledge that seems to come from nowhere.

Wisdom is a spiritual knowledge based on nothing material or created. All spiritual knowledge is transcendent and eternal. Meditation is the main method used to draw perfect wisdom from the pool of the unified First Principle. In silence and tranquillity, sparks of unalterable truth appear. Intuitive truth or spiritual wisdom remains the same through ages; they never change. Aware of this reality, the awakened never stops searching the maze within for the light, which enlightens all of mankind. Wisdom is the creator of comprehension and happiness

Why isn't spiritual knowledge relative?

WISE ONE

Someone who possesses a real knowledge of the world.

The wise one often is seen by the rest of the world as a mild eccentric who has lost all sense of reality. It is understandable that someone who has realized that the world is illusory and totally unsatisfactory can look a little bizarre to the eyes of our sleeping society. The wise man, after having dominated his thought process, realizes the futility of matter and of all things of this world. He is no longer affected by electronic gadgets, beauty products, luxury clothing, social conventions, temporary glory or the intellectualism of the world; which still fascinate the sleeping masses of people. The ignorant believes he knows everything and thinks he is progressive while the wise man only believes he is a searcher among other searchers. He knows very well that all human beings are on the same path leading to the same eternal blinding reality. He knows that no one can understand what he is, nor is ready to understand it, and that each individual walks his own path. He meditates on the void and shares his experiences with those who demonstrate an interest. He knows that the goal is still some distance away.

What is the impact of sensations on human beings?

WORD

Sound used by the brain to express the sensations perceived by the various body senses (vision, touch, smell, hearing, etc.).

Words are only sounds used to express the inexpressible. One must be conscious that as soon as the truth is expressed in words, its true sense is lost. The searcher must listen to the words trying to explain reality, while always keeping in mind that he will have to experiment them personally by meditating. One must never follow a teaching that asks to believe without experiment. The wise man prefers silence to words, and uses them only when he judges that he cannot do otherwise. Silence is truth, words are often only the sound of confusion.

Why does a bird sing even when there is no one to listen?

WORLD

Everything comprised in the universe.

The world is an infinite field of dualities all somewhat opposed to one another. Everything that exists in this world is bound together by its opposite, positive by negative, truth by false, etc. The antithesis is the glue that cements this world together, without it the illusion would disappear. This duality also allows the existence of time by producing motion, by proposing a beginning and an end. The world is the kingdom of confrontations and transformations where everything has a contrary, an opposite, the created and uncreated, ignorance and wisdom, real and illusion, potentiality and manifestation, etc. If duality were to disappear, the world would vanish. But when the wise man explains the world from his stand point, he declares that every one of these dualities which seem to be opposing one another are in fact one and the same unity, indivisible and unalterable, called reality. In his attempt to discover the truth, the adept only has to understand one of these dualities in order to understand and assimilate the whole universal duality. The adept looks first for peace because he knows that from quiescence emerges the truth.

Why is the wise man refraining from changing the world?

May this book bring you what you are seeking?

Julien Bouchard

About the Author

During his more than thirty year international career Julien Bouchard has worked and visited numerous of countries in Asia, Middle-East, South America, Central America, Europe, etc. All those voyages were not solely done for professional purposes since they were also the object of philosophical and spiritual researches especially in India and in the northern region of Nepal.

He studied several civilisations and religions; he managed numerous large scope electrical development projects counting several hundreds of persons. He took advantage of these privileged periods to study the behaviours of others as well as his, facing every day life and a variety of problematic and conflicting situations.

He practices meditation since more then 45 years and at the beginning he visited ashrams in India and monasteries in Nepal where he was initiated to the some Buddhist philosophies and practices. His goal was to find a simple method of meditation. A method with the least human and time tempering, a method in its purest form. In order to succeed he had to conduct a research that took him on a time journey and finally, during a trekking trip in the northern regions of Nepal, he met a Master from the Kargyûpta school (Adept of the apostolic succession).

The teaching of this Master was based on the MahaMudra (the Great Symbol). One of the most ancient and purest forms of meditation known today. It was first set forth by a wise Indian named Saraha sime times in the first century before J.-C., and at that time the Great Symbol was already known to be very old according Master Tilopa's texts dated around the 11th century after J.-C.

The Great Symbol was exported to China from India as soon as the 1st century after Jesus-Christ, where this discipline took the name of Chan, then it was further exported to Japan where it is known by the well publicised name of Zen. Of course, Chan and Zen are disciplines based on the Great Symbol, but they were subjected during the ages to a lot of man's modifications and additions. The Great Symbol is thus the ancestor of Chan and Zen, and the purest and simplest form of meditation known today.

Julien wrote this book in order to set forth his personal experience.

"I wish a good journey to the honest reader on the way to the ultimate truth, the THRUTH that comes as a flash and sets the searcher within the light of silence."